ULYSSES

Ulysses

HUGH KENNER

Revised Edition

The Johns Hopkins University Press
Baltimore and London

Revised edition © 1987 The Johns Hopkins University Press
Printed in the United States of America

First published in 1980 in the Unwin Critical
Library series: General Editor, Claude Rawson
© George Allen & Unwin (Publishers) Ltd, 1980

Revised edition first published in 1987 by
The Johns Hopkins University Press
701 West 40th Street
Baltimore, Maryland 21211
The Johns Hopkins Press Ltd., London

LIBRARY OF CONGRESS CATALOGING-IN-PUBLICATION DATA
Kenner, Hugh.
  Ulysses.
  Bibliography: p.
  Includes index.
  1. Joyce, James, 1882–1941. Ulysses. I. Title.
PR6019.09U6723   1987   823'.912   86-27773
ISBN 0-8018-3489-9
ISBN 0-8018-3384-1 (pbk.)

For Adaline and Fritz

And it was a sight worth seeing to behold the several souls choose their lives. And a piteous and a laughable and amazing sight it was also. The choice was mostly governed by what they had been accustomed to in their former life . . .

It so happened that the soul of Odysseus came forward to choose the very last of all. He remembered his former labours and had ceased from his ambition and so he spent a long time going round looking for the life of a private and obscure man. At last he found it lying about, ignored by every one else; and when he saw it he took it gladly, and said that he would have made the same choice if the lot had fallen to him first.

Plato, *The Republic*, X-620
trans. A. D. Lindsay

CONTENTS

Scheme of References

1	Preliminary	1
2	'O, an Impossible Person!'	6
3	Uses of Homer	19
4	Immediate Experience	31
5	The Hidden Hero	43
6	Stephen's Day	55
7	The Arranger	61
8	The Aesthetic of Delay	72
9	Oceansong	83
10	Maelstrom, Reflux	93
11	Metempsychoses	107
12	Death and Resurrection	118
13	Lists, Myths	134
14	The Gift of a Book	146

APPENDICES

1	The Date of Stephen's Flight	161
2	Bloom's Chest	164
3	The Circle and the Three Nines	166

Critical Sequels	169
Bibliography	174
Index	180

SCHEME OF REFERENCES

Page references in parentheses follow quotations. All editions of *Finnegans Wake* have the same pagination. For *Dubliners* and *A Portrait of the Artist as a Young Man* I have used the Penguin editions (revised texts, 1976); an identifying letter, D or P, precedes the number when there can be a question of which book is intended. References to *Ulysses* employ the scheme established by the revised critical edition of 1984, supervised by Professor Hans Walter Gabler (Garland Publishing, Inc., New York and London, 3 vols.); thus 7.584 means line 584 of episode 7 (Aeolus). While pagination may vary from publisher to publisher, typesetting from master computer tapes ensures that lineation of the Gabler text does not change.

Superior figures refer to notes at the end of chapters, asterisks to notes at the foot of the page.

CHAPTER 1

Preliminary

A day in June is a very long day indeed at 53° North latitude. In Dublin in 1904, Standard Time and Summer Time still years in the future, local time had the sun rise on 16 June at 3.33 and not set until 8.27. Two or three hours past sunset, on such nights, one can still make out newspaper headlines by skyshine, and at no time between dusk and dawn does the northern sky really darken.

The sun rises and the sun goes down, says Ecclesiastes, and hastens to the place where it rises; it is the lot of man, beneath its circuit, to see no thing that has not been before. To look at the never new with ever new hope is one conceivable form of sanctity and, as days in Catholic countries are identified with saints, 16 June now draws pilgrims to Catholic Ireland for Bloomsday, the day of a man who was never down for long.

His distinction is to have been fit to live in Ireland without malice, without violence, without hate. Like certain other saints he had only an ideal existence. It has been difficult for Ireland to go about breeding such citizenry, but an Irishman, James Joyce, conceived of Bloom, his gift to Ireland and the fulfilment of his old promise to forge abroad, in the smithy of his soul, the uncreated conscience of his race. Bloom was also a cuckolded Jew, and Ireland's gratitude has not been marked, though it now permits itself sidelong self-congratulation on having produced James Joyce.

Ulysses, the Book of Bloom, was commenced in Trieste about 1914, written there and in Zürich and Paris during the next seven years, published in Paris, 2 February 1922 on the author's fortieth birthday, and promptly created what the gutter press loves, a scandal. 'SCANDAL OF "ULYSSES",' read hoardings for the *Sporting Times* ('The Pink 'Un'), in which one could read that the contents of this book were 'enough to make a Hottentot sick'.[1] Hottentots in those days were British subjects.

In a Britain alive to her responsibilities, HM Customs at Folkestone early in 1923 confiscated and presumably burned 499 copies of *Ulysses*, one short of the entire third printing. In Cambridge a young lecturer named F. R. Leavis requested permission to import one copy; the Office of the Director of Public Prosecutions promptly supplied the Vice-Chancellor of the University with a police report on the percentage of women attending Leavis's lectures. The Director of Public Prosecutions also described *Ulysses* as 'incredibly filthy', and offered the Vice-Chancellor the opportunity to inspect it.[2] For more than ten years, during which other writers responding to smuggled copies made it the most influential English-language work of the twentieth century, *Ulysses* could not legally be brought into any English-speaking country in the northern hemisphere save Ireland, where they never banned it but relied on booksellers not to stock it. ('We don't have *that*,' some still affirm quietly, though obtaining the Penguin edition in Dublin today presents no real difficulty.)

It was not at all clear what kind of book it was. Alfred Noyes, author of *The Highwayman*, conceived that no foulness conceivable to the mind of man had not been 'poured forth into its imbecile pages', which he also found 'bad simply as writing', and 'obscure through sheer disorder of the syntax'.[3] There was much other spluttering. Ignoring it, T. S. Eliot, who was later to call James Joyce 'the greatest master of English since Milton',[4] addressed himself to the book's parallel between antiquity (Homer) and modernity (1904), in which he saw a way of ordering 'the panorama of anarchy and futility that is the contemporary world'.[5] Ezra Pound dismissed the Homeric parallel as *affaire de cuisine*, more important to the chef than to the diner; it was as encyclopedic realism, in succession to *Bouvard et Pécuchet*, that he valued the book.[6] A French critic, Edmond Jaloux, was reminded of sixteenth-century France: 'On y trouve l'aspect encyclopédique des grandes œuvres de cette époque, leur souci de connaître la vérité, leur volonté de pénétrer la vie toute entière et ses sciences au moyen d'un truchement spirituel, cette horreur de la dissimulation, de l'escamotage qui sont si sensibles chez un Montaigne, chez un Rabelais.'[7]

As for Joyce himself, during the years when the work was in progress he had been accustomed to tell new acquaintances that he was writing a book based on the *Odyssey*. Yet nothing he said in amplification of this would have led anyone to expect the queer book that resulted. (There was a time, we now think, when he didn't expect it himself.) *Ulysses* seemed, to most readers able to pick up a copy, not a mirror of Homer, not a story at all, but something as featureless as a telephone directory. Decades later a cardinal insight, elaborated by several researchers, concerned the unexpected extent to which Joyce based it on the Dublin section of *Thom's Official Directory of the United Kingdom of Great Britain and Ireland*, all stray copies of the 1904 edition of which have consequently vanished into research libraries.

Succès de scandale encouraged a few features to coalesce out of the murk. The unpunctuated forty pages at the end were soon understood to be a woman's monologue. The long section that looks like a play, easily skimmed for outrages, was evidently a phantasmagoria, justifiable by learned mentions of the Walpurgisnacht in Goethe's *Faust*, the *Tentation* of Flaubert, the iconography of Bosch. A visit to a privy might be pointed to as an instance of perfectly lucid narrative. And one character, Stephen Dedalus, was carried forward from Joyce's earlier *A Portrait of the Artist as a Young Man*, where he whored and had high-flown thoughts. Still, the reviewer for the *New York Times Book Review*, a neurologist named Collins, thought it plausible that only he and the author had ever read *Ulysses* through twice.[8]

For printed words on a page – any words, any page – are so ambiguously related to each other that we collect sense only with the aid of a tradition: this means, helped by prior experience with a genre, and entails our knowing which genre is applicable. No one in 1715 would have known what to make of Mr Pope's *Iliad* who did not know that it was translated from Homer, and numerous eighteenth-century poems would seem wholly chaotic did we not know what to expect of Pindaric odes. Swift disorientated his readers by confusing the genre signals: we know to call *Gulliver's Travels* and *A Modest Proposal* 'satires', but new readers were led to think the former a travel-book, the latter a projector's pamphlet, and had to reorientate themselves forcibly some pages or paragraphs later. Wordsworth had hoped to orientate readers of his 1799 collection by adducing the genre of the literary ballad; but the distance between their experience of broadside ballads and 'The Thorn' or 'We Are Seven' proved too great for many purchasers, who as Eliot has acutely remarked found the poems difficult and called them silly.[9] 'Difficult' here means excessively removed from generic controls.

Ulysses has one clue, a title, which does not help at all if we flip its pages in quest of Greek heroes, and another clue, the resemblance of its first page to the first page of a novel, which does not aid us for long if we expect novels to keep narrative, dialogue, comment and reverie rhetorically and typographically distinct. Other genres, too, were tried and found unhelpful: the dirty book, the neurological treatise fiction-alised. *Ulysses* is the first of the great modern works that in effect create for themselves an *ad hoc* genre – today we may also instance *The Waste Land, The Cantos, Molloy* – and so entail an *ad hoc* critical tradition. Understanding this clearly, Joyce was soon prompting his critics. He assisted Valery Larbaud to put the phrase 'interior monologue' into circulation, and many sequences cleared up when readers knew that that was what to call them. He also urged Eliot to circulate a phrase coined in conversation, 'two plane',[10] but Eliot never got around to it.

In 1931 Stuart Gilbert's *James Joyce's 'Ulysses'* made its appearance as a quasi-authorised guide. It was based on a typewritten *schema* Joyce had prepared ten years earlier for the guidance of Larbaud; others had been allowed to profit from this subsequently, all under the injunction that it must be kept private. Gilbert's readers, who saw most of it, were thus the first to receive explicit knowledge of not only what was happening on that Dublin day, hour by hour, but also under what Symbol, Colour, Bodily Organ, presided over by what Art, rendered by what Technic, in accordance with what Homeric parallels. Gilbert had also a good deal of esoteric Buddhism to offer, more likely his enthusiasm than Joyce's. He seems to have been solemn and naïve, which was unlucky because *Ulysses* is neither.

Joyce had listened while Gilbert read from his typescript, had supplied hints, corrected some downright errors. He didn't restrain the flights of esoterism, being pleased apparently by new evidence that his book contained more than deliberation had put into it.[11] Gilbert's book encouraged a generation of commentators to look for large-scale patterns, which wasn't a total mistake.

The next guide in which Joyce had a finger was published in 1934: Frank Budgen's *James Joyce and the Making of 'Ulysses'*. Budgen was a rare man, a man the wary Joyce trusted; an ex-sailor, a painter by profession, a born writer though untouched by literary ambition. He had known Joyce in Zürich during a period (1918–20) when six of the eighteen episodes of *Ulysses* were being drafted. Interweaving reminiscence with commentary, he makes the strange book seem an eminently natural one for a normal man to have conceived, rooted as it is, like Budgen's apprehension of it, in everyday fact. Its centre, for him, wasn't system or correspondence but Leopold Bloom, a beset indestructible man. Bloom was accessible to Budgen as he wrote, *Ulysses* spread open before him. Conversations from a dozen years in the past, which on his pages have the immediacy of *Ulysses* itself, were in part remembered, in part synthesised from Joyce's letters and from note-sheets with which Joyce began to ply him as soon as the memoir was under way. For hard biographical detail the book is less than wholly reliable (its single most famous story, alas, can't be quite accurate).[12] As an introduction to *Ulysses* it is still unsurpassed.

Partly, this is because there is so much quotation. Like Gilbert, Budgen was compelled to assume a reader who had never seen *Ulysses* and was prevented by law from obtaining a copy. Episode by episode, therefore, he supplied orienting information and sample passages, of a kind that would now be elided into a page reference. Had *Ulysses* been available to British readers in 1934, *James Joyce and the Making of 'Ulysses'* would have been a slighter book: a book of anecdotes. And in 1936 *Ulysses* did become available in the United Kingdom, as since 1933 it had been in the United States.

At about this time James Joyce, long entoiled in *Finnegans Wake*, left the Book of Bloom to fend for itself. The main lines were laid down: the Homeric parallel explicated, the titles of the episodes placed on record, the book's rationality affirmed and, above all, thanks to Budgen, the centrality of Bloom. 'A complete man,' Joyce had told Budgen; 'a good man'. Fiction's good men are few.

NOTES

1 Cited in Herbert Gorman, *James Joyce* (New York, 1939), 296. The hoarding is visible in the photo opposite p. 298.
2 Ronald Hayman, *Leavis* (London, 1976), 8.
3 Noyes's review in the *Manchester Sunday Guardian* is cited by Gorman, 295.
4 In a conversation reported by F. O. Matthiessen, *The Achievement of T. S. Eliot*, 3rd edn (New York, 1959), 135.
5 T. S. Eliot, '*Ulysses*, Order and Myth', *Dial*, November 1923, 480–3.
6 Ezra Pound, 'James Joyce et Pécuchet', in his *Polite Essays* (London, 1937), 82–97.
7 From *Revue de Paris*, cited in Gorman, 303.
8 Cited in ibid., 302.
9 T. S. Eliot, *The Use of Poetry and the Use of Criticism* (London, 1933), 150.
10 Joyce, *Letters*, III, 83. His next remarks are shrewd: 'Mr Larbaud gave the reading public about six months ago the phrase "interior monologue". . . . Now they want a new phrase. They cannot manage more than about one such phrase every six months – not for lack of intelligence but because they are in a hurry.'
11 That different observers will see different phenomena is guaranteed by *parallax*, a principle Joyce explicitly installed by name in the book itself, where the word is used six times.
12 This is the anecdote about a day's work on two sentences of 'Lestrygonians', which Budgen claims to have heard Joyce recite in their final form, though as the Rosenbach manuscript reveals he'd thought an earlier, more conventional version sufficiently final to copy out. Frank Budgen, *James Joyce and the Making of 'Ulysses'* (London, 1972), 20.

CHAPTER 2

'O, an Impossible Person!'

What the first readers of *Ulysses* were meant to know of its author may be gathered from *A Portrait of the Artist as a Young Man*, in which a youth named Stephen from a moneyless Irish Catholic home undergoes a Jesuit education, opts against the priesthood and for what he calls 'Life' – which connotes living somewhere else – develops a subtle dogmatism about aesthetics, defines the terms of a struggle in which 'silence, exile, and cunning' will be his weapons, and on the last page is poised to fly abroad, 'to encounter for the millionth time the reality of experience and to forge in the smithy of my soul the uncreated conscience of my race'.

We learn all this, at any rate, about Stephen, and to some extent we know it of Joyce, too. To what extent? While there can be no doubt that the book mirrors James Joyce's childhood and adolescence, we cannot feel confident that the mirroring is steady and whole. The book's method is insidious; told in the third person until the last few pages, where a transcription from Stephen's diary supervenes, it mimics a tranquil narrative detachment while in fact confining us to Stephen's view of everything.

For decades there have been readers aplenty to accept Stephen's view, and it is reasonable to ask if the *Portrait* provides sanctions for doing anything else. The question is of more than biographical interest, since Stephen, grown a year or two older, is a principal character in *Ulysses*, too, and what we are to make of him there depends a good deal on whether he has the author's complete indulgence. Stephen's way of experiencing and judging may seem so thoroughly to pervade the *Portrait* that there is no way he can be appraised: whatever he says or does seems utterly reasonable.

A written style, however: that is something to appraise, once we become aware of it; and the *Portrait* makes us highly aware of style by the unusual device, much extended and complicated in *Ulysses*, of changing the style continually, from the Stein-like sub-style of the first pages to the wrought periods of the last.

Every reader perceives that as Stephen's experience increases the prose grows more resourceful. At first we find short words and para-tactic sentences:

To remember that and the white look of the lavatory made him feel cold and then hot. There were two cocks that you turned and water came out: cold and hot. He felt cold and then a little hot: and he could see the names printed on the cocks. That was a very queer thing. (11)

And here, from a late page, is the cry of circling birds:

He listened to the cries: like the shriek of mice behind the wainscot: a shrill twofold note. But the notes were long and shrill and whirring, unlike the cry of vermin, falling a third or a fourth and trilled as the flying beaks clove the air. Their cry was shrill and clear and fine and falling like threads of silken light unwound from whirring spools. (224)

The difference is a measure of Stephen's increased adeptness: for the language, without our being quite told so, is really his, and we are to understand that the simile of whirring spools originates in his mind. The canons of imitative form would be satisfied were the style simply to mature as the subject ages. But in the *Portrait*, equivocally, intermittently, we are to think of Stephen as *responsible* for the style: certainly at moments of perceptual intensity, when it tends to exhibit effects we can sense him admiring.

Though he outgrows admirations, they circumscribe him while they are indulged. Thus shortly before he enters the University he has a period of conspicuous indulgence in *chiasmus*: 'The towels with which they smacked their bodies were heavy with cold seawater: and drenched with cold brine was their matted hair' (168). Subject$_1$ was [predicate]: and [similar predicate] was likewise Subject$_2$.

In celebrating its rituals of finality, *chiasmus* leaves after-vibrations of sententiousness by which the young man does not seem to be troubled. 'There's English for you,' part of his mind is saying, and his fondness, at this period, for this figure – 'The clouds were drifting above him silently and silently the seatangle was drifting below him' – as well as for variations on it – 'An ecstasy of flight made radiant his eyes and wild his breath and tremulous and wild and radiant his windswept limbs' – affects his very perceptions with a certain staginess, something to bear in mind when we come to the celebrated paragraph in which a girl standing in a tidal stream becomes the apparition of a wild angel, 'the angel of mortal youth and beauty, an envoy from the fair courts of life'. For the paragraph that describes her, and studiously half-turns her into a bird, is written with ostentatious deliberation and brings itself to climax with a *chiasmus*: 'But her long fair hair was girlish: and girlish, and touched with the wonder of mortal beauty, her face.' *Chiasmus* is not conspicuous again in the book.

This girl, encountered near the end of the fourth chapter, embodies the future of multiform possibility on which Stephen has staked everything. He accords her so much significance because he is already excited; afflatus is sustaining paragraph after paragraph; now we hear of 'the holy silence of his ecstasy'. It is a silence induced by the following:

> A girl stood before him in midstream, alone and still, gazing out to sea. She seemed like one whom magic had changed into the likeness of a strange and beautiful seabird. Her long slender bare legs were delicate as a crane's and pure save where an emerald trail of seaweed had fastened itself as a sign upon the flesh. Her thighs, fuller and softhued as ivory, were bared almost to the hips where the white fringes of her drawers were like featherings of soft white down. Her slateblue skirts were kilted boldly about her waist and dovetailed behind her. Her bosom was as a bird's soft and slight, slight and soft as the breast of some darkplumaged dove. But her long fair hair was girlish: and girlish, and touched with the wonder of mortal beauty, her face. (171)

Assenting to Stephen's joy, we may let this prose work on us as it seems to want to, and later think it bad and overdone, Joyce trapped by the need, or the will, to make more of the experience than it will yield. But these are thoughtless readings. We ought to be asking what the passage *is*. And once the *chiasmus*, or some other sign, has prompted us to scan it curiously it comes to seem a young man's copybook page: not exactly an experience we are to share with Stephen, but something like a piece he might have written out afterwards, practising his new vocation.

'Her bosom was as a bird's soft and slight, slight and soft as the breast of some darkplumaged dove.' We may note the chiasmic detailing, also the omitted comma which makes the first clause say 'soft and slight as a bird's', not 'as a bird's in being soft and slight', but say the simpler thing the more portentously. We should reflect that Stephen would have been 16,[1] and would be working from the kind of preliminary outline in which his Jesuit masters had drilled him. So a topic sentence proposes the optical fact, a girl, and a second sentence rolls up its sleeves to state what the paragraph will elucidate, that she seems changed by magic into the likeness of a seabird. Four more sentences deal with this statement as though it were a proposition to be demonstrated; each, beginning with 'Her', affirms something birdlike of a separate part of her body, the scan proceeding upward, her legs, her thighs, her waist, her bosom. Then an orderly 'But', when we come to hair and face, affirms the unvanquished categories of girlishness, with the solemnly cadenced *chiasmus* to achieve finality.

This passage, like the narrative sequence of which it is an element, is as nicely calculated as the poem on Parnell which a journalist named Hynes recites at the end of Joyce's story 'Ivy Day in the Committee Room'. The rightness of the poem as Joyce concocted it has been justly celebrated ever since Padraic Colum drew attention to the way real feeling breaks through its hand-me-down idiom.[2]

> *He lies slain by the coward hounds*
> *He raised to glory from the mire;*
> *And Erin's hopes and Erin's dreams*
> *Perish upon her monarch's pyre.*

No one has ever surpassed James Joyce's skill at contriving plausible limits for expressive competence, and like Hynes's poem Stephen's paragraph careers near the brink of parody without detriment to our awareness that something enchanting has happened.

What happened next was that the girl turned her head toward Stephen and discovered that he was looking at her; after a long exchange of stares she then lowered her eyes and commenced paddling about with her foot, and blushed. This is re-created as follows:

She was alone and still, gazing out to sea; and when she felt his presence and the worship of his eyes her eyes turned to him in quiet sufferance of his gaze, without shame or wantonness. Long, long she suffered his gaze and then quietly withdrew her eyes from his and bent them towards the stream, gently stirring the water with her foot hither and thither. The first faint noise of gently moving water broke the silence, low and faint and whispering, faint as the bells of sleep; hither and thither, hither and thither; and a faint flame trembled on her cheek.

We should recall that the year is about 1898, and that she is posed like a naughty beauty on a cigarette card of that period; her skirts tucked up and her bare legs on show. Pictorially considered, this apparition is thoroughly conventional *Kitsch*. Socially considered, she is a very cool young woman indeed for those times; there are hints in *Ulysses* that a girl at leisure on the beach may even be of dubious virtue. (Leopold Bloom sees three girls on Sandymount strand, and two of them, or their namesakes, later turn up in Nighttown.)

Symbolically, she is easier to assimilate; she combines a conventional late-nineteenth-century emblem, Woman Epitome of the Ennobling, with the bird-motif that twines its way through the *Portrait*, from the vengeful eagles of the opening sequence to the birds of augury watched outside the library and the emblematic kinsmen who shake 'the wings of their

exultant and terrible youth' in the antepenultimate entry in Stephen's
diary. A charming awkwardness, even, may inhere in his effort to
combine these emblems, bird and girl, so soon after finding a prophetic
force in his own strange surname, which is Dedalus.

> Now, at the name of the fabulous artificer, he seemed to hear the
> noise of dim waves and to see a winged form flying above the waves
> and slowly climbing the air. What did it mean? Was it a quaint device
> opening a page of some medieval book of prophecies and symbols, a
> hawklike man flying sunward above the sea, a prophecy of the end
> he had been born to serve and had been following through the mists
> of childhood and boyhood, a symbol of the artist forging anew in his
> workshop out of the sluggish matter of the earth a new soaring
> impalpable imperishable being? (169)

We may say that the *Portrait* is unified by Stephen's twenty years'
effort to substitute one father for another. In the first sentence his father,
of the 'hairy face', is telling him a story about a moocow. That father
descends – '. . . a small landlord, a small investor, a drinker, a good
fellow, a storyteller, somebody's secretary, something in a distillery, a
taxgatherer, a bankrupt and at present a praiser of his own past' (241) –
and in the book's last sentence the word 'father' points past him, aloft:
'Old father, old artificer, stand me now and ever in good stead.' Now
Stephen is praying, as it were, to his name-saint, the pagan Dedalus,
a father whose example represents liberty from the father who has gone
down so far in the world. Appealing from father to father was a habit
formed early. In the first chapter, after Father Dolan beats him, Father
Conmee promises him safety. In the third chapter Father Arnall's
sermons scare him witless and a nameless Father grants him absolution
As these priestly examples indicate, fatherhood is rather a role than an
estate; to shift fathers is for the son, too, to shift roles, to be no longer
the son of a drunken bankrupt but heir to the vocation of the fabulous
artificer.

In Chapter IV a different possibility is dangled before him: he may
think of becoming the Reverend Stephen Dedalus, SJ. He would owe
allegiance to the Holy Father, and be himself Father Dedalus. But no
sooner does the Director of Studies formulate this possibility than Stephen
knows it is unreal, and he finds himself wondering at 'the remoteness of
his soul from what he had hitherto imagined her sanctuary, at the faint
hold which so many years of order and obedience had on him when once
a definite and irrevocable act of his threatened to end forever, in time
and eternity, his freedom' (161). And as he picks his way homeward
through the slum where the Dedaluses live now he smiles 'to think that
it was this disorder, the misrule and confusion of his father's house and

the stagnation of vegetable life, which was to win the day in his soul' (162).

We learn from these important sentences that Stephen has for a long time vaguely assumed that the priesthood lay ahead.[3] Now that he knows he will never be a priest, the alternative appears to be his father's 'misrule and confusion'.

It is in the final part of Chapter IV that a new alternative to 'misrule and confusion' presents itself. His schooldays are behind him; entry to the University has been arranged; he feels an elated freedom; his soul (he soon phrases it) has 'arisen from the grave of boyhood'. And the revelation comes: 'Yes! Yes! Yes! He would create proudly out of the freedom and power of his soul, as the great artificer whose name he bore, a living thing, new and soaring and beautiful, impalpable, imperishable' (170).

It is then that he sees the girl, and almost smothers whatever it was he saw beneath an appliqué of bird-phrases. If this written-out bird-girl is an instance of the 'new and soaring and beautiful', the artificer is off to a doubtful start. Still, the life of an excited 16-year-old seems to have acquired a momentum.

What he writes in the fifth chapter isn't better: a Swinburnian villanelle, very much of the nineties, to a Temptress who might have been painted by Gustave Moreau –

> And still you hold our longing gaze
> With languorous look and lavish limb! (223)

– 'lure of the fallen seraphim', in fact, to whom go up 'smoke of praise', a world-wide 'eucharistic hymn', and an uplifted 'chalice flowing to the brim' in which beneath the trappings of studio satanism we can just discern a naughty nineties wine-glass: wine and woman and song, no less. The account of the poem's composition permits us the dry observation that Stephen is writing, still in bed of a morning, in the afterglow of a wet dream. In France the Symbolist Movement, villanelle-makers at its fringes, was staffed by lapsed Catholics in quest of efficacious words of power, and Stephen, too, thinks of himself as 'a priest of eternal imagination, transmuting the daily bread of experience into the radiant body of everliving life' (221). So the old destiny and the new have fused.

Stephen's other achievements in this final chapter include the outlines of a theory of the beautiful and an extended prose style which still courts Newman and Pater but can make do tellingly with the short sentence. 'Talked rapidly of myself and my plans. In the midst of it I unluckily made a sudden gesture of a revolutionary nature. I must have looked like a fellow throwing a handful of peas into the air. People began to look at us. She shook hands a moment after and, in going away, said she hoped I would do what I said.' That is from Stephen's diary entry for 15 April, and if it has a little fun with her hope that he would do what he said it has fun with the figure he was cutting, too. 'Welcome, O Life,' he writes on the 26th, and the prayer to the Old Father is dated the 27th. Stephen's departure from Ireland is surely imminent and, if it is 1902, Ascension Day is eleven days off.[4]

Had James Joyce died in mid-1914, leaving the *Portrait* for post-humous publication, it would no doubt be the kind of minor masterpiece, like Alain-Fournier's *Le Grand Meaulnes*, that is accorded enthusiastic rediscovery from time to time without ever quite commanding attention. Fitting it to the Joyce canon would present no problems, since the rest of the canon would consist only of the thirty-six poems of *Chamber Music* which it is easy to imagine Stephen writing, and the fifteen stories of *Dubliners* which are perfectly compatible with the *Portrait* in presenting Dublin as a city to get out of. Some reader of all three books might occasionally ponder the fact that the careful documentary prose of the stories predates the bird-girl rhapsody.

> Mrs. Mooney was a butcher's daughter. She was a woman who was quite able to keep things to herself: a determined woman. She had married her father's foreman and opened a butcher's shop near Spring Gardens. But as soon as his father-in-law was dead Mr. Mooney began to go to the devil. He drank, plundered the till, ran headlong into debt. It was no use making him take the pledge: he was sure to break out again a few days after. By fighting his wife in the presence of customers and by buying bad meat he ruined the business. One night he went for his wife with the cleaver and she had to sleep in a neighbour's house. (61)

That compresses much character, incident and observation into a few lines, and why the man who had written it in 1905 should eight or nine years later be writing of a bosom 'as a bird's soft and slight, slight and soft as the breast of some darkplumaged dove' is a question we can imagine being answered in several ways, supposing this comparatively minor author seemed worth the speculation. There might not even seem to be a question; such a reader, in his nearly Joyce-less library, might actually prefer the darkplumaged prose and imagine a Joyce who before his unlucky death at 32 had evolved from mean little sentences all the way to a rhetoric of some amplitude. But we have the advantage over that reader that we have learned to prize a tautness and economy of little words and cunning syntax as a consequence of the revolution of taste at the centre of which stands *Ulysses*, and it is now as impossible to imagine a twentieth-century literature without *Ulysses* as to imagine a twentieth-century physics without Relativity.

It is *Ulysses* that compels the attention the rest of the canon routinely receives: that has trained the readers who can see how much is achieved in *Dubliners*, or are willing to venture amid the lianas and mocking mirrors of the *Wake*. And, in being a book in which Stephen figures again, *Ulysses* reacts with the *Portrait* in complex ways. Is his being back in Dublin a grim joke of fortune? Or is he to find only here the Life to which he bade welcome? At any rate, he has tumbled from aloft into a very different sort of book, one he cannot dominate as he dominated the *Portrait*. He walks out of it near the end, as if out of the universe.

The *Portrait* is a book of vignettes and inner symmetries, so compliant to the fluid play of Stephen's memory that the reader must exert attention, against the suasions of the text, to keep even some rudimentary grasp on chronology. A publisher rejected it in 1916 for being 'discursive, formless, unrestrained' and needing to be 'pulled into shape'.[5] It had cost Joyce years of effort to pull it out of the shape in which the unfinished first version, *Stephen Hero*, had implicated it, and if a first-time reader is unlikely to perceive that in Chapter I everything between the first row of asterisks and the second, from 'The wide playgrounds . . .' to '. . . the water's edge', takes place in a twenty-four-hour span, or if the cunning with which the three episodes and diary of Chapter V reverse the overture and three episodes of Chapter I went unnoticed for sixty years,[6] Joyce had achieved what he thought the book required, a fluidity with a rigour deep beneath it. Time and place are equally understressed. It is only the death of Parnell that establishes what part of the nineteenth century we are in, and Dublin, when the Dedalus family moves there from Bray, is presented with no special vividness: a large squalid commercial city with some local history like all cities.

But the calculated vagueness of the *Portrait* answers the imperatives of a nearly solipsistic novel. In *Dubliners* (written 1904–7) Joyce had specified times, places, idioms so stubbornly the book's publication was delayed for years while publishers fretted over single words that registered quiddities of dialogue ('. . . if any fellow tried that sort of a game on with his sister he'd bloody well put his teeth down his throat, so he would') or designated actual pubs by name ('Nosey Flynn was sitting up in his usual corner of Davy Byrne's'). Joyce declined to delete this one 'bloody' from 'The Boarding House', though elsewhere in the book there were other 'bloody's' he would sacrifice 'with infinite regret', because 'the word, the exact expression I have used, is in my opinion the one expression in the English language which can create on the reader the effect which I wish to create', and he declined to delete mention of Davy Byrne's and several other pubs from 'Counterparts', though in other stories he had used fictitious pub-names, because they served as ports of call in a rain-soaked Odyssey: 'the names are real because the persons walked from place to place',[7] and to alter them, he implied, would be like inventing fictitious substitutes for Genoa, Istanbul, Marseilles. In fiction certain things at least had to be *so*, and in *Ulysses* the list of what could not be altered grew enormously longer. Some time after *Ulysses* was published Joyce told Arthur Power:

> In realism you are down to facts on which the world is based: that sudden reality which smashes romanticism into a pulp. What makes most people's lives unhappy is some disappointed romanticism, some unrealizable or misconceived ideal. In fact you may say that idealism is the ruin of man, and if we lived down to fact, as primitive man had to do, we would be better off. That is what we were made for. Nature is quite unromantic. It is we who put romance into her, which is a false attitude, an egotism, absurd like all egotisms. In *Ulysses* I tried to keep close to fact.[8]

In *Ulysses*, clocks and church-bells keep us aware of the hour, a stenographer's typewriter clicks out day, month and year ('16 June 1904'), newspapers specify local and world events, and feet move on clearly named streets past clearly named houses and places of business, several hundred with specified and verifiable addresses.

All this has an immediate effect on our sense of Stephen Dedalus, whose mind in the old way can transport us instantly from Sandymount strand to Paris, but whose body, now subject to the necessity of getting some six miles from Dalkey (10.30 a.m.) to the strand (11.05 a.m.), would have been borne on the Dalkey tram from Castle Street, Dalkey, to Haddington Road, thence on the Sandymount line to Tritonville Road. Though the book does not particularise this journey it permits us to work it out, and the Stephen who must take the new electric trams[9] to be in definite places at definite times is no longer in command of the new book the way his psyche was in command of the *Portrait*.

A worked example may be in order. Stephen is free to leave his post at Mr Deasy's school early because it is Thursday, a half-day, and the latter half of the half-day is for hockey, starting 'at ten' (2.92). After the boys file out he spends a few minutes with a boy named Sargent, and rather longer with his headmaster Deasy, who types in his presence the final sentences of a letter. The two conversations and the business with the typewriter delay him till perhaps 10.30. He is next seen near Watery Lane (6.39) from the carriage of a funeral procession which was to start at eleven (5.94) and has been under way perhaps five minutes; he would then be walking from the tram-stop in Tritonville Road to the beach. So he has come from Dalkey (six miles) in about half an hour; the logistic details can be deduced from a tram-map.[10]

Though no reader need feel obliged to perform such researches, anyone can welcome their corroboration of the sureness we feel underlying each page of the book. Joyce obeyed a principle Hemingway later enunciated, that a writer's omissions will show only when he omits things because he doesn't know them, and he worked out elaborate *schemata* so as to be able to suppress them. Except for the funeral cortège, with which we ride swaying and rattling clear across the city with frequent indications of time and place ('Are we late?' asks Martin Cunningham; Paddy Dignam has an appointment with the grave), Joyce only once (10.113) takes us aboard the wheeled conveyances his characters use so freely. An abrupt cessation of action here, an abrupt resumption there – such is his staccato notation: the cut, not the dissolve. The effect, for a reader trained on the *Portrait's* suave transitions (where cuts signify the passage of days, or years) is one of calculated disorientation: Where are we now? How did we get here?

We see Stephen Dedalus leave Deasy's school in Dalkey; the eye traversing a narrow white space on the page next picks him up on the strand framing sentences about ineluctable modalities (3.1). Especially when we reflect that he must have just alighted from a tram, we can guess why he should be musing on entrapment in a space–time continuum, moving 'a very short space of time through very short times of space' the interstices of which Joyce plotted with such rigorous care it is possible to account for the entire day, 8 a.m. to midnight, of a secondary character, Buck Mulligan, whose onstage appearances are only four in number and widely separated.[11]

Deasy's typewriter, two telephones, the brand-new electric trams, some talk of motorcars – these epitomise a Dublin that has changed since Stephen walked its streets in the *Portrait.* Machinery is interpenetrating the ancient, stagnant city. More important, gadgetry epitomises a shift of emphasis between the two books. In *Ulysses*, as Joyce's friend and one of his best commentators, the late Frank Budgen, shrewdly observes, people have 'just that social time sense that is part of the general social mentality of the period, and no more. This arises out of the necessity for coordinating their daily social movements. . . . James Watt invented the steam engine, and the steam engine begat the locomotive, and the locomotive begat the timetable, forcing people to . . . think in minutes where their great-grandfathers thought in hours. . . . The discoveries of the astronomer and the mathematician have less immediate effect on [social time-sense] than the electrification of the suburban lines.'[12]

Now, all this was true, if less egregiously true, of the Dublin of the *Portrait*, the last chapter of which precedes the action of *Ulysses* by no more than a couple of years. Joyce opened that chapter, though, by explicitly stressing Stephen's indifference to the space–time grid.

– How much is the clock fast now?

His mother straightened the battered alarmclock that was lying on its side in the middle of the mantelpiece until its dial showed a quarter to twelve and then laid it once more on its side.

– An hour and twentyfive minutes, she said. The right time now is twenty past ten. The dear knows you might try to be in time for your lectures. (174)

Lost in his thoughts, he sets out on a walk of over two miles to the University, and has not gone halfway when a clock beats 'eleven strokes in swift precision'.

Eleven! Then he was late for that lecture too. What day of the week was it? He stopped at a newsagent's to read the headline of a placard. Thursday. Ten to eleven, English: eleven to twelve, French; twelve to one, physics. (177)

He sees almost nothing of the city's busy morning life. His passage past Trinity and along the awninged and thronged bustle of Grafton Street – a route Bloom traces in *Ulysses*, on pages thronged with sensuous particulars (8.401–640) – is obliterated by much revery and reminiscence from which a flower-seller's hand on his arm arouses him. He arrives too late for the English class, or the French. As if in anticipation of the norms of *Ulysses*, the only class Stephen can attend that day is physics, where on borrowed paper he copies 'spectrelike symbols of force and velocity', and hears words about an ellipsoidal ball and about the currents that induce magnetism in coils.

Ulysses lets us know that its doings are transacted in a designated zone on the surface of the magnetic ellipsoidal earthball, near the intersection of its 53rd parallel of latitude, north, and its sixth meridian of longitude, west (17.2303). It is 1904, 16 June (10.376). The sun rose at 3.33 a.m. local time, will set at 8.27 p.m. The action of the book begins at 8 a.m. atop the Martello tower at Sandycove. And the book is no more than a few pages old when we commence to divine that Stephen, returned from Paris, has become a drinker like his father Simon.

He has not changed fathers after all; and, no longer sustained by the myth of sonship to the fabulous artificer, he is becoming another improvident Dublin character. People notice his resemblance to his father, the voice, the eyes; and he and Si Dedalus, pursuing their separate ways the length of the book, pursue them in parallel, never meeting, drinking, drinking. 'Chip of the old block!' (7.899) cries one of the company when Stephen suggests a pub. He uses up about a pound, drinking and treating, in a day when stout was twopence a pint and one could live on less than a pound a week. One time when father and son almost meet there is a suggestive parallelism of behaviour. Stephen's persistent sister Dilly extracts from her father 14*d* to feed the family (10.678–708). Just a few pages later (10.855) Stephen encounters her at a book-cart. Her intellectual cravings shadow his; she has spent a penny on Chardenal's French primer. He has at that moment over three pounds in his pocket (14.286). He indulges in eloquent unspoken words, pitying them both, but does not offer her a penny.

In neighbouring chapters we even see father and son performing: Si Dedalus in the Ormond Bar (11.658–760) in glorious song at the insistence of cronies, Stephen in the National Library (episode 9) fortified by three whiskeys (9.533) and performing with no less virtuosity his lengthy *Hamlet* turn, earlier scheduled for a pub. The Stephen of this book would appear to be headed toward as predictable a future as any of the young men in *Dubliners*, several of whom turn up in *Ulysses* as if to verify the sure workings of destiny. Corley is still the sponger of 'Two Gallants', Lenehan still the agile leech, while being son-in-law to Mrs Mooney of 'The Boarding House' as we might have expected drives Bob Doran to periodic benders. A great dreary stagnant mechanism, locked in space, locked in time, the city slowly turns its cogs and millwheels; men down their pints and emit their witticisms on schedule, and a married woman who isn't busy with children is very lonely.

But the air is bright, colours sparkle, the city has a carnival glitter, and in a long book free of the drizzle and cold that dominated so much of *Dubliners* we shall be spending many hours with a prudent citizen, a non-toper, a non-idler, who observes everything that goes on and has no quarrel with clock and tram necessities. He is Leopold Bloom. *Ulysses* is his book (he is 'Ulysses'), he dominates it, and Stephen is now a secondary character. And if the *Portrait* may be summarised as Stephen's effort to substitute one father for another, *Ulysses* may be (most imperfectly) summarised as the story of Bloom's futile effort to treat Stephen as a son. Stephen in *Ulysses* is no longer in search of a father, as he was in the *Portrait*. He is obsessed by a dead mother, and as for fathers, living or mythic, elected or adoptive, his present instinct is to get clear of them.

NOTES

1   Joyce (born 2 February 1882) was 16 in the summer that preceded his matriculation into the University. Not that Joyce's calendar is always a safe guide to Stephen's; see Appendix 1.

2   In his preface to the Modern Library *Dubliners*, dated October 1926. 'It is an amateurish and conventional piece of rhetoric, and yet, amazingly enough, a real grief and a real loyalty break through the hand-me-down

verse. . . . He must have entered into Hynes's mind before he could recreate the verses that have just the exact heat, just the exact flourishes that a passionate and semi-literate man would give to his subject according to the literary convention which he knew.'

3 cf. 'All through his boyhood he had mused upon that which he had so often thought to be his destiny and when the moment had come for him to obey the call he had turned aside, obeying a wayward instinct' (165).

4 Again, *if* it is 1902, as Joyce seems to have once intended. Appendix 1 explains why he changed to 1903, though the revisions were never quite completed. To let Stephen commence his flight on Ascension Day of whatever year would have been heavy-handed, but the connection asked to be made and while he was considering 1902 'eleven' would have seemed a good way to make it. Eleven is a recurrent Joyce-number. Bloom's son in *Ulysses* lived 11 days and would be in his eleventh year if he were alive on Bloomsday. The last phrase in *Finnegans Wake* has 11 words, and the text encodes variations on 11 throughout. By one gloss, 11 signifies renewal by inaugurating a new decade, and Joyce may have noticed that 1881, the year of his conception, is divisible by 11.

5 Richard Ellmann, *James Joyce* (New York, 1959), 416–7. The reader was Edward Garnett.

6 It was Hans Walter Gabler who spotted this chiasmatic structure. See his essay in Thomas F. Staley and Bernard Benstock, *Approaches to James Joyce's 'Portrait'* (Pittsburgh, Pa, 1976), 25–60.

7 *Letters*, II, 136, and II, 312.

8 Arthur Power, *Conversations with James Joyce* (London, 1974), 98.

9 The tram of an idyllic scene in the second chapter of the *Portrait* (69–70) is horse-drawn, but by 1904 Dublin had the most advanced electric tram system in Europe.

10 Expertise in the space–time continuum of *Ulysses* characterises some of the best recent Joyce scholarship. The analysis above is paraphrased from Clive Hart and Leo Knuth's *Topographical Guide to James Joyce's 'Ulysses'* (Colchester, 1975), 24. See also Clive Hart's essay and chart in the Clive Hart and David Hayman *James Joyce's 'Ulysses'* (Berkeley, Calif./London, 1974), 181–216, where minute by minute the movements of some thirty characters in the sixty-five-minute 'Wandering Rocks' episode are accounted for.

11 See Hart and Knuth, 35–6.

12 Budgen, 131–2.

CHAPTER 3

Uses of Homer

At this point exposition must acknowledge certain difficulties, epitomised by the fact that for nearly fifty years The Search for a Father has been a recurrent phrase in *Ulysses* criticism. Sponsored by Stuart Gilbert, loosely grounded in an ironic phrase of Buck Mulligan's,[1] it draws apparent sanction from the Homeric parallel to which the title of *Ulysses* points. For Stephen is Telemachus, and does not Telemachus seek his father Ulysses? 'Like Stephen,' Gilbert wrote in 1930, '. . . Telemachus sets out from Ithaca to Pylos in quest of his father.'[2] Gilbert's unstated premise is that Homer tells us what Stephen is doing: a natural error of emphasis at a time when finding any way to grasp the book at all was a reader's major problem. But here as often – as, obviously, with Penelope's fidelity – the parallel is a dangerous guide to what is actually happening. We need to observe what the characters are up to before we can ask what to make of the Homeric presence.

Finding out what the characters are up to – in most novels a routine tracing of the narrative – can be unexpectedly difficult in *Ulysses*. For one thing, characters are out of sight for long periods, during which they are spending their time in ways Joyce was quite clear about. Had he written the Shakespeare plays he would have known how many children Lady Macbeth had, and their ages, and what course of study Hamlet pursued at Wittenberg. When he expects us to fill gaps he leaves clues that are barely sufficient; thus when we re-encounter Stephen (14.192) after nearly seven hours his drunken state and the amount of money we can deduce he has spent (by subtracting what he now displays – 14.286 – from what he was paid – 2.222, point to a way of filling up that time that is later confirmed by a list of pubs (15.2518) and by his still later statement that he didn't dine at all (16.1572).

For another thing, what happens in plain sight is sometimes so sparely narrated we must piece its epiphenomena together, and is sometimes almost concealed by linguistic energies that are affirming motifs of their own. It is easy to make large mistakes, and not surprising that a bold man like Harry Blamires[3] has made some little ones, incident to his useful effort to supply a 260-page narrative paraphrase of the entire book. 'There's eleven of them' (14.1562) we read amid a confusion of revellers leaving a pub, and Mr Blamires, noting 'the true apostolic number', wonders where an eleventh man came from.[4] But 'eleven' refers to the strokes of the closing-time clock. 'Time all. There's eleven of them. Get ye gone. Forward, woozy wobblers! Night. Night.'

And, finally, Joyce has not the melodramatist's trust in motivation, which more often than we may have been aware has served the novelist as a narrative lubricant. Popular novels – easy to write and read – are peopled with beings who each want one clear thing, and so plotted as to entangle these lines of desire. The thief wants to save his skin, the sleuth wants to catch the thief, the lady wants her jewels returned, the hero wants to impress the lady: at any juncture in however complex a weaving of these threads we need only glimpse one of these characters looking left and right in the street to divine what is happening, and narration can be episodic without confusing us. *Ulysses* contains one character, Blazes Boylan, who wants one clear thing, to bed Molly Bloom. He will succeed because he is a cardboard seducer, modelled on the swashing adulterers in the novels with which Molly occupies her time. He can even place a red carnation between his teeth (10.334) and keep it there while he saunters down Grafton Street (10.1150). So when we encounter the following scene –

> The blond girl in Thornton's bedded the wicker basket with rustling fibre. Blazes Boylan handed her the bottle swathed in pink tissue paper and a small jar.
> – Put these in first, will you? he said.
> – Yes, sir, the blond girl said. And the fruit on top. (10.299)

– we are not bewildered for a moment: he is buying Molly an offering. Subsequently, at another reading, we may enjoy penetrating the spare 'Thornton's', expandable with the aid of *Thom's Official Directory* (1904) into 'J. Thornton, 63 Grafton St., fruiterer & florist to H.M. the King, H.E. the Lord Lieutenant, and H.R.H. the Duke of Connaught, K.G., etc.', and conclude (with Professor Hart, who turned up this information[5]) that Boylan is treating Molly to the best. But we needn't, to follow the story.

Likewise a number of minor characters are governed whenever we chance to encounter them by desire for more drink, or for a good tip on the horse-race, or both. They vary the narrative surface and present no problem.

But, in the absence of an overarching quest after woman, drink or money, a character glimpsed in a vignette may puzzle us. Thus Corny Kelleher, whom we first encounter as an undertaker (6.92), is next displayed for half a page (10.206) in the doorway of his establishment doing nothing of import. Constable 57C pauses to pass the time of day and then imparts cryptic words: 'I seen that particular party last evening.' The vignette ends here and we are left quite blank unless we recall a rumour about Kelleher, 'police tout' (5.14), further encoded (8.441) as 'Corny Kelleher he has Harvey Duff in his eye'. (Harvey Duff was the police informer in *The Shaughrann*, a play less well known now than it was to Joyce's generation.) Once these details are correlated, Corny's intimacy with a policeman is comprehensible. More important, we can understand why several hundred pages later (15.4811) officers on the night beat greet him by name and disappear when he gives them the hint.

And so an auctorial purpose emerges. Joyce needed a way to get rid of these officers so Stephen would not be arrested for drunken assault and could be taken in charge instead by Bloom. But typically, at this moment of Kelleher's maximum usefulness to the plot, none of the careful groundwork is recalled and nothing overt reminds us of the man's leverage. We must simply watch how everyone behaves and draw on copious memory.

The 'motivated' characters in *Ulysses* – the Boylans, Bob Dorans, Lenehans, not to mention the insanely patriotic 'Citizen' – are apt to be figures of fun; 'motive', for Joyce, is comedy's simplification. The more we know of anyone the harder it is to say what he is about, he is about so many things, and the harder also to specify why he does any of them. This fact has two important consequences. Even with considerable narrative assistance the first-time reader is often unsure what exactly Leopold Bloom is doing, and the expositor finds exact summarising statements surprisingly difficult to frame.

Consider the transaction with Bloom's letter. Early in the book's fifth episode Mr Bloom furtively slips a card from the lining of his hat, feigns an elaborate carelessness, enters Westland Row post office, presents the card and receives an envelope addressed 'Henry Flower, Esq.' (5.25, 5.62). So he is receiving letters under a pseudonym. None of this is at all difficult to follow, though the narrative phrases are embedded in sharply noted revery and some five hundred words of Joyce's must be traversed with more attention than a chapter of Ian Fleming's.

What follows is characteristic. Bloom regains the street, opening the envelope without removing it from his pocket. The next words are: 'McCoy. Get rid of him quickly. Take me out of my way. Hate company when you.' Whereupon the letter drops wholly out of the text (out of Bloom's mind?), and if this is our first experience of *Ulysses* we may be forgiven if we have quite forgotten it by the time it is spread out before us nearly six pages later (5.241). Some small talk with McCoy has intervened, and some strolling, and gazing at hoardings, and a memory of how moved his father was by a performance of *Leah*; also ruminations on horses and on cabmen. . . . Is it correct to say that he is all the while in search of a secluded place to read? If he is, then why is so evident a purpose, which would have lent narrative urgency to all those distractions, allowed to drop out of mind?

There are several answers. Looking closely, we can perceive Bloom's overriding anxiety, that no one who knows him shall see him doing anything in the least unusual: hence the attention he bestows on doing perfectly ordinary things. Thus, when he wonders if McCoy may be following him, 'Mr Bloom stood at the corner, his eyes wandering over the multicoloured hoardings. Cantrell and Cochrane's Ginger Ale (Aromatic). Clery's Summer Sale. No, he's going on straight' (5.192).

Drawing back a little, we next reflect that Bloom is putting in time before a funeral, more than an hour in which he will also order some prescription lotion, buy soap, have a bath, and get out to Sandymount. Collecting his *poste restante* letter is one of the hour's minor objectives, not to be invested with narrative tension. (The correspondence with Martha – on the whole a tepid amusement – at no time bulks large in his scheme of things.)

Taking a still longer view, we remember how this hour is placed in the day. In a state of near-nescience, Bloom is wandering almost at random, thinking of everything but the main thing he found out an hour before, that Boylan will cuckold him this afternoon. This he must not dwell on. Much of his aimlessness in the vicinity of Westland Row is referable to an interaction between the need not to think of Boylan and the desire not to be noticed himself, neither of which can be articulated intelligibly.

And we may withdraw to a farther remove, where the episode's Homeric parallel, Lotos-Eaters, appears to take charge of much of its random detail: the warmth, the directionless walk,[6] the gelded horses munching in their nosebags, the communicants in the church Bloom passes through, the chemist's chloroform and poppysyrup, the lemony smell of the soap, the anticipated warm bath. At this remove questions of purpose fade away, and we contemplate a pure array of narcotic elements, the narrative structure nearly unnoticeable, deeds and doers turned into a drift of symbols.

This is decorous when the Homeric theme is narcosis, but is apt to occur whatever the Homeric theme, and years of concentration on the large-scale patterns, commencing with Gilbert's Homeric emphasis of 1930, have fostered an expositor's *Ulysses* in which characters sleepwalk through a grand design laid down by the Ionian Homeridae, and very little happens save the display of eighteen successive *tableaux vivants*.

Such a design has the advantage of being easy to diagram. Joyce himself while the book was in progress would invariably describe it to strangers in Homeric terms. 'I am now writing a book based on the wanderings of Ulysses,' he told Frank Budgen at their second meeting (summer 1918). 'The Odyssey, that is to say, serves me as a ground plan. Only my time is recent time and all my hero's wanderings take no more than eighteen hours.'[7] It is hard to think of three sentences better contrived to turn an unwritten book into something that could be talked about. Later, if you were a critic struggling simultaneously with the queer book and with the need to describe it for readers who had not seen it, you would find the parallel more manageable than the text. Joyce, who knew the value of informed articles, prepared his famous *schemata* for just such contingencies. One went to Carlo Linati in late 1920 to help him write an article. A year later Valery Larbaud received a somewhat different one to help him prepare a lecture. It was emphasised that they were not to be shown around. In the *Ulysses* manuscripts Homeric indications were confined to the title. The eighteen chapter-headings – catch-words to identify the dominant correspondence of the moment – turn up only in letters, *schemata* and reports of Joyce's conversation. The book readers were to see would hint at a hidden plan only on its title-page: a neat instance of Joyce's trust in synecdoche.

Restored to currency by Gilbert in 1930, the episode-titles have since become so familiar we sometimes forget they are not part of the text. Their usefulness points up one of the salient peculiarities of *Ulysses*: the identity each of its eighteen episodes assumes, by contrast with the relatively anonymous chapters of normal novels. 'Episode', a word Joyce used consistently, suggests something more bounded than a chapter, and one episode apiece was assigned to eighteen critics for a volume to commemorate the book's fiftieth anniversary. One critic per episode would seem a bizarre subdivision of attention for normal fictions but it is right for *Ulysses* and would have seemed right to Joyce, who wrote to Linati: 'Each adventure is so to say one person although it is composed of persons – as Aquinas relates of the angelic hosts.'[8]

The episodes' differences from one another are deeply rooted in Joyce's stubborn conception and plainly manifested in the verbal textures: scan a few lines, and you know where you are in the book. 'Each adventure (that is, every hour, every organ, every art being interconnected and interrelated in the structural scheme of the whole) should not only condition but create its own technique.'

As the word 'adventure' indicates, his first thoughts about the book were rooted in his adolescent reading of Charles Lamb's *The Story of Ulysses*, where the heading of the first chapter reads:

The Cicons. – The Fruit of the Lotos-Tree. – Polyphemous and the Cyclops. – The Kingdom of the Winds, and God Aeolus's Fatal Present. – The Laestrygonian Man-eaters.

Lamb's highly readable retelling for children disregards Homer's folding-back of time-schemes, embedding of narratives within narratives, son

seeking father, father seeking home, gods deliberating, interfering. In
Lamb's version there is no son seeking a father at all. Nor are any
scenes set anywhere but on earth. Lamb's concentration is wholly on
Ulysses, his ordering of the incidents is chronological, and his unit of
attention is the adventure.

Encountered by Joyce at twelve, this version so impressed itself on
his exceptional memory that he seems to have read versions of the Greek
text as though they were expansions and rearrangements of Lamb.
When he planned *Ulysses* the 'adventure' was his unit, and the core of
the book consists of twelve episodes in chronological order, each based
on one adventure, each independently elaborated and bounded.

An episode of *Ulysses* is a space–time block of words, approximately
one hour long on its time axis, and extended in Dublin space as little
as a few yards ('Penelope') or up to four miles ('Hades'). It normally
lingers some time in one or more enclosures – Davy Byrne's pub, an
office in the National Library – and normally ends with a principal
character moving on to some other place. (But the three main structural
divisions all end with a *stasis*: Stephen looking back at a ship–3.503–
Bloom standing over Stephen–15.4955–Molly drifting off to sleep–
18.1609. Thus the first episode of all, called 'Telemachus', opens in
sunlight atop the Martello tower, shifts to a dim tower room, then
conducts us down the sunlit path to the Forty-Foot Hole where Mulligan
swims; as it ends we are following Stephen away.

The shifts are kaleidoscopic, and readers acquire the illusion of having
travelled all over Dublin City. In fact Stephen and Bloom between them
cover, by tram, by coach and on foot, nearly thirty miles in the course
of Bloomsday. Like Homer, Joyce keeps his protagonists moving.

Several episodes – 'Lestrygonians', 'Cyclops', 'Eumaeus' – have a
kind of sonata structure: movement along streets, an indoor lingering,
street movement again. In only two ('Proteus', 'Nausicaa') are we never
indoors at all; in only one ('Penelope') never outdoors. Yet protagonists'
minds are seldom constrained for long and, though Molly Bloom in
the last moments of 'Penelope' lies abed near day-break, we are trans-
ported on the final page to a high outdoor sunlit place which is
somehow both Gibraltar and Ben Howth, with spread out below us the
kingdoms of the earth: Spain, Ireland, distant Dublin, the Irish Sea,
the Mediterranean and the open Atlantic into which Dante imagined
Ulysses himself to have sailed away that last time.

Blocking out movements and places, blocking out episodes, these
seem to have been for Joyce concurrent processes. In the eighteen
episodes of his final scheme[9] the Homeric titles point less to analogy
of incident or character than to analogy of situation: the journey to
the land of the dead, a funeral; Circe's bestial metamorphoses, delirium
in a whorehouse. Then sequences had to be juggled for plausibility; since

not just for plausibility

I TELEMACHIA

	Name	Locale	Time*	Main Protagonists
1	Telemachus	The tower, Sandycove	8.00– 8.45 a.m.	Stephen, Mulligan, Haines
2	Nestor	The school, Dalkey	9.45–10.30 a.m.	Stephen, Mr Deasy
3	Proteus	Sandymount strand	11.00–11.45 a.m.	Stephen

II ODYSSEY

	Name	Locale	Time*	Main Protagonists
4	Calypso	Chez Bloom	8.00– 8.45 a.m.	Bloom, Molly
5	Lotos-eaters	Westland Row	9.45–10.30 a.m.	Bloom
6	Hades	Cortège, Cemetery	11.00–12 noon	Bloom, mourners
7	Aeolus	Newspaper office	12.00– 1.00 p.m.	Stephen, Bloom, talkers
8	Lestrygonians	Streets, Davy Byrne's	1.00– 2.00 p.m.	Bloom
9	Scylla and Charybdis	Library	1.45– 3.00 p.m.	Stephen, librarians, Mulligan
10	Wandering Rocks	Streets	2.55– 4.00 p.m.	Everybody
11	Sirens	Ormond Bar	3.38– 4.30 p.m.	Bloom, Si Dedalus, drinkers
12	Cyclops	Barney Kiernan's pub	4.45– 5.45 p.m.	Bloom, drinkers, 'The Citizen'
13	Nausicaa	Sandymount strand	8.00– 9.00 p.m.	Gerty MacDowell, Bloom
14	Oxen of the Sun	Hospital, pub	10.00–11.00 p.m.	Bloom, Stephen, medicals
15	Circe	Brothel	11.15–12.40 p.m.	Bloom, Stephen, whores *et al.*

III NOSTOS

	Name	Locale	Time*	Main Protagonists
16	Eumaeus	Shelter	12.40– 1.00 a.m.	Bloom, Stephen
17	Ithaca	Chez Bloom	1.00– 1.45 a.m.	Bloom, Stephen, Molly
18	Penelope	Bedroom	1.45– 2.20 a.m.	Molly

*In Joyce's *schemata* idealised times allot each episode a round hour. This table uses the more exact times derived by Clive Hart from internal indications (*Topographical Guide*, 23–5). I end 'Ithaca' and start 'Penelope' a little earlier than he does, to give Molly some time before 2 a.m. is heard chiming (18.1232). In general Joyce packs the hours full, and Bloom has a long, fast-paced exhausting day.

funerals are morning affairs in Catholic Dublin, 'Hades' comes before 'Circe', though it was Homer's Circe who directed Odysseus to Hades.

Pondering his central analogies, Joyce devised lesser correspondences which seem to have had heuristic uses. Sometimes they helped him choose among a hundred ways of specifying some detail. Sometimes they fenced with system the mere accidents of experience: drawing continually on events from his own life but aware that what had merely happened could have happened a thousand ways, he liked interlocking reasons for the version he chose. Where on the map of Dublin to assign an address for the dead man, Paddy Dignam? Unlike many minor characters, the fictional Paddy needs an address for the funeral cortège to start from, and it needs to be near the shore so Bloom can have his glimpse (6.39) of Stephen heading from tram to strand. Now, Stephen is thereabouts because, no longer resident in the tower, he has been half-thinking of going to his mother's people, the Gouldings. Their prototypes, the Murrays, with whom Joyce stayed after *he* was evicted from the tower in September 1904, lived in Fairview near the north shore of the Liffey, and Fairview would have made a plausible address for Dignam. It's attractive to guess that Joyce pondered it; Stephen could have walked near the beach he walked on in the *Portrait*, and Bloom, when his second trip to the Dignams' brought him to the same beach, could have gazed on Gerty MacDowell ('Nausicaa') where Stephen gazed on the bird-girl.

But the four rivers of Homer's underworld entailed bringing Dignam's cortège successively across the Dodder, the Grand Canal, the Liffey, the Royal Canal; so Dignam's home had to be placed east of the Dodder, near the city's southern shore, where *Thom's* yielded a vacant house at 9 Newbridge Avenue, Sandymount (16.1249). So Joyce was spared empty compliance with what had merely happened.

This determination of a site for 'Proteus', 'Nausicaa' and the start of 'Hades' gave Stephen a shorter tram-ride from Dalkey at the cost of an unduly long funeral route for Bloom. The author had to trot Corny's horses very briskly indeed to haul dead Paddy clear across the city from Sandymount northward to Glasnevin in the time available. ('We are going the pace, I think, Martin Cunningham said. God grant he doesn't upset us on the road, Mr Power said': 6.367.)

'They are not to be thought away,' Stephen muses (2.49) of events that are done with, and readers of the achieved *Ulysses* can hardly imagine any of its major aspects being otherwise, so many details support them. Once 'Nausicaa' had been located on Sandymount strand, Joyce had Star of the Sea Church nearby for religiose counterpoint, and the Mirus Bazaar fireworks at Ballsbridge for *obbligato* to Bloom's erotic provocation, and could have the cortège of 'Hades' cut north-west across the city to reverse the viceregal cavalcade's gesture in 'Wandering

Rocks', south-east across the city. This is to say that once he had made a decision he was resourceful in squeezing everything possible from it; but other values could have been squeezed from other decisions, and there was a time when none of these matters had been determined, node after node still suspended amid multiple possibilities, each freighted with implications and accidental benefits.

Here the lesser Homeric correspondences will have banished indecision, furnishing reasons for things to be so and not otherwise. With Homer's aid events were branded, fettered, 'lodged in the room of the infinite possibilities they have ousted' (2.50) − a phrase on time and history Joyce wrote early, not long after making a great many such decisions.

Sometimes we can see correspondences help him invent bits of business. A final snub for Bloom, who is snubbed so often in 'Hades'? The example of Ajax, who had lost a judgement to Ulysses and whose ghost stalked away from the hero without a word, apparently prompted the idea of letting Bloom be snubbed by someone he had once bested. So John Henry Menton was invented, and the bowling game Bloom won all those years ago by a fluke, and Menton's stiff discourtesy today when Bloom has pointed out the dinge in his hat; also the two women in Homer's account will have prompted 'Molly and Floey Dillon, linked under the lilactree, laughing' (6.1013). It stands on its own, a plausible little incident, and 'Menton: Ajax' in the table of correspondences tells us nothing save how it was probably arrived at. Not liking to have even trivia hang from just one cord, Joyce also invented (for 'Eumaeus') a parallel incident in which Bloom returned the great Parnell's hat and was thanked (16.1514).

Minor correspondences abound, most of them mocking mirrors. Odysseus kissed the soil of Ithaca; Bloom kisses Molly's rere. Melanthius' vitals were fed raw to dogs; Corley is offered a chance at a job teaching Deasy's schoolboys. And where Nestor tames horses Deasy runs a school, which in making the boys colts as well as curs would seem inconsistent were it not amply plain that Joyce rearranged his analogies *ad lib*.

In passing, as it were, from one playlet to another characters can change Homeric roles. Molly Bloom plays Calypso, also Penelope. As Calypso she is hidden beneath the bedclothes (*kaluptein*, 'to cover up') and has for visible surrogate '*The Bath of the Nymph* over the bed. Given away with the Easter number of *Photo Bits*: splendid master-piece in art colours. . . . Not unlike her with her hair down: slimmer' (4.369). When the Calypso's Isle of Episode 4 becomes the Ithaca of Episodes 17–18, Molly will be Penelope and the Nymph will pertain to the Cave of the Sea-Nymphs where Homer's Odysseus had done sacrifice a thousand times: sacrifices given Joycean inflection in 'Circe', where she puts in a speaking appearance to hint at spilled seed:

THE NYMPH:
(*covers her face with her hands*) What have I not seen in that chamber?
What must my eyes look down on? (15.3284)

This reapportioning of roles not only looks forward to *Finnegans
Wake*, but also points up a premise of *Ulysses* itself, that a relatively
limited number of structures defines the acts and relationships of people.
In one of the Homeric structures usurping suitors are despoiling the
substance of Ithaca and laying siege to Queen Penelope's affections, so
Telemachus sets off in quest of his father. In *Ulysses* Mulligan plays the
usurper in Stephen's intellectual kingdom, Boylan the usurper in Bloom's
marital bed. One Ithacan situation has become two Dublin ones with no
personnel in common, nothing at all in common except a structure, and
when Stephen/Telemachus sets out for the day it is not to seek a father
but to drink like the father whose destiny he fears he will never escape.
As for Bloom/Odysseus, he is not so much striving to get home as
finding many reasons not to go home just yet, there being no indication
when the adulterer is likely to have left. These reversals of a prototype's
intention appear to concern Joyce less than the wide applicability of a
prototypical pattern.
    Not only are patterns repopulated in *Ulysses*; a keen eye for pattern
can conflate many books. Usurpers, an absent hero, a young man in
trouble: that describes *Hamlet*, too, and Stephen's discussion of the
play ('Scylla and Charybdis') in equating a ghost by death with a ghost
by absence (9.174) in effect equates the *Hamlet* pattern with the
Odyssey pattern, though Stephen has no idea he is in a book called
Ulysses, nor that he is helping its readers perceive his 'Hamlet hat'
(3.390) and Hamlet-like suit of solemn black as appropriate costume
for this book's Telemachus. An avenger come back 'from the dead' to
rout adulterous usurpation, that is the role not only of Ulysses but of the
Stone Guest in *Don Giovanni*, and when Bloom hums 'in solemn echo'
the Stone Guest's recitative (8.1040) he is trying on unbeknownst the
role of avenging Ulysses.
    Autre temps, autre mœurs; Ulysses in 1904 does not rout spoilers,
slaughter suitors, hang collaborationist maids. Nevertheless, the Homeric
parallel is neither a reproof to his ineffectuality nor a pasticheur's
exercise. If it does not magnify Bloom, as Yeats's perception of a
haranguing Helen ('Was there another Troy for her to burn?')[10] enlarges
Maud Gonne, still it lends him the enhancement of an emphasised
contour. In repeating the deeds of Ulysses, Bloom's most ordinary deeds
acquire definition, distinguished from countless similar Dublin deeds.
When we listen in to the musings of Tom Kernan the tea salesman, we
hear two pages of interior monologue (10.718–798) similar to that
of Bloom the ad canvasser, but something still is lacking, several things:

for one, the defining contour of Ulysses steering past Lestrygonian perils. Kernan is just Kernan.

And as surely as Yeats thought Maud Gonne was Helen reborn we are to think that Bloom is no imitation Ulysses but Ulysses reborn. Bloom *is* Ulysses again. Maud could be Helen thanks to metempsychosis, a doctrine sufficiently current then in Dublin for Bloom to have an explanation ready (4.341), though the easier word 'parallax' defeats him (8.110).

> – Some people believe, he said, that we go on living in another body after death, that we lived before. They call it reincarnation. That we all lived before on the earth thousands of years ago or some other planet. They say we have forgotten it. Some say they remember their past lives. (4.362)

That speech – the book's first internal clue to the meaning of its own title – doesn't ask us to accept the doctrine (which Bloom himself, in quest of an example, proceeds to muddle with 'metamorphosis'), and the doctrine won't explain Bloom unless we think it as real as we think Bloom. By adducing it Joyce gained not a rationale but (1) a hard word for Bloom to explain to Molly, (2) a chance to state early in his book the theme of previous lives, (3) a dig at the Yeatsians, whose ability to perceive Helen in a hortatory beauty didn't entail the eyes to see Ulysses in an unnoticeable commercial traveller, despite Plato's prompting in that prime metempsychotic text, the myth of Er (*Republic*, X). Fancy Yeats noticing Bloom! Yeats's and not his, Joyce implies, is the merely literary exercise.

No, Bloom and Ulysses are not identical in order that metempsychosis may be validated. They are identical in not existing save as manifestations of human creative power, products of an artistic process that is like a natural process, and that intuits in many times comparable situations, whether in the mind of Homer of Chios or in the mind of James Augustine Joyce. Both, far from the scenes of their stories, created their heroes and re-created an epic geography, Joyce with the aid of *Thom's Official Directory*, and Homer, as Joyce read in Victor Bérard, with the aid of Phoenician voyagers' *periploi*. Both were guided by the circumstances they knew (warfare, seafaring, marvels; commerce, perambulation, novelties). Both were compelled by immutable human givens: that men are born of women, espouse women, beget children, rear them, lose them; that the dead – parents, children, spouses – are buried and mourned; that fortune takes men afield; that women grow lonely; that predators gather, that distraction may turn to desire; that sons may join with fathers, or decline to join them; that outrage may bring revenge, or abstention from revenge; that there is a home, and that it is good to be there. If *Ulysses* resembles the *Odyssey*, that is at bottom no mystery. Joyce early perceived, in Chapter II of the *Portrait*, that even *The Count of Monte Cristo* resembled the *Odyssey*. How much more was a work not entitled to be Odyssean on which a fabulous artificer expended seven patient years?

So the large pattern. As for the lesser correspondences, many of them are trivial. Some, if we chance to know them, lend definition, some contrast. Joyce listed many, did not list many, and some that we see he may not have thought of at all. Their dubious immanence adds fun to our endless exploration of his book. Ulysses returned to Ithaca had still his strength, Bloom at age 38 has fallen from his; but when the unremarkable drooping trajectory of Bloom's urination in 'Ithaca' reminds the implacable catechist how when a schoolboy he 'had been capable of attaining the point of greatest altitude against the whole concurrent strength of the institution, 210 scholars' (17.1195), it would be a pity not to let that heroic arc remind us of Odysseus' power manifested in his great bow.

NOTES

1 'O, shade of Kinch the elder! Japhet in search of a father!' (1.561). This jest pertains to Haines's misunderstanding of the pronouns in an earlier remark of Mulligan's about Stephen's theory of *Hamlet*. *Japhet in Search of a Father* was an 1835 novel by Frederick Marryat. Though the allusion seems recondite now, we are to imagine that this was a boy's book for Mulligan. Many Marryat titles abounded in cheap reprint as late as the 1930s.

2 Stuart Gilbert, *James Joyce's 'Ulysses'* (New York, 1931), 87.

3 Harry Blamires, *The Bloomsday Book* (London, 1966).

4 ibid., 165.·

5 Hart and Knuth, 70.

6 Hart and Knuth (25-6) show that traced on the map Bloom's meanderings in this episode delineate two large question marks.

7 Budgen, 15.

8 *Letters*, I, 147.

9 We are naïvely surprised to learn that so firm a book was ever subject to uncertainty. But in mid-1915 (*Selected Letters*, 209) he envisaged 22 episodes, grouped 4-15-3; in May 1918 (*Letters*, I, 113) he told Harriet Weaver there would be 17, grouped 3-11-3; by 1920 (*Letters*, I, 145) he had settled on the present 3-12-3 grouping. So one episode was not even envisaged until after May 1918. Michael Groden, *'Ulysses' in Progress* (Princeton, NJ, 1977), 33, is surely correct in surmising that this was 'Wandering Rocks', which not only marks a pause in the action but corresponds to no adventure of Ulysses. It was drafted in the spring of 1919.

10 W. B. Yeats, 'No Second Troy', *Collected Poems* (London, 1952), 101.

CHAPTER 4

Immediate Experience

Some things were clear to Joyce extremely early. At 22 he wrote to his brother 'Damned stupid', after reading 'The Wild Goose' in George Moore's *Untilled Field*. 'A lady who has been living for three years on the line between Bray and Dublin is told by her husband that there is a meeting in Dublin at which he must be present. She looks up the table to see the hours of the trains. This on [the Dublin, Wicklow & Wexford Railway] where the trains go regularly; this after three years. Isn't it rather stupid of Moore.'[1]

Moore, who didn't live on the DW & WR, would have had to look up that train, but he should have reflected that his character wouldn't have. *The writer should be alert to what his characters would know.*

There is a corollary, less obvious. Characters in fiction are frequently made to stir up knowledge they'd have left tranquil, or exchange remarks they'd not have uttered, for the sake of imparting some fact to the reader. By Joyce's principle this is disallowed. It warps the characters. Indeed, with exceptions to be carefully deliberated, *the reader should not be told what no one present would think worth an act of attention.*

So 'descriptive' details will not define a neutral 'setting': they will alert us to what someone present did, noticed, thought important. From *A Portrait of the Artist as a Young Man*:

> In a few moments he was barefoot, his stockings folded in his pockets and his canvas shoes dangling by their knotted laces over his shoulders: and, picking a pointed salteaten stick out of the jetsam among the rocks, he clambered down the slope of the breakwater. (170)

Where his stockings are, where his shoes are and how they are secured, these are matters to which Stephen has just been paying attention so they come to our attention likewise. We are not told the colour of his trousers because, within the scope of the present narrative, that detail hasn't mattered, to him. (But in *Ulysses* it does matter, and when Stephen rejects Mulligan's offer of grey trousers (1.120) it is because he is choosing to wear only black, in mourning and also in emulation of mourning Hamlet.)

From *Ulysses*, Bloom's first morning walk:

He crossed to the bright side, avoiding the loose cellarflap of number seventyfive. The sun was nearing the steeple of George's church. Be a warm day I fancy. Specially in these black clothes feel it more. Black conducts, reflects, (refracts is it?), the heat. But I couldn't go in that light suit. Make a picnic of it. (4.77)

Bloom's awareness comprises all this; that is why we can slip into his inner monologue so smoothly. To cross to the bright side was a deliberate act; likewise to avoid the loose cellarflap, the city-dweller needing as many kinds of alertness as a Fenimore Cooper Indian. Sun brings the coming warmth to his mind, so the black clothes enter his awareness, and the reason for rejecting the light ones.

And here Joyce shuns the temptation to let us know that Bloom is dressed for a funeral. A man who says to himself 'But I couldn't go to a funeral in that light suit' is either a different man from Bloom, fussier and more categorising if he is in Joyce's kind of book, or else he is in a slacker kind of book – the kind in which people look up trains they would have known about – and his thoughts are being phrased not to shape our sense of him but to impart narrative information. That kind of book demands less of us, and tells us less.

In this book it is enough just now if we anticipate a function where a light suit would be frivolous. Clarification will come by natural stages. A page later: 'Stop and say a word: about the funeral perhaps. Sad thing about poor Dignam, Mr O'Rourke' (4.118). Five more pages, and things are quite explicit:

> She doubled a slice of bread into her mouth, asking:
> – What time is the funeral?
> – Eleven, I think, he answered. I didn't see the paper. (4.318)

When he does see a paper we encounter more of this scrupulousness. Bloom buys it and consults it during a gap in the narrative. At 5.48 he unpockets it and rolls it into a 'baton' to tap his leg with, in a fantasy of ambulant leisure. At 5.143, feigning elaborate casualness to mislead a bore, he unrolls it and scans an ad which we later discover (8.138) was printed beneath the obituaries; the inference may be that he'd not delved farther.* At 5.534 he offers to abandon it to Bantam Lyons: 'I was just going to throw it away.' (And horse-player Lyons takes this for a tip on Throwaway, a fact that will have comically magnified consequences.) So Bloom spent a penny (17.1459) solely to verify one fact of immediate practical import, where-

---

The Freeman's Journal carried births, marriages, deaths and small advertisements on the front page; if we happen to know this, we know that Bloom need not have so much as opened it. If we don't, we're in no trouble.

upon the *Freeman* became first a 'baton', then potential waste paper (but knelt on at the funeral – 6.586 – and not finally discarded till late afternoon – 11.1123). For all his minute curiosity Bloom seems not to be a newspaper reader – another piece of information for the reader of *Ulysses*, conveyed wholly by omission. And Joyce, with his mind on Bloom, is rigorous in forgoing the opportunity for 'period' detail which the newspaper would have afforded a less exacting writer. If Bloom doesn't read it, we can't be told about it.

Much later (16.1232) Bloom does scan the headlines of a late-edition *Telegraph*, but elects to read only the account of the Dignam funeral, where his own name is misprinted, 'L. Boom'. Subsequently, killing time, he glances through a racing story on page 3 while Stephen is drawing morose delectation from the foot-and-mouth-disease letter on page 2; from this we may deduce if we like that when the elements of the Dublin Trinity are assembled at last the Son sits at the left hand of the Father while the Word engages them both.

Thematic implications of this sort are frequent in the later pages of the book, and frequently whimsical. So many sorts of minor consistency – as that newspapers, in this book, seem to go with funerals, the funeral episode being followed immediately by one set in a newspaper office – hint at a vast order, presided over by an intelligence that keeps track of each scrap of waste paper as Providence discerns the fall of sparrows. We are free to muse on the shabby lot of urban man, passing through the jaws of death with for Recording Angel the casual *Telegraph* reporter (whom we observe – 6.878 – in the act of collecting mis-information). All such reflections are our responsibility. The author's responsibility as Joyce conceived it was not to frame *sententiae* but to create, like God, the huge system, seemingly bounded, in which we glimpse such orderly recurrences. As he did not write it straight through but revised and elaborated, so we cannot read it straight through save with intent to reread.

There are drawbacks to the method, clearly. It must fragment and distribute through a long text what would have been elements of a single ambient awareness. It puts us to the trouble of collating scraps, and put the writer also to immense trouble in devising plausible ways to tell us simple things. Its compensating advantages are three. (1) By restricting with its logic a narrator who could otherwise tell us anything he liked, it circumvents a fundamental question most fiction must outface: Why we should be detained with serial preliminaries when we might be hearing their outcome? (2) It strews our way with hundreds of small revelations, microplots to impel us through the long presentation. When we divine that Bloom must be going to a funeral, that, on its minor scale, is as much an event as his going there. (3) By tacitly observing the constraints on someone who is present, it both defines the present person in many little cumulative ways, and permits a sharp vividness, as though we were present also.

Of what use, a Descartes might ask, is the senses' sharp vividness, when minds may entertain clear ideas? And Joyce will let Stephen answer: Hold to the now, the here, through which all future plunges to the past (9.89). The now, the here, are where *I* am. Reality is immediate experience, and in a book is the immediate experience of language, streaming through what *Finnegans Wake* will call 'the eye of a noodle' (143).

Ulysses opens with words obedient to corporeal reality, stately plump Buck Mulligan, playacting:

> Stately, plump Buck Mulligan came from the stairhead, bearing a bowl of lather on which a mirror and a razor lay crossed. A yellow dressinggown, ungirdled, was sustained gently behind him on the mild morning air. He held the bowl aloft and intoned:
> – *Introibo ad altare Dei.*
> Halted, he peered down the dark winding stairs and called out coarsely:
> – Come up, Kinch! Come up, you fearful jesuit! (1.1–8)

No one is here but Mulligan, so though this is third-person narrative we are confined to Mulligan's sense of himself. (Otherwise put: a narrator is mimicking Mulligan). Since the Buck is Hellenophile – 'Mulligan', as he will soon remark, is a dactyl – the first nine words mimick a Homeric hexameter:

Státelý | plúmp Búck | Múllĭgăn ‖ cáme frŏm thĕ | stáirhéad | béaring |

He *bear*s the bowl, a more conscious act than a mere carrying. He is aware of the colour of his dressing-gown; priests' vestments, on days when no other colour was specified, were gold and white. Ungirdled (the cincture not tied as it would be for the priest's ritual affirmation of chastity), it leaves him frontally naked, his private parts on display for mild air to caress; he is aware of that, too. And 'intoned' is deliberate; preparing to shave, he is also playing at the Black Mass with its naked priest. Joyce sensed, we may discern, that the book should begin with someone who is deliberately, theatrically, beginning his day, and beginning it with an act of mockery.

The words Mulligan intones are from the Prayers at the Foot of the Altar, then (1904) inseparable from the Mass.* Mulligan (whose name

---

*Joyce likely assumed that this at least would never change so long as *Ulysses* would be read. But he didn't foresee the Second Vatican Council, and even Catholics require a footnote now.

by the way isn't 'Buck' but 'Malachi', just as Stephen's isn't 'Kinch')
is tastelessly pretending to be a Black Mass celebrant, who is going
through the motions of an Irish priest, who is reciting from the *Ordo*,
which quotes from St Jerome's Latin version of Hebrew words ascribed
to a Psalmist in exile: 'Va-a-vo-ah el mizbah elohim': 'I will go up to
the altar of God' (Psalm 42:4 Vulgate; 43:4 King James). So we might
set the first words spoken in *Ulysses* inside six sets of quotation marks –

' " ' " ' " *Introibo ad altare Dei*," ' " ' " '

– a multiple integument of contexts to contain this Hebrew cry for help
amid persecution. (It is spoken by the least persecuted man in the book.)
On a later reading we may also remark the appropriateness, for the book
of Bloom, of an initial statement in disguised Hebrew, and note, too,
that as the Roman priest adopts the role of the Psalmist, so Irish political
consciousness in those years was playing the role of the captive Chosen
People, with Great Britain for its Babylon or its Egypt (cf. 7.828–869).

'O God sustain my cause,' Ronald Knox's version of the Psalm begins,
'give me redress against a race that knows no pity; save me from a
treacherous foe and cruel'. Bring me to thy holy mountain; and there I
will go up to the altar of God . . . Buck Mulligan means none of this;
he means to mock.

At the foot of the altar a server should reply 'Ad deum qui laetificat
juventutem meum': 'to God who brings joy to my youth' ('God the
bringer of triumphant happiness,' writes Knox). But the server in
Ulysses is laggard, and Stephen Dedalus will not speak those words
until fifteen hours later, when he is entering the quarter of the whores
and gives *deum* a change of gender (15.122). That is for the future,
and most likely for remark at a future reading. For now, we may note
that Stephen's advent introduces a new pair of eyes through which
Mulligan can at last be seen:

Stephen Dedalus, displeased and sleepy, leaned his arms on the top
of the staircase and looked coldly at the shaking gurgling face that
blessed him, equine in its length, and at the light untonsured hair,
grained and hued like pale oak. (1.13)

He also introduces a convention of unspoken comment, seeing Mulligan's
'even white teeth glistening here and there with gold points' and reflecting Chrysostomos'. 'Golden-mouthed': there were two Greeks of that
nickname, one an orator, one a saint. More pertinently, the pope who
sent the English mission was called in Ireland Gregory Goldenmouth.
This, the book's first Greek word, might have been an epithet for nimble-
tongued Ulysses and anyway is a typically erudite Stephen-joke. It is

also the book's first flicker of interior monologue. No such notation attaches itself, ever, to any word of Mulligan's, who throughout *Ulysses* has no unspoken thoughts whatever: as it were, no inside. The 'bone-setter', the 'medicineman', he is as stonily *objective* as the tower atop which he commences the day by disporting. A stage-Irishman, who opens the book by stepping onstage, he speaks as though cued by stage-directions, 'coarsely', 'sternly', 'briskly', 'gaily', and at his periodic reappearances is always the actor.

He makes his next extended appearance (9.485) in an episode devoted to discussion of Shakespeare's stage, where his entrance is captioned 'Entr'acte', and his last one (14.651) in a costume-drama of narrative manners each mutation of which affords him a new role. He then disappears into the night, headed back to his tower 'that beetles o'er his base into the sea' (1.567) like Hamlet's Elsinore (*Hamlet*, I, IV, 71). He is happiest *enacting* spontaneity, not improvising but reciting.

So ready indeed is Mulligan with quotations, one would think he, not Stephen, was the *littérateur* in residence. It is he, moreover, who introduces theme after theme. His first words introduce, at six removes, the Jew in exile. His next quotation is from Homer's Greek. It is he, not Stephen, who intones the song from Yeats that will attend Stephen like a *leitmotif*. He invokes Swinburne, mocks Wilde, alludes (in a German word) to Nietzsche.

His metamorphosis into a role is explicitly caught:

> Buck Mulligan at once put on a blithe broadly smiling face. He looked at them, his wellshaped mouth open happily, his eyes, from which he had suddenly withdrawn all shrewd sense, blinking with mad gaiety. He moved a doll's head to and fro, the brims of his Panama hat quivering, and began to chant in a quiet happy foolish voice. (1.579)

What he chants this time is 'The Ballad of Joking Jesus', and to Haines's surprised 'O, you have heard it before?' Stephen drily rejoins, 'Three times a day, after meals': the wording of a prescription, in a jibe at Mulligan the Medico. Whether playing Christ as he drops his gown ('Mulligan is stripped of his garments', from the motto of the Tenth Station of the Cross) or playing the Fool, 'blithe in motley' (9.486) in the National Library – 'Puck Mulligan, panamahelmeted, went step by step, iambing, trolling' (9.1125) – or conjuring up mock-Gothic spooks to make half-drunken medicals roar with delight ('But Malachias' tale began to freeze them with horror. He conjured up the scene before them. The secret panel beside the chimney slid back': 14.1010), always on stage, the stately plump Buck in his primrose vest ('God, we'll simply have to dress the character': 1.515) plays parts like a chameleon and plays onlookers like fish ('Why don't you play them as I do?': 1.506) in roistering affirmation of Mulligan's Law, the first principle of Dublin, that all is style, is appearances, is show. 'Usurper,' breathes Stephen (1.744). Mulligan usurps Stephen's place, stage-centre; usurps, with his mockery, Stephen's anguished unbelief; usurps, quoting classroom Greek and facile Swinburne, the office of the Hellenising bard.

'He fears the lancet of my art', Stephen tells himself, 'as I fear that of his. The cold steel pen' (1.152). Stephen's 'art', though, much of the time, is to appropriate and redirect the words of others, a game he can only play because Mulligan is literate. They have just been bandying misquotations from Wilde. Later Stephen cancels a rendezvous with Mulligan by sending a telegram: a lordly gesture, since the telegram travels only a few hundred yards, from College Green to the pub called the Ship where Stephen is expected to perform the mad Irish literary critic. We learn what the telegram said when Mulligan reads it aloud in the National Library:

> – Telegram! he said. Wonderful inspiration! Telegram! A papal bull!
> He sat on a corner of the unlit desk, reading aloud joyfully:
> – *The sentimentalist is he who would enjoy without incurring the immense debtorship for a thing done.* Signed: Dedalus. Where did you launch it from? The kips? No. College Green. . . . Telegram! Malachi Mulligan, The Ship, lower Abbey street. O, you peerless mummer! O, you priestified Kinchite! (9.548)

In a pub late at night, showing the 'mummer's wire' round afresh, he adds the detail that it was 'cribbed out of Meredith' (14.1486), as it was, from *The Ordeal of Richard Feverel*, where in Chapter 25 of the Tauchnitz edition Joyce evidently used[2] we read:

> 'Sentimentalists,' says the PILGRIM'S SCRIP, 'are they who seek to enjoy, without incurring the Immense Debtorship for a thing done.'
> 'It is,' the writer says of Sentimentalism elsewhere, 'a happy pastime, and an important science, to the timid, the idle, and the heartless: but a damning one to them who have anything to forfeit.'

'The timid, the idle, and the heartless': that is pretty much Stephen's view of Mulligan,[3] to whom the words in the telegram would say, 'You want the entertainment of exhibiting my telegram to Haines, but are unwilling to pay me in any coin, and notably not in respect'.

With points of reference at our disposal that were not available to Stephen, we may paraphrase more freely: 'This morning's black mass was easy mockery for you; it is I (having something to forfeit) who am prepared to contemplate a mistake which can last as long as eternity

[Cf. *Portrait*, 247], and when T. S. Eliot writes a quarter-century hence
of a man (Baudelaire) that he "was capable of a damnation denied to
the politicians and the newspaper editors of Paris", I shall hope to claim
that I am some such man. We are both in a book, *Ulysses*, in which the
first adjective applied to me was "displeased". I was watching your silly
performance at the time. Can you commence to understand the force of
that adjective?'

All this loses point if Mulligan does not know the context, with its
reference to the timid, idle and heartless; but the spotting of the
quotation comes from him (14.1486), and we can guess that *Richard
Feverel*, in its time a famously 'clever' and 'difficult' book, serves him
and Stephen for the sort of allusion-game they played (1.143) with Wilde.

We perceive Buck Mulligan almost exclusively with Stephen's exacer-
bated nerves, and he is fairly dull the one time he is briefly on view
with neither Stephen there to be teased nor Stephen's hostile patience
to mediate our perceptions. That once (10.1043–1099) he is a lay figure
in a fiction. When Stephen is near he is show without inside, but
sparkling show.

Stephen by contrast comes to seem little but inside. His myopic eyes
focus on a 'threadbare cuffedge' (1.106), while for the distant blur they
see – 'a dull green mass of liquid'* – his mind effortlessly substitutes the
bowl of white china that held his dying mother's vomit, 'green sluggish
bile'. How her ghost came to him 'in a dream silently' (1.102; 1.270)
makes a more vivid scene than anything his eyes see (and accords with
his interest in *Richard Feverel*, early in which Richard wakes up 'to see
a lady bending over him': called a ghost, but really his absent mother,
returned). Repeatedly and at increasing length his chemistries of words
usurp what is there to be seen, what there is to hear. From that first
flicker, 'Chrysostomos', his interior monologue gradually expands to
engulf all other reality.

By the third of the three brief opening episodes we are so irretrievably
installed in Stephen's consciousness that, though the world, as he assures
himself, is 'there all the time without you: and ever shall be, world
without end' (3.27), we can never be quite sure what it contains –
nor for that matter how clearly Stephen can see it. A woman on the
beach 'swung lourdily her midwife's bag', so identified apparently for
no better reason than that Stephen wants it to be one, in order that it
may contain 'a misbirth with trailing navelcord, hushed in ruddy wool'.
A visit not made – 'I pull the wheezy bell of their shuttered cottage'

---

*A myope's distant sea, and a brilliant early example of Joyce's scrupulous
care for the limits of a character's perceptions. Stephen's eyes apparently focus
at about eight inches, and when we eventually learn (15.3628) that he broke
his glasses 'yesterday' and so has been without them the whole of Bloomsday
we must reassess everything he seems to have seen.

(3.70) – or a drink remembered from another time and city – 'Noon slumbers. Kevin Egan rolls gunpowder cigarettes through fingers smeared with printer's ink (3.216) – exists on the page with exactly the authority of the immediate actual: 'Broken hoops on the shore; at the land a maze of dark cunning nets; farther away chalkscrawled backdoors and on the higher beach a dryingline with two crucified shirts' (3.154). This mixes what he knows from other walks with what weak eyes can discern at high noon, when the iris closes down and diminishes circles of confusion. And Egan's 'gunpowder cigarettes' are not some dangerous Paris fad like absinthe, they denote Stephen's fancy that whatever the old dynamiter lights is a fuse:

> The blue fuse burns deadly between hands and burns clear. Loose tobaccoshreds catch fire: a flame and acrid smoke light our corner. (3.239)

This flare in a café niche becomes in Stephen's mind, hence on the page, the 'flame of vengeance', with its 'shattered glass and toppling masonry' that had assaulted Clerkenwell Prison thirty-seven years previously. (Hence Egan's exile; he had been a maker of political statements in the Irish mode.) In the theatre of Stephen's mind women with a bag enact midwives, Egan for ever enacts a dynamiter, drying shirts enact the Crucifixion. He himself in his 'Hamlet hat' and black suit enacts Hamlet. In Paris the same hat had been his 'Latin quarter hat' (3.174); he remembers wearing it, 'Proudly walking. Whom were you trying to walk like? Forget: a dispossessed.'

That is one meaning of the third episode's title, 'Proteus': people, places, even hats shift roles. Another is that men re-enact what their ancestors had been: 'The cords of all link back, strandentwining cables of all flesh' (3.37); 'You're your father's son,' Egan had said in Paris. 'I know the voice' (3.229). And near this strand where I stand now, where starving Dubliners in AD 1331 swarmed forth to hack great fish to pieces, 'I moved among them on the frozen Liffey, that I, a changeling, among the spluttering resin fires. I spoke to no-one: none to me' (3.307). Language, too, mutating, protean, enacts unpredictably. 'Irlandais' is misheard as 'Hollandais' (3.220), and though the former is a person the latter turns out to be a cheese. Language makes what we can perceive. Hare, buck, bear, wolf, calf, fox, pard, panther are some of the words that create a chameleon dog (3.333–364). Modern words, 'bald' and 'millionaire', couple with some fourteenth-century words of Dante's, 'maestro di color che sanno', to create a provisional Aristotle (3.6). Shakespeare's 'that on the unnumbered pebbles beats' helps create Sandymount Strand (3.148).

So all melts into Stephen's mind and into words. There is no coupling of name to thing; there is, rather, a swerving approximation of two experiences, one sensual, one textual, as of hyperbola and asymptote. *Lear* is to be read by analogies with walking in Sandymount now (how else would its words acquire meaning?) and Sandymount is now to be verbalised with the aid of *Lear* (where do words come from save from former usage?). 'These heavy sands are language tide and wind have silted here' (3.288), and 'signatures of all things I am here to read', a phrase itself formulated with the aid of a quotation, the title of Jakob Boehme's seventeenth-century *Signatura Rerum*. Things have voices also:

> Listen: a fourworded wavespeech: seesoo, hrss, rsseeiss, ooos. Vehement breath of waters amid seasnakes, rearing horses, rocks. In cups of rocks it slops: flop, slop, slap: bounded in barrels. And, spent, its speech ceases. It flows purling, widely flowing, floating foampool, flower unfurling.
>
> Under the upswelling tide he saw the writhing weeds lift languidly and sway reluctant arms, hising up their petticoats, in whispering water swaying and upturning coy silver fronds. Day by day: night by night: lifted, flooded and let fall. Lord, they are weary; and, whispered to, they sigh. Saint Ambrose heard it, sigh of leaves and waves, waiting, awaiting the fullness of their times, *diebus ac noctibus iniurias patiens ingemiscit.* (3.456)

Day and night, wrote Saint Ambrose the hymnologist, creation groans over its wrongs. No doubt Ambrose had read Romans, 8:22, with an ear trained by leaves and waves, their words serving to elucidate God's word. And his fine Latin cadence says what they strive to say, as the scrupulous – comic – onomatopoeia ('seesoo, hrss, rsseeiss, ooos') of the fourworded wavespeech does not. Whoever supposes that what is experienced should be naïvely recorded supposes that the writer's discipline is the onomatopoeist's. Not that to write out the wavespeech was a negligible feat. It testifies to ingenious attention, and within two pages we shall be attending to a fourworded catspeech, not 'Meow' and 'Purr' but 'Mkgnao!', 'Mrkgnao!', 'Mrkrgnao!' and (milk bestowed at last) 'Gurrhr!' Later the book's final episode will revolve a fourworded womanspeech, by correlation with which we may eventually discover without surprise that 'Gurrhr!' in Cat means 'Yes'.*

---

*What Joyce's trained ear and resourceful pen transcribed with the aid of 5 consonants, a vowel, a diphthong and an aspirate was of course not meant to represent the cat's full vocabulary, which according to recent research (Muriel Beadle, *The Cat* (1977), p. 186) entails 9 consonants, 5 vowels, 2 diphthongs, an umlaut and an *a:ou* sound which 'begins as *a* while the mouth is open but ends as *ou* while the mouth is gradually closed'.

So the discipline at which Joyce hinted when he observed a careless-ness of George Moore's has rigorous, often unexpected consequences. One of them is the tendency of language-patterns to pre-empt other offices of narrative. In this book's first sentence Buck Mulligan was acting; by the third episode, it is commonplace to remark, the chief actor has become the language. This structural rhythm, corresponding to a movement from the exterior world to the interior, persists through-out Joyce's writing and shapes *A Portrait of the Artist as a Young Man, Ulysses* and *Finnegans Wake*, each of which, contrary to what Stephen (P 215) designated as art's natural progression, begins in the third person and ends in the first. Each of the three main parts of *Ulysses* repeats this rhythm, commencing with Narrative (Young, Mature and Old respectively, says the *schema*) and ending with Soliloquy ('Proteus', 'Penelope') or with Hallucination ('Circe'). What is Out There gives way to what is In Here, in re-enactment of the primal narrative act whereby Event becomes Word. For events in a book, and notably in this book, are events perceived and worded as if by someone present, and perceiver gradually engulfs perceived as words replace visible acts.

In the *Portrait* Joyce had confined each phase of his five-parted narrative within the growing consciousness of Stephen Dedalus, the *style indirect libre* growing more resourceful as Stephen grows. To achieve a third-person opening he commenced the book with a story about a moocow, spoken by Stephen's father; the first-person close consists of excerpts from Stephen's diary, its written sentences supplanting the spoken words of the first page. Part of the indirection of *Ulysses* is its play with our assumption that it is going to repeat the preoccupations of the *Portrait*: a second and much longer book about Stephen Dedalus, the young artist (we might naturally suppose) at a further stage of maturation. Once more, after a third-person opening, Stephen is intro-duced on the first page; once more it is Stephen's darting subjectivity that soon takes charge of the narrative. Within fifty pages we are so entoiled in his subjectivity that nothing much is happening save internal events, alterations of cadence and image, gestures of a mobile ego. The book is commencing to be claustral, our pace of ingestion slow. Rich and brilliant though the linguistic sequences are, we may quail at the prospect of no more than their brilliance throughout such a long book as we hold in our hands.

At this moment a new part commences. In the book's first major surprise a new character is introduced, a man with the principal role in this book of roles, whom the Protean language will first mimic and later will find itself powerless to obliterate as he enacts Ulysses and never knows it: 'Mr Leopold Bloom. . . .'

NOTES

1 *Letters*, II, 71.
2 (Leipzig 1875), I, 262. Annotators generally cite chapter 28 of the first edition (1859), where the word 'Reality' appears after 'enjoy', and the omission of this word from Stephen's version has been speculated on. But it was Meredith who cut it when he revised the novel drastically for Tauchnitz and conflated the first four chapters into one. For his final version (1896) he cut yet another chapter, and in this the quotation appears in chapter 24. Since these revisions were made in silence, Joyce couldn't have known the sentence he has Stephen borrow ever spoke of 'Reality' unless he performed a collation between his Tauchnitz and what had become a rare book. The way of the annotator is strewn with thorns.
3 'A coward's mask,' Joyce had written of the boisterousness of this character in a draft he later discarded: Richard Ellmann, *James Joyce* (1959), 390. Though Mulligan's physical courage ('He saved men from drowning': 3.317) is unquestionable.

CHAPTER 5

The Hidden Hero

His advent has been heralded by Mr Deasy, who alleges of dying England that Jews are in all the highest places, including finance and the press, eating up (it is their way) the nation's vital strength (2.348). These propositions prove to fit Leopold Bloom with inadvertent accuracy. As to high places, he lives on Eccles Street, to which all roads lead upward; its north-western end is the highest place within the 1904 municipal boundaries of Dublin. As for finance and the press, he is employed by the *Freeman's Journal*, moreover on its money-making rather than its editorial side, though as ad-man he makes futile efforts to affect the content of the news columns, where he tries to plant 'puffs' for his clients. And, as for eating up the nation's vital strength, we know from the *Portrait* (203) that Ireland is 'the old sow that eats her farrow', and we shall shortly be watching Bloom consume a pork kidney. Since Mr Deasy had also said that there were no Jews in Ireland, Bloom has somehow escaped his gaze, as he also escaped that of *Thom's*, where 7 Eccles Street in 1904 is listed as vacant.

The census of 1901 places 2048 Jews in Dublin.[1] Since its criterion was religious affiliation, this count, too, would not have included Bloom, who was never circumcised (13.979), was baptised a Protestant in consequence of his father's apostasy, and moved still farther from the tents of Judah when he underwent Catholic baptism in October 1888 prior to his marriage with Marion Tweedy (17.542). And whether Jewry would at any time have acknowledged him is doubtful: Jewish affiliation is traced through the mother, and Leopold's mother Ellen Higgins Bloom had herself an Irish mother, Fanny Hegarty (17.537). So he undergoes the disadvantages of a Jewish name and appearance unsupported by any claim to solidarity with an interwoven community. (That may be why he has taken up Freemasonry.) He lived among Jews as a boy, on and around Clanbrassil Street on the south side of the river, but at 38 he looks back on his Jewish friends – Owen Goldberg, J. Citron, Philip Moisel, Julius Mastiansky, others – as belonging to his remote past. The same seems true of all his friendships now, though like any Dubliner he has much acquaintance. He is rather frequently disregarded and snubbed, though with no special malice. The Irish can be great overlookers of non-Celts.

Since the publication of *Ulysses* in 1922 Bloom has been further

victimised by cliché. He gets called 'the little man', though at 5 feet
$9\frac{1}{2}$ inches (17.86) he exceeds, as Ulysses should, the average Dublin
height.* Nor is he anonymous of feature; 'he was very handsome', Molly
recalls (18.208) of their courting days, and 'splendid set of teeth he
had made me hungry to look at them' (18.307). He is quietly witty,
too, and when not preoccupied as on Bloomsday by intolerable worry
he can be what Dublin much prizes, a man ready of tongue (12.893).
Least of all is he what he is easily taken for, the forgotten man with no
economic niche, weaver of a fiscal rope of sand. At a time when, as
Sean O'Faoloin tells us in *Vive Moi!*, a Cork policeman maintained a
family on a pound a week, Bloom has five guineas' income immediately
foreseeable (8.1060) plus cash in the bank worth six months of
Stephen's wages and, moreover, could buy and sell most of the people
he deals with on Bloomsday did he care to liquidate insurance and
securities that total nearly £1500 (17.1855). Ireland, he affirms, is his
country (12.1431), but he is not so Irish as to drink his modest income
up.

   Stature, relative wealth, an exalted dwelling-place, handsome features,
polysemous wit, a famously beautiful wife: Bloom may be said, albeit
misleadingly, to possess these salient attributes of his prototype the
Homeric chieftain. Not that we receive any encouragement to think of
him in that way. The essential facts come inconspicuously and late:
Bloom's height, for instance, when the long book has not many more
pages to run and the hero (engaged, it is true, like Ulysses, in 'a
stratagem') is climbing over an area railing. Next, the datum is repeated
in a demeaning context, as if it were an advertisement for a stray dog:

   £5 reward, lost, stolen or strayed from his residence 7 Eccles street,
   missing gent about 40, answering to the name of Bloom, Leopold
   (Poldy), height 5 ft $9\frac{1}{2}$ inches, full build, olive complexion, may have
   since grown a beard, when last seen was wearing a black suit.
   (17.2001)

Penelope of Ithaca composed no such notice, and £5 under-values the
absent hero whose worth the Phaeacians valued at thirteen bars of gold,
as many cloaks and tunics, a sword of silver and bronze and ivory, a
gold intaglio wine-cup, other treasures (*Odyssey* VIII, 392–431). No,
Ulysses will let us suppose in the first Bloom pages that a commonplace
man is getting breakfast for his wife, and will proceed to modify this

---

*Lionel Trilling was the first to point this out (*Sincerity and Authenticity*
(1972), 90). We can get at Dublin demographic norms obliquely. In Bloom's
time, when most British infantrymen were Irish, the average recruit measured
5 feet $4\frac{1}{2}$ inches, and Dublin Municipal Policemen, with a minimum height of
5 feet 9 inches, looked like 'giants' to the general public.

impression of ordinariness so imperceptibly we may need to combine exceptional attention with various outside knowledges, as of the elevation of Eccles Street, the size of Irishmen, the worth of a turn-of-the-century pound sterling, to perceive anything out of the way at all. Joyce is as cunning as his mythical hero, whose normal strategy was to withhold his identity.

Mulligan, we have noticed, is all outside; the book does not grant him a hint of inner life. Stephen by the end of 'Proteus' has become virtually all inside, the great bright world subsumed into his phrasemaking. Bloom at first is a balance; we move in and out, in and out, the 'out', however, closely in touch with the 'in', prompting, controlling.

> – Milk for the pussens, he said.
> – Mrkgnao! the cat cried.
> They call them stupid. They understand what we say better than we understand them. She understands all she wants to. Vindictive too. Cruel. Her nature. Curious mice never squeal. Seem to like it. Wonder what I look like to her. Height of a tower? No, she can jump me.
> – Afraid of the chickens she is, he said mockingly. Afraid of the chook-chooks. I never saw such a stupid pussens as the pussens.
> – Mrkrgnao! the cat said loudly. (4.24)

Though on a later reading we may think we glimpse Molly, *femme fatale*, behind 'she', and Bloom's masochism in the unsquealing mouse, still at first reading none of this is arcane the way Stephen's thoughts tend to be arcane, woven if not of wind then of insubstantialities, fine words, swift perverse associations, the mind enamoured of its own prestidigitation.

The way of Stephen's mind is something new in fiction, one reason completing *A Portrait of the Artist as a Young Man* cost Joyce ten years of trouble though he had written most of *Dubliners* in fourteen months. Achieved with such toil, the short novel's *style indirect libre* can perform with seeming ease and in the same movement both narrative and something more elusive than 'characterisation', the portrayal of one unique sensibility's individuating rhythm. To characterise, since Theophrastus, has been to classify, to offer the typical: Volpone is the Fox, Scrooge is the Miser, the Pardoner is the Avaricious Hyprocrite. Though to enliven and individuate a type was Shakespeare's miraculous gift, still the type is there, discernible: Falstaff the Fat Roisterer, Hamlet the Melancholic. But Stephen Dedalus: is he the Artist? That is not satis-factory, nor is the Sensitive Youth, nor the Tortured Apostate. He is difficult to speak of because he seems so delicately individuated by style that we, not the author, must impose the categories with which discussion proceeds. And in the first three episodes of *Ulysses* that style undergoes prodigious leaps of development. The dazzling 'Proteus', with its crystalline inventions – 'The new air greeted him, harping in wild nerves, wind of wild air of seeds of brightness' (3.266) – hardly a sentence resembling anything English has known before, a lucid, edged, energised particularity, in keeping company with the new century's most inventive new poetry nearly persuades us that fiction as we have known it is obsolescent, that new domains of sensibility, not character, lie open, that 'prose-poem', even, may connote something shapely.

Whereupon:

Mr Leopold Bloom ate with relish the inner organs of beasts and fowls. He liked thick giblet soup, nutty gizzards, a stuffed roast heart, liverslices fried with crustcrumbs, fried hencod's roes. Most of all he liked grilled mutton kidneys which gave to his palate a fine tang of faintly scented urine. (4.1–5)

Though neither Smollett nor Dickens any more than Henry James would have written down that last word, we seem back in their domain. Is Mr Bloom a caricature? Have we perhaps a parody of dead-end naturalism, as the deadly documentation proceeds – 'His hand took his hat from the peg over his initialled heavy overcoat and his lost property office secondhand waterproof' (4.66)? He exists, does Mr Bloom, comfortably in fiction's familiar world of nouns, all those *things* jostled by their attributes, all cerebration either an expository flight or a fly's crawl over the obvious.

And we seem to be being told everything, held as were early cinema audiences by the novel fascinations of watching the perfectly common-place take its course in an unfamiliar medium. A writer who can get down a cat's word accurately – 'Mrkrgnao!' – or make us *see* a mere tea-kettle on the fire – 'It sat there, dull and squat, its spout stuck out' – is compelling us to read what we had never thought to read with atten-tion, an account of a man getting through his own front door (a dozen lines of text!) on his way to purchase a mere breakfast kidney. ('Illiterate, underbred,' thought Virginia Woolf.[2]) We seem to follow him to the butcher's and back home step by step. Our attention lulled by so much urban specificity, we may not notice him getting back into the house, and a few pages later Joyce raps the desk for a lesson. Bloom on his way to the privy is made to reflect:

Where is my hat, by the way? Must have put it back on the peg. Or hanging up on the floor. Funny I don't remember that. (4.485)

Novelists normally don't know where characters' hats are. The heady experience of frequenting a novelist who does know may encourage us to turn back, expecting to find out more about Bloom than Bloom knows himself. If we do, this is what we find:

> Quick warm sunlight came running from Berkeley Road, swiftly, in slim sandals, along the brightening footpath. Runs, she runs to meet me, a girl with gold hair on the wind.
> Two letters and a card lay on the hallfloor. He stooped and gathered them. Mrs Marion Bloom. His quickened heart slowed at once. Bold hand. Mrs Marion.
> – Poldy!
> Entering the bedroom he halfclosed his eyes and walked through warm yellow twilight towards her tousled head. (4.240)

So there has been a skip in the narrative. We never did see Bloom pass through that door, nor take his hat off and dispose of it.

As to why we do not see him entering the door, what we see is in general what he is conscious of, and he does not bestow attention on passing back *in*, the way he did on how to leave it unlocked when he went *out*. Also he has had a bad scare ('Grey horror seared his flesh') and has no mind for the mechanics of entry; all he wants is 'to smell the gentle smoke of tea,* fume of the pan, sizzling butter. Be near her ample bedwarmed flesh. Yes, yes.' What scared him was a premonition of death. In grey air under a covered sun, suddenly a member of 'the oldest people' wandering from 'captivity to captivity', he had felt 'age crusting him with a salt cloak' and had had to remind himself that he was alive (4.232).

As to the hat: when he entered his 'quickened heart' was slowed by another unpleasant jolt: the envelope addressed 'Mrs Marion' in a 'bold hand'. Not only is 'Mrs Marion' a presumption that there is no Mr Leopold worth considering, but also the 'bold hand' is recognisably Boylan's, and we are having our first experience with the principle that any irruption of Boylan into his perceptual field has the effect of suspending Bloom's faculties. That is why he is not aware of what he did with his hat, and his 'Funny I don't remember that' affirms that we have here a silence of a special kind, a hiatus of perception, not an elision to speed the story up.

So the cry, 'Poldy!', breaks in upon a blankness for which the book has no notation to offer, and the next thing Bloom knows he is in the bedroom, approaching her 'ample bedwarmed flesh', walking through 'warm yellow twilight', warm as the sunlight that greeted him in the street, yellow as the sunlight's gold hair on the wind.

*Ulysses on Calypso's isle was near death from longing to see but the smoke rising from his home: *Odyssey*, I, 57–9. Joyce's use of incidental Homeric phrases has never been studied.

This sequence of narrative skips is something to examine, and the effect of 'Where is my hat by the way' is to nudge us back to examine it. 'Calypso', the first Bloom episode, abounds in little skips of that sort, hiatuses, narrative silences. There is much that the Blooms do not say to each other, much also that the book does not offer to say to us. Pondering such instances, we may learn how largely *Ulysses* is a book of silences despite its din of specifying, and may notice how eloquent is the Blooms' rhetoric of avoidance and also the author's. Some of the most moving things the book has to say are things never said.

Consider, for instance, that we are not present at an affair of some moment, the day's leavetaking. Bloom will be gone all day, and this is unusual; his job is undemanding and he is (Molly testifies) normally underfoot:

> he ought to chuck that Freeman with the paltry few shillings he knocks out of it and go into an office or something where hed get regular pay or a bank where they could put him up on a throne to count the money all the day of course he prefers plottering about the house so you cant stir with him any side whats your programme today (18.503)

Knowing that the writer of the 'bold hand' will be coming by, knowing what this portends, it would be callow and un-Bloomlike to just slip out the front door. Having left the jakes, he did go back up to take leave of her, he must have. And he would have meant to retrieve his latchkey, too, from the trousers in the bedroom wardrobe, though given the emotional import of the scene it is not surprising that he in fact forgot it again, and is some time remembering that he forgot.

The text has details to sustain our sense of the probable. Joyce clearly did think out such a scene, and very pointedly did not write it: a scene during which Bloom learns, what was not explicit earlier, that Boylan is coming at four, and Bloom says that he will not be home early, will dine out and perhaps go to the Gaiety. 'At four she said', we learn early in 'Sirens' (11.188), and she didn't say that in our hearing any time in 'Calypso'. True, there were other things she didn't say in our hearing, notably 'Met him pike hoses', and if that were all we had to go on we might suppose she specified 'at four' during one of those little narrative skips. But no, we'd best assume she said it at the second meeting, the one with the cards, the one Bloom remembers while he talks with McCoy perhaps half an hour afterward. 'Who's getting it up?' asks McCoy, preternaturally tactless, and Bloom thinks:

> Mrs Marion Bloom. Not up yet. Queen was in her bedroom eating bread and. No book. Blackened court cards laid along her thigh by sevens. Dark lady and fair man. Letter. Cat furry black ball. Torn strip of envelope.

Love's.
Old.
Sweet.
Song.
Comes lo-ove's old . . . . (5.154)

Not up yet. ('Who's getting it up?' Not up *yet.*) The cat is on her bed, the cat we saw starting upstairs as Bloom left for the privy (4.468).

This is the scene we are after, and lest we think he's remembering some earlier day, not today, we are apprised that the torn strip of Boylan's envelope is still in sight. And the cards are the cards Molly recalls in 'Penelope' – 'yes wait yes hold on he was on the cards this morning when I laid out the deck union with a young stranger neither dark nor fair' (18.1313).* As for 'going to the Gaiety', 'I said I' is all Bloom imparts to himself in 'Hades' (6.185); Molly again is more explicit: 'he said Im dining out and going to the Gaiety' (18.81).

So they had that talk, and we hear of it in bits, and some of the bits are eighteen hours surfacing. It's by no means a trivial scene that we've failed to witness; they both know that when they meet again things will be irreversibly altered between them. Why, then, are we excluded from the bedroom of the Blooms during those last minutes together? If Joyce were the implacable realist we're sometimes told about, he would have forced us to watch.

But he is not; he is a connoisseur of performances. Social and psychic reality, for Joyce, are aspects of performance. In *Finnegans Wake* a very small troupe of players – perhaps six, plus supernumeraries – fills the air with hundreds of voices, congests the page with thousands of names. Speech for Joyce, as for men of the Renaissance, is the distinctively human act. Silence, a failure of role, is the stuff of drama (so Shakespeare, compared to Ibsen, is merely 'literature in dialogue' – *Critical Writings*, 39).

What a role is for any actor knows; it tells you what to say next. As such it is Joyce's equivalent for the formulas which by Milman Parry's hypothesis told Homer what to say next; Homer, like Bloom, like everyone, was improvising aloud and needed to run no risk of being left speechless. Joyce understood as early as *Dubliners* that it is not only the bard for whom speechlessness is a peril; it is anyone at all confronted by anyone else's expectations. Nothing creates more social awkwardness than the sudden simultaneous silence of everyone present, and roles can prevent this from ever happening.

If I am Boylan, man of the world, I say things like 'That'll do, game

---

*Bloom's 'dark lady and fair man' goes by the look of the cards, where all Jacks have yellow hair; Molly's 'neither dark nor fair' must stem, like 'young stranger', from rules of interpretation.

ball' and 'What's the damage?' – things like that (10.304, 325). If I am a
stately buck, I say 'God, isn't he dreadful?' and 'The mockery of it'
(1.51, 34). These two men of the future are great successes, thanks to their
skill at imposing their roles on the situation. Boylan's very hand can
speak with authority, as in the wordless riposte Molly recalls with
disfavour: 'no thats no way for him has he no manners nor no refinement
nor no nothing in his nature slapping us behind like that on my bottom'
(18.1368). It was evidently eloquent at the time.

Failures of role are instructive. Mulligan's deserts him once, when
Stephen casts back at him words it˙ had once prompted, 'It's only
Dedalus whose mother is beastly dead', and the Buck blushes as he says,
'Did I say that? Well, what harm in that?' (1.202) Boylan's deserted
him when he learned the result of the Gold Cup and tore up his tickets
in a tantrum (18.423): less, one supposes, because he has lost £20
than because he feels made a fool of.

Stephen Dedalus apprises us that silence may *be* a role. A student
of silence, exile and cunning, he sometimes talks nonsense, sometimes
has nothing to say, is sometimes grossly offensive, and throughout the
book is preparing to disappear. If other men say nothing when a role
fails, he is preparing a role which shall consist in saying nothing.

And Bloom? Bloom has numerous roles, *Odysseus polyhistrion*, and
does not know that one of them is Ulysses. Opposite the cat, his day's
first interlocutor, he plays the kindly catkeeper, Leo pride of the ring.
Opposite the Cyclops, he is an Eloquent Jew who could talk of a straw
for an hour and talk steady (12.893). Opposite Molly, he is the
unctuous lightbreakfastbringer, the pedagogue of Metempsychosis, the
complaisant absentee, the man who won't be there, the – but this role
is unscripted – incipient cuckold. What do you say to let your wife know
that you know why Boylan is coming? No answer. And no scene.

Joyce writes nothing that is not already written. Like the Homer of
Samuel Butler's imagination he does not like inventing, chiefly because
he thinks human beings seldom invent, and the painful scene is unwritten
because its silences will have outscreamed its speeches. A silence. What
time is Boylan coming? At four. A silence. I shall be late. A silence.
I think I shall dine out ('dine out', good God, 'dine out') and perhaps
go to the Gaiety ('the Gaiety!'). This is not a normal morning. Normally
their dialogue is scripted, as when Molly asks him the 'destination
whither, the place where, the time at which, the duration for which,
the object with which' (17.2296) in the case of temporary absences
projected as well as effected. That has become *her* role, the intent shrew,
and she has played it for nine months, ever since Milly's puberty. But
we cannot imagine her having the immense coolness to run through that
catechism this morning. So both are roleless, awkward, and we are
shown no performance.

And we ought to observe how much silence pervades such of their conversation as we do hear. They are agreed to pretend that Blazes Boylan is coming to hear Molly sing. They agree to regard the projected concert tour – Molly with Boylan! – as a fund-raising project. They are agreed that Molly may put Boylan's letter not quite under the pillow, and that Leopold will see it, and that she will see him see it, and that neither will comment. They agree that 'Mrs Marion' will pass without remark. They are so much agreed on all this that they even agree to let the time of Boylan's arrival be unspecified – a casual drop-in merely – until (in that hidden interview) either Bloom asks for the time of the assignation or Molly volunteers it, on the shared understanding that Poldy must know how long to stay out of the house. Their conversation is guided by a set of agreements not to ask, not to comment.

'At four she said.' Though Boylan as it happens arrives late, 4 p.m. does mark a division in *Ulysses*, between the end of 'Wandering Rocks' and the start of 'Sirens'. This division is important enough to be signalled in several ways, not least by the advent of engulfing stylistic idiosyncrasies. Examining it on the plane of naturalistic action, we may say that it demarks two phases of Bloom's day. Up to 'Wandering Rocks' he is moving through a day's routine, benumbed by impending cuckoldry, whereas after 'Sirens' he is in free fall, routine and cuckoldry equally behind him, occupied chiefly with staying away from the house as long as he can, and evading the question how long that had better be. (He mustn't meet Boylan, and will prefer not to talk to Molly. When will she be asleep? 'Must be getting on for nine by the light. Go home. . . . No. Might be still up': 13.1212.)

But, until 4 p.m., benumbment. For eight hours Bloom goes through engrossing motions, busily curious, blocking off from his thoughts what ought to be the novel's principal topic, the Boylan–Molly liaison. From 'Calypso' to 'Wandering Rocks', *Ulysses* exemplifies a kind of fiction Ernest Hemingway is sometimes credited with inventing: the kind which foregrounds meticulously rendered detail which we may be misled into taking for the real theme. Such fiction can mislead. 'Big Two-Hearted River' was admired for years because it seemed to render with such immediacy a fisherman's absorption in his sport. That the theme of the whole story was what Nick Adams was not thinking of, was screening off from his mind by preoccupation with the little rituals of fishing, this was years in coming clear. *Ulysses*, similarly, was long regarded as an eccentrically detailed account of a man spending a Dublin day: 'the dailiest day possible', it was even called. Not at all. The man is virtually in shock.

In 'Lotos-Eaters' Bloom, embarked on his day, is adrift, erratic; he has nearly two hours to put in before the funeral, and there are welcome distractions: picking up his clandestine mail at the post-office box, idling in a church, buying soap, ordering Molly's lotion, indulging in a bath. The Boylan topic comes up once (raised by the unwelcome McCoy) and is at once suppressed; Dublin's lotos-anodynes are powerful in mid-morning.

In 'Hades' Blazes Boylan is actually sighted, saluting the cortège; Bloom instantly 'reviewed the nails of his left hand, then those of his right hand. The nails, yes' (6.200). He does not need to pursue this for long; in the rest of the episode death itself is an engulfing distraction. So, in the following episode, is business. Fussing with the absurd complications posed by Keyes' trivial ad – Can the crossed-keys design be obtained? Will 'puffs' be forthcoming? Can Keyes be persuaded to renew for a sufficient span? – he has room for but a single hasty thought of Eccles Street: 'I could go home still: tram: something I forgot' (7.230).

By 1 p.m. he has run out of distractions. There is nothing to do but walk and eat lunch, and the thought of Boylan assails him again and again.

– Will Boylan infect Molly? (8.102)

– How Boylan's fingers touched Molly's two Sundays past:

Touch. Fingers. Asking. Answer. Yes.
Stop. Stop. If it was it was. Must. (8.591)

– Nosey Flynn's 'Isn't Blazes Boylan mixed up in it?'; whereupon

A warm shock of air heat of mustard hanched on Mr Bloom's heart. He raised his eyes and met the stare of a bilious clock. Two. Pub clock five minutes fast. Time going on. Hands moving. Two. Not yet. (8.789)

– How having lightly lunched he can dine at six: 'Six, six. Time will be gone then. She...' (8.852).

– And, horrors, Boylan himself, walking straight toward him. 'Straw hat in sunlight. Tan shoes. Turnedup trousers. It is. It is.' This crisis absorbs fully 200 words. His breath is short; his heart troubles him; his hands search pockets in a dumbshow of misdirection ('I am looking for that. Yes, that'). He ducks out of sight into the museum gate (8.1168).

Ventral and sexual hungers, this episode implies, are intertwined. With his mind on lunch Bloom at one moment lingers for half a page amid memories of his idyllic time with Molly, sixteen years ago now, amid the rhododendrons atop Howth (8.899), and at another moment is virtually pursued by erotic fancies prompted by a window display (8.631). This episode, 'Lestrygonians', and this one alone bears out what one might have expected to be the premise of the book, that Bloom is a man driven by Boylan's spectre. From no episode, indeed, is Boylan wholly absent, but Joyce knew better than to let his menace grow dominant. A postcard he sent his brother in 1907 from Rome illustrates amusingly the habit of mind that served *Ulysses* so well. He has been to hear *Götterdämmerung*, and 200 crisp words convey the evening: the neighbour who smelt of garlic and got sleepy; the man who said Wagner's music was splendid but intended only for Germans; the horse which 'being unable to sing, evacuated'; the devotees with scores; the people humming 'correctly and incorrectly the nine notes of the funeral motive'; everything but the music, save for one phrase. A malicious little masterpiece, the card situates us vividly at the perform-ance, yet permits Wagner's opera to be present only by indirection, between sentences.[3] Wagner created that evening as Boylan creates the quality of Bloom's day; Boylan, too, is absent from *Ulysses* most of the time.

And, so far as presence is conveyed by explicit textual attention, Bloom eventually commences to be absent as well. In 'Scylla and Charybdis', where he puts in time at the Library hunting down the design for Keyes' ad, we barely see him, though we can trace his move-ments from little clues. And in 'Wandering Rocks' he is accorded one vignette out of nineteen.

Here he is immobile, savouring porn. At the midpoint of the hour before the dreaded rendezvous, he is attending to his last errand for Molly, who had asked for another book. So in this last of the 'natural-istic' episodes we leave Bloom amid the circulation of indifferent Dubliners, devouring what may pass for an account of what is on the threshold of occurring:

> Yes. This. Here. Try.
> – *Her mouth glued on his in a luscious voluptuous kiss while his hands felt for the opulent curves inside her deshabille.*
> Yes. Take this. The end. (10.610)

Though Shakespeare, even when read with the aid of a glossary, has in the past shed little light on difficult problems (17.390), today the ancient technique of *sortes Virgilianae* ('he read where his finger opened') has disclosed a radiance in *Sweets of Sin*: a book in which the situation at home is mirrored. He has found what perhaps he did not know he was looking for, turning over the volumes at more than one bookseller's.

So Bloom's day until four; or, by Mr Clive Hart's precise calculations, until 3.18. We take leave of him absorbed in sexual fantasies, immobile amid indifferent mobilities, one citizen among dozens, among thousands, his private miseries translated into a few vulgar words in a book. 'Hands felt for the opulent.' His hands hold a block of bound paper labelled *Sweets of Sin*: a book within a book. He will shortly put down the inflated rental, a shilling, and take the drab pages with him into the next hours' aimlessness.

NOTES

1 Louis Hyman, *The Jews of Dublin* (Shannon, 1972), 60. This author's pertinacity was unflagging; he is notable for having run down Dlugascz, a Triestine Jew whom Joyce in one of his whimsical departures from verity installed in a porkbutcher's shop on Dublin's Dorset Street.
2 Virginia Woolf, *A Writer's Diary* (New York, 1954), 49.
3 *Letters*, II, 214.

CHAPTER 6

Stephen's Day

The book's switch of attention to Bloom, we have noted already, counts as a major event. Not only has there been no hint that such a person exists, but there has also been nothing in the lengthening Stephen Dedalus saga – one whole book, plus three chapters of this one – to apprise us that persons exist, that a world exists, beyond the domain of Stephen's perceptual field. So portentous is Bloom's appearance that the sun in the sky is set back, and the day of *Ulysses* commences over again at 8 a.m.

His advent is like the introduction of a dark sun into a system of errant bodies. His superior gravitational field assumes control, and it becomes convenient to plot orbits with reference to him. So *Ulysses* is Bloomocentric. In particular, after he and Stephen finally meet, two seemingly impersonal episodes, 'Eumaeus' and 'Ithaca', are perceptibly tilted toward Bloom's view of things. Thus such a word as 'inexplicable' means 'not understood by Bloom'. But we are apt not to notice this tilt, and when Stephen, declining Bloom's offer of a bed for the night, is said to do so 'inexplicably' (17.955), we may want to echo Buck Mulligan's exasperation with Stephen, 'O, an impossible person' (1.222).

Still, Stephen's long day is not as inexplicable as all that, and though he is out of our sight for hours at a time we can make a fair effort at reconstructing its continuities.

(8.00–8.45 a.m.) Up, 'displeased and sleepy', to the top of the tower, where Mulligan is playing at his tiresome mockeries. It has been a bad night. The third man, Haines, raved in his sleep about shooting a black panther. Since Haines has a guncase handy, and Stephen took to wearing black when his mother was buried a year ago, Stephen's terror is understandable. And he continues to be haunted by his mother – has dreamed at least once of her coming from the grave to bend over him – and galled by his state of dependence on Mulligan, who not only paid the rent* and calls the tunes, but assumes *droit de seigneur* over Stephen's

---

*I owe to Arnold Goldman the suggestion that Stephen's unspoken words 'It is mine. I paid the rent' (1.631) are to be read in Mulligan's voice, between invisible quotation marks, as words Stephen can already hear Mulligan speaking when he demands the key. For it is unlike Stephen to assert ownership in consequence of payment – that is the way of the Mulligans and Deasys. Moreover, when Haines asks whether rent is paid for the tower, it is Mulligan

school pay as well. By the end of breakfast it has been established that he is to entertain Haines with his *Hamlet* performance, that they are to meet at the Ship at 12.30, and that he himself is powerless not to do what Mulligan tells him. ('And twopence, he said, for a pint. Throw it there. Stephen threw two pennies': 1.724.) As he leaves he says to himself, 'I will not sleep here tonight. Home also I cannot go.'

(9.00–10.30 a.m.) He has walked into Dalkey, and we find him in the classroom hearing recitations of history (Pyrrhus) and literature ('Lycidas') and worrying about determinism: Were the things that never happened in any sense possible, seeing that they never were? In short, was the aborting of his escape to Paris fated, and is he fated to be here? Pyrrhus is remembered for his Pyrrhic victory; the flight to Paris may have been one of those. As for Lycidas, his original, Edward King, drowned in the same Irish Sea Stephen crossed to return to his mother's bedside, but gained immortality 'Through the dear might of him that walked the waves', also through the might of his acquaintance who wrote the poem. Stephen has abandoned Christ, and his Milton is likely to be Mulligan.

Here in the classroom history and poem alike are mazes for boys to stumble through. They have one recourse: children of affluent Dalkey, they feel safe in cheeking Stephen. Talbot's 'recitation' of 'Lycidas' is a reading from an ill-concealed book, and Stephen mildly lets him know that he knows this and isn't going to forbid it (2.80). On the other hand, a boy someone else has ordered to recopy algebra problems from the board receives liberating guidance; Stephen shows him how to do them himself. ('The soul is the form of forms', and Sargent's soul can now encompass algebraic forms.)

Stephen treats this job as a squalid secret, incompatible with the artist's welcome to Life. Mulligan, who knows about it, has been let think the pay is more than it is ('Four shining sovereigns, Buck Mulligan cried with delight': (1.296). Others who help him drink it up are told he gets his money for poems (11.265; 14.287), perhaps Stephen's way of compensating himself for his omission from AE's anthology (9.20). In cold fact he receives from Mr Deasy, the day after the 15th of each month, £3 12s 0d for services rendered, each ritual of

---

who promptly answers with the exact amount, twelve quid. And this is a preposterous amount for us to think of Stephen getting together at any time. Five months ago he borrowed a guinea (2.257) from AE when he was hungry, and promptly spent most of it in a harlot's bed (9.195). On his wage of £3 12s 0d he could have amassed twelve quid (hardly eating) in four paydays, but there has been only one payday before this one (2.233) – the first of 'three times' was a bargaining session – and his acknowledged debts to 10 people total £25 17s 6d (of which £9 is owed to Mulligan) plus socks, shoes, ties, two lunches, five weeks' board.

payment reconfirming his servitude. Today Deasy's commission – to get a letter about foot and mouth disease into the press – affirms the practical man's valuation of 'literary friends'. 'I will try,' Stephen says, 'and let you know tomorrow. I know two editors slightly' (2.413). This undertaking, punctiliously carried out, will shape his day till mid-afternoon.

We should note the punctiliousness; Stephen can be 'impossible', but is not necessarily so on principle. We should note, too, that in the terminology of *Finnegans Wake* he spends many hours playing Shaun the Post, delivering letters, while Mulligan is permitted to play Shem the Penman, literary and insufferable. Though Joyce saw these two as opposed dynamic principles, their taxonomy is still not well understood. Thus in *Finnegans Wake*, II, ii, marginalia to a schoolbook are supplied by the polarised brothers, and commentators agree that phrases like '*Bet you fippence, anythesious, there's no purgatory, are you game?*' belong to Shem (Stephen), but 'THE LOCALISATION OF LEGEND LEADING TO THE LEGALISATION OF LATIFUNDISM' must be ascribed to Shaun (Mulligan), in accordance with an unformulated premise that Joyce allied art with infantilism and anti-art with pedantry. But Latinisms in *Ulysses* come from Stephen, easy blasphemies from Mulligan; roles and psyches need not map one another in an obvious way, and the parody of professorship in the book is surely Stephen's virtuoso impersonation of a Shakespeare commentator, which 'poet' Mulligan professes to find incomprehensible.

(10.30–12 noon) By tram to Haddington Road, where he has a choice; and when we next spot him (6.39) – 'a lithe young man, clad in mourning, a wide hat' – he has chosen not to take the connecting tram to the city centre but to walk toward Sandymount. Having time to kill before the rendezvous at the Ship, he has apparently decided, without enthusiasm, to investigate the chances of lodging with Aunt Sara. But he does not, without really deciding not to ('I have passed the way to Aunt Sara's. Am I not going there? Seems not': 3.158). He walks eastwards along a spit of sand, talking to himself; reaffirms that he will not return to the tower (3.276); scrambles on to higher rocks to let the incoming tide flow by, composes a quatrain, lies back on the rocks, apparently masturbates,* and sitting up to look back sees a Calvary emblem: three moving masts with 'crosstrees' (3.504).

The quatrain is about Death, a pale vampire, coming as his dead mother came to him by night. It is also a poetic defeat, being no more than a stanza of Douglas Hyde's *Love Songs of Connacht* with a few

---

*See David Hayman, 'Stephen on the rocks', *James Joyce Quarterly*, XV, 1 (Fall, 1977), 5–17. In one of the many parallels between 'Proteus' and 'Nausicaa', Bloom on the rocks on the same beach does the same things hours later.

words changed. Translating Irish, Hyde was obligated by the Irish past; beset by the Irish present, Stephen is coerced by Hyde, and the vampire comes, like the poem, in the nightmare from which he is 'trying to awake' (2.377). Whatever he can say seems derived from what someone has said before, one reason the first word of this episode is 'ineluctable'. 'Cousin Stephen, you will never be a saint,' he has told himself (3.128), doubtless intending also what Dryden is sometimes supposed to have told Swift: 'Cousin Swift, you will never be a poet.' And 'Here, I am not walking out to the Kish lightship, am I?' (3.267) means that neither like Christ nor like Milton will he walk the waves. All his thought derives from himself, returns to himself; thus thoughts about heresies have actually been about paternity, Arius offering the attractive possibility that the bond of son with father may be an elective one. But there is no eluding the 'strandentwining' cables of heredity, and when he turns his thoughts to Aunt Sara's people his 'consubstantial father's voice' (3.62) takes abrupt possession of his mind, brutal with a contempt he himself has not willed. Richard Feverel was destroyed by his struggle to escape the tyranny of a rationally benevolent father; Stephen's deepest fear appears to be that his father, though turned indifferent, may destroy him through a tyranny of the blood. Drunkenness, improvidence, failure, may these be inherited?

His father controls his genes, his mother his dreams; Ireland shapes his opportunities. Intricately though he has twisted and turned, he is like a character in *Dubliners*, that book of traps.

(12.00–12.30 p.m.) A quick walk via Ringsend and the river to the centre of town, and he has now decided not to go to the Ship: he can cut that bond at least. Having money, he conceives the first of his day's grand gestures: a telegram which will encode the message, 'You want to enjoy my performance without paying me in any sort of coin.' He addresses it to the Ship from College Green post office, which means that a boy will carry it about four short blocks, then himself takes the boy's route northward across the Liffey toward the *Evening Telegraph* office, at some point joined by Mr O'Madden Burke. People with no fixed occupation have the knack of joining him.

(12.30–1.30 p.m.) One errand is accomplished: the editor assures him (7.586) that Deasy's letter will go in. Stephen next contrives his Parable of the Plums, and Professor MacHugh enjoys it; no one else hears it (7.1061). At 1 p.m. he and five others enter Mooney's, only a few doors from the Ship. Stephen spends some shillings (9.535) treating, with money he says is a fee for 'the labour of his Muse' (11.265). In this company he poses as paid author, which helps explain Crawford's effort to recruit him for the paper.

(1.30–4.00 p.m.) Stephen and the parasite Lenehan move their drinking one block to the other Mooney's (3 Eden Quay), whence Stephen takes his leave, the warmer by three whiskeys (9.533), to deliver the other copy of Deasy's letter to AE at the *Homestead*. Probably he went to the *Homestead* office (22 Lincoln Place, near Bloom's bath) and was sent the further few hundred yards to the Library, where AE was to be found in the Librarian's office. By the time the narrative locates Stephen again AE has received the letter and had it explained to him (9.316), the talk has turned to *Hamlet*, Stephen has called this sacred play a ghost-story, and there has been some sceptical friction which the Quaker librarian is composing (9.1). Before long Stephen is launched on a version of the lecture he dodged giving for Haines at the Ship. Midway his nemesis enters – Buck Mulligan, whom he'd thought safely ditched.

Despite the Buck's heckling, Stephen forces himself through his *Hamlet* re-creation, without holding AE to the end or satisfying the most exacting auditor present, the essayist John Eglinton, in W. B. Yeats's opinion 'our one Irish critic'. He and Mulligan then walk together from the Library as far as the gates of Trinity, where the Buck goes on to the DBC to meet Haines (10.1043) and Stephen lingers to chat (10.338) with an Italian acquaintance. This man tries to persuade him he should turn to singing; he would make money with his voice: 'But instead you are sacrificing yourself.' Stephen replies, 'A bloodless sacrifice,' but agrees to think about it. He then wanders off alone down Fleet Street, parallel with the Liffey. He meets his impoverished sister (10.855) but does not offer her money. Intellectual cravings are stirring in her, too; she has spent a penny on a French grammar. He and she, he proposes in a lurid set-piece, are drowning together in Dublin's mad sea. He is perceiving a parallel with something he imagined in the morning, an effort to save a drowning man as Mulligan once did:

I would want to. I would try. I am not a strong swimmer. . . . If I had land under my feet. I want his life still to be his, mine to be mine. A drowning man. His human eyes scream to me out of horror of his death. I . . . With him together down. . . . (3.323)

Now his pity for his sister Dilly takes the following highly wrought form:

She is drowning. Agenbite. Save her. Agenbite. All against us. She will drown me with her, eyes and hair. Lank coils of seaweed hair around me, my heart, my soul. Saltgreen death.
We.
Agenbite of inwit. Inwit's agenbite.
Misery! Misery! (10.875)

Turning his pity and guilt into heady rhetoric, he shirks the morning's 'I would try', though there are still some three pounds in his pocket. He will do his drowning in pubs.

The sea is a torpid Sargasso, bearing him in listless arcs. Unlike Ulysses/Bloom, engaged on voyages of sweep and amplitude, Stephen hasn't strayed more than a few hundred yards from College Green in the centre of Dublin since he arrived there just past noon and sent the telegram. By mid-afternoon it is clear to him that he has thought, talked and misconducted himself into virtual non-existence. He has no place to stay, he is close to having no job. The literary establishment – Eglinton, AE, the librarians – treat him as an uncomfortable fantastic. His poems will not be in AE's 'sheaf of our younger poets' verses' (9.290), and it is Mulligan, not he, who will be going to George Moore's gathering of 'the best wits of the town' (14.780). There is no allure in two options that have been offered: to sell his voice, to do something vulgar for the newspapers. With the sun still high on this almost longest of days, he may as well succumb to his destiny and start drinking in earnest.

So he hangs about in mid-town, drinking and treating in the Moira and Larchet's: drowning. He is, no doubt about it, Si Dedalus' son, and by the time we next encounter him past 10 p.m. he will not have dined but will have gone through thirteen shillings altogether, five days' pay, with the binge still young (14.285).

CHAPTER 7

The Arranger

A line across the page divides, nine and nine, the first extant list of *Ulysses* episodes, the one Joyce sent John Quinn in September 1920 (*Letters*, I, 145). Correspondingly, the words 'End of First Part of *Ulysses*' appear on the last page of the Rosenbach fair copy of Episode 9, 'Scylla and Charybdis'. If we append to this half its coda, 'Wandering Rocks', we have a ten-episode block, homogenous in its style[1] and reasonably self-contained in its themes and actions. It is instructive to linger on this fragment. What should we make of *Ulysses* if it had ended with 'Wandering Rocks'?

We should have, by contrast with the book we know, a moderately orthodox novel of under 100,000 words, its ten chapters each of fairly normal length. The interior monologue, tactfully introduced, would be its striking technical feature: that and a certain penchant for abrupt scene-shifting (and both have precedents in Meredith). It would follow, contrapuntally, Stephen Dedalus and Leopold Bloom from 8 a.m. till mid-afternoon, when the ostensible business of each is done for the day. Bloom, fussing with Keyes's ad, is tacitly acquiescing in cuckoldry. Stephen, placing Deasy's letter with editors, is unresistant to the role of bullockbefriending bard.

We might say, two *Dubliners* stories intercut. Bloom's story – the cuckold-to-be drifting round the city, triumphant only in procuring the porn book his wife wanted – may even be based on the 'Ulysses' story Joyce thought of writing late in 1906; the ironic point of the title is simply the faithlessness of Penelope.[2] Stephen's story – the 'artist' ruminating, drinking, and placing someone else's letter to the press – resolves, with ironies of its own, 'A Little Cloud', the last *Dubliners* story Joyce wrote before he conceived 'The Dead'. Its artist, though formidably talented by contrast with the story's Little Chandler, has seemingly made his restless peace with the world's Ignatius Gallaghers. Intertwining these two stories, our ten-episode *Ulysses* affirms the usual *Dubliners* message, the futility of Dublin aspirations. A marriage that has come to be defined by masochistic non-interference, a vocation that has lapsed into acquiescence in being, like it or not, a drunken father's bibulous son – these are a Dublin marriage, a Dublin vocation. Ulysses' consort will welcome a brawny suitor; Telemachus is driven by his consubstantial father who is not in heaven nor yet secure in his kingdom. And the tenth episode draws back as though to locate and also lose these two in a fragmented Dublin like that of *Dubliners*, where many other lives are taking their course while Church and State command the passer-by's assent.

How Joyce might have talked about *Ulysses* had he planned to end it here is a question not quite beyond speculation; its governing note is irony, relentless irony, like the governing note of *Dubliners*, and we may remark how he refrained from summarising *Dubliners* stories. In numerous letters he alluded to them in passing and by title, once or twice hinting that a plain blunt reader would miss much that they contained, but thematic summaries he avoided. The theme of a *Dubliners* story and the graph of its happenings are apt to be entirely different things; it is pointless to say that in 'Grace' four good-hearted men talk a fifth into amending his ways. For their talk is a monstrous collage of misinformation, and the sermon to which they lead their friend is ingratiatingly unedifying, and as for the title, 'Grace', if mysterious grace works like this, summoning Tom Kernan to no more than Father Purdon's preaching, then it is (is it not?) the free gift (*gratia*) of an unworthy God. Groping to summarise, we are back with the word 'irony', and to any questions about a much longer work in this vein Joyce's answer might well have been a thin-lipped smile.

But Joyce did discuss *Ulysses*; always, as we have seen, with reference to the Homeric parallel. This, we may now note, commences to direct the action only in the second half of the book, where its working-out establishes the requirement that Ulysses and Telemachus shall meet. If its function in a ten-episode *Ulysses* is ironic, in the eighteen-episode *Ulysses* it is coercive. Remove it, and nothing is left to obligate what only chance procures, some kind of confrontation between the two figures who when we last discern them in 'Wandering Rocks' are each as shut away in private concerns as two characters in the same book might possibly be. Save in a non-Aristotelean universe, one might suppose, their conjunction could not be plausibly arranged.

And Joyce planned from the start that his principal characters should meet. In 1920 (*Letters*, III, 31) he told John Quinn that 'Ithaca' and 'Penelope' – Bloom with Stephen; Molly's thoughts – had been sketched since 1916, his first year of undivided work on *Ulysses*. Later his first biographer, Herbert Gorman, was to hear that 'preliminary sketches for the final sections' dated from early 1914.[3] Whatever their date, they preceded the toil that began at the beginning. Joyce then elaborated the first half of the book in what he was to call 'the initial style' (*Letters*, I, 129), a manner backed by fluent practice with *Dubliners* and the *Portrait*. This took until early 1919 – say, three years – and with no disrespect to a prodigious feat of writing we may call it relatively rapid work for a man who had struggled during $5\frac{1}{2}$ years on the five-chapter *Portrait*. Fourteen *Dubliners* stories and twenty-five chapters of *Stephen*

Hero had taken but a year and a half; the *Dubliners* irony is useful if one must produce, and it helped him produce unelaborated versions of the early sections of *Ulysses* with some facility. If once in a while two sentences took all day,[4] we may be sure that on other days long passages were blocked out with little hesitation. (At two lines a day, *Ulysses* would have taken forty years.)

And now, at midpoint, new invention was incumbent. Bloom and Stephen were to converge, and one thing needed was a set of narrative conventions that would keep an eye on two main characters simultaneously without acquiescing in Victorian fictionist's puppetry. 'Aeolus', the first episode in which Stephen and Bloom are both present though not at the same time, was one precedent. Joyce had already stressed the artifice of its surfaces, making the first sentence of his first version read:

Grossbooted draymen rolled barrels dullthudding out of Prince's stores and bumped them up on the brewery float. (7.21)

This already seems to foresee the sentence he was later to insert after it:

On the brewery float bumped dullthudding barrels rolled by grossbooted draymen out of Prince's stores.

Though Bloom is within earshot of the din, the syntactic artifice is not meant to reflect the working of his busy mind: rather, a self-sufficient geometry as indifferent to his presence as are whatever Newtonian equations can describe the momentum of dullthudding barrels. Subsequent to its *Little Review* publication (October 1918) Joyce was greatly to extend the artifice of 'Aeolus', multiplying its rhetorical figures, emphasising their conspicuousness, breaking the text sixty-three times with captions, even introducing the episode with yet more paragraphs of Bloomless material, the tramcars, the bootblacks.[5] 'Rhetoric', which is something less personal than pervasive talk and gives a collective identity to disembodied facility with words, corresponds, as it blows through the episode's interstices, to a certain Dublin indifference on the part of the talkers, anonymous as the wind 'that changing its direction changes its name'. Petty errands, unconsummated, blow Bloom in and out, unattended to, and no one but Professor MacHugh hears out Stephen's parable.

In 'Wandering Rocks' – apparently an addition to plans that had seemed firm as late as May 1918[6] – Joyce extended the principle of pervasive indifference, again inserting Stephen and Bloom into separated parts of the one episode but entrusting the whole to a narrator whose grim delight is to monitor with clock and map the space–time whereabouts of more than thirty characters simultaneously. All these people, plus the many who jostle them and the viceregal cavalcade that sweeps east and then south-east across the city, make a composite synecdoche for Dublin; here as in 'Aeolus' a rhetoric that can manage more than one centre of awareness is still grounded in Dublin itself.

Once accustomed in 'Wandering Rocks' to a narrator with a good deal more in mind than getting on with two men's fortunes, we shall not be allowed to overlook his autonomy again. It is as though a giant were slowly coming awake. In 'Sirens' he manifests two more degrees of freedom. For the first time 'style', some game the narrator is playing, is more expressive and more apparent than narration, forcing us to pay close attention if we would be sure what the characters are doing. And, in a manner reminiscent of 'Wandering Rocks', details commence to find their way on to the page without regard for the consciousness of anyone present, thoroughly subverting the premise of the initial style. In 'Wandering Rocks' such details had been cross-links of synchronicity. In 'Sirens' their origin is in former time, coming as they do from earlier parts of the book. Bloom munches, and the page comments:

> Leopold cut liverslices. As said before he ate with relish the inner organs, nutty gizzards, fried cods' roes.... (11.519)

'As said before' looks back to the first of all the Bloom sentences:

> Mr Leopold Bloom ate with relish the inner organs of beasts and fowls. He liked thick giblet soup, nutty gizzards, a stuffed roast heart, liver slices fried with crustcrumbs, fried hencod's roes. (4.1)

And, lest the retrospect be missed, the 'Sirens' narrator soon repeats, 'Bloom ate liv as said before'. Some pages later we find Bloom furtively answering Martha's letter. He pens a postscript, 'I feel so sad today. So lonely,' and reflects:

> Too poetical that about the sad. Music did that. Music hath charms. Shakespeare said. Quotations every day in the year. To be or not to be. Wisdom while you wait.

Whereupon the narrator interpolates:

> In Gerard's rosery of Fetter Lane he walks, greyedauburn. One life is all. One body. Do. But do. (11.904)

And Bloom, as if he had either heard this remark or not heard it, continues, 'Done anyhow': meaning he has written what he has written. The narrator has paraphrased and interpolated thoughts about Shakespeare which Stephen framed but did not speak two hours before (9.651). Some mind, it is clear, keeps track of the details of this printed cosmos, and lets escape from its scrutiny the fall of no sparrow.

The intrusion of this consciousness is perhaps the most radical, the most disconcerting innovation in all of *Ulysses*. It is something new in fiction. It is not the voice of the storyteller: not a voice at all, since it does not address us, does not even speak. We do not hear its accents, we observe its actions, which are performed with a certain indifference to our presence: actions such as pasting captions across the pages of 'Aeolus' in such wise as to render impossible a straightforward vocal performance of that talk-ridden episode.

For the tale of Bloomsday is not in the old sense, nor in any sense, 'told'; it is mimed in words arranged on pages in space. We are urged to read aloud and tripped up if we try. The arranging presence (David Hayman, the first critic to dwell on its intrusions, has even suggested that we say 'the Arranger'[7]) enjoys a seemingly total recall for exact forms of words used hundreds of pages earlier, a recall which implies not an operation of memory but access such as ours to a printed book, in which pages can be turned to and fro. Like an author's ideal reader, this Arranger keeps remembering, savouring the choice verbal bits.

We have mentioned a certain indifference to our presence; and yet surely 'Bloom ate liv as said before' is marginally aware that we are present to be irritated. 'A harsh and awkward narrator,' Clive Hart writes of the spirit behind 'Wandering Rocks', 'whose difficult personality is the most salient thing about the chapter'.[8] 'Wandering Rocks' was Joyce's earliest exploitation of the Arranger – the captions in 'Aeolus' extended his presence retroactively at a late stage of revision – and it is noteworthy that in 'Wandering Rocks' the Arranger's difficult personality manifests itself in snares scattered for the reader. 'Mr Bloom's dental windows' (10.1115) is a familiar example: a small gratuitous puzzle, apt to annoy if noticed. It will be an exceptional reader indeed who will calmly hold this detail in abeyance until it is resolved some eighty-five pages later in a snatch of dialogue about the Bloom we know:

– Isn't he a cousin of Bloom the dentist? says Jack Power.
– Not at all, says Martin. Only namesakes. (12.1638)

True, we can imagine a reader from whom 'Mr Bloom's dental windows' would have instantly invoked the actual Marcus Bloom, dentist, who practised in 1904 at 2 Clare Street: a reader who would have known that vanished, pre-Rebellion Dublin as intimately as do Joyce's Dubliners. But not even in 1922 can there have been many left alive who both commanded such lore and were capable of reading 250 pages into the difficult *Ulysses*. No, the Arranger can be sure that we readers are probably visiting, and he treats us, when he deigns to notice our presence, with the sour xenophobic indifference Dublin can turn upon visitors who have lingered long enough for hospitality's first gleam to tarnish. Mr Hart has also detected in the Arranger the spirit of Dublin itself, 'endowed with a distinctive personality', 'capable of a great deal of malice, of deliberate *Schadenfreude*'.[9] That spirit does not mind if we misunderstand wholly and never know it, standing unhelpfully by as we read of non-fictional Father Conmee's encounter with a Mrs Sheehy we may not understand is also non-fictional:

— Very well indeed, father. And you, father?
Father Conmee was wonderfully well indeed. He would go to Buxton probably for the waters. And her boys, were they getting on well at Belvedere? Was that so? Father Conmee was very glad indeed to hear that. (10.18)

If we do not know (as we almost certainly do not) that the boys in question, Richard and Eugene Sheehy, were of Joyce's (hence Stephen's) generation and long since out of Belvedere, the Arranger will leave our ignorance undisturbed and will not by the twitch of an eyelid prompt us to remark that we weren't allowed to hear what it was that absent-minded Father Conmee was very glad to hear.[10] Our innocence will doubtless occasion disgusted comments when we are out of earshot; the Dublin habit of jeering at Joyce enthusiasts has its precedent inside the book itself, where it is an aspect of the Irish citizen's acculturated scorn for anyone whose information or whose sense of things does not coincide precisely with his own.

This is to resay what we began by noticing, that the Arranger's role in the book seems to have been prompted by the needs of two episodes in which neither Stephen nor Bloom but an engulfing Dublin is dominant. Besides civic ubiquity, though, the Arranger has another hall-mark, virtuosity. He epitomises the Dublin knack for performance. Astute readers will have sensed some alien presence well before 'Aeolus'. Who transcribed the voice of Bloom's cat with such precision? Certainly not Bloom, who utters (4.462) a common 'Miaow'. Whose phrase registered Bloom's gait in his rush toward the burning kidney, 'stepping hastily down the stairs with a flurried stork's legs' (4.383)? The same Arranger's, surely, who in contriving the phantasmagoria in 'Circe' will make a trolley's gong speak, 'Bang Bang Bla Bak Bludd Bugg Bloo,' and have Bloom, as he blunders out of the way, raise 'a policeman's whitegloved hand' (15.189). Bloom has no white glove and imperson-ates no policeman; the whitegloved hand is an expressionistic vividness, in an episode where every passing analogy is rendered visible and audible. By parallel logic the kidney in 'Calypso' might have called out as loudly as that trolley and the stork have been as visible as that glove, but the Arranger was not ready to show his hand so early.

In the heyday of the initial style he was content to lie low, imparting at need the little graphic touches whose innovative economy every reader admires:

The felly harshed against the curbstone: stopped. (6.490)

The priest began to read out of his book with a fluent croak. (6.594)

Mr Bloom walked unheeded along his grove by saddened angels, crosses, broken pillars, family vaults, stone hopes praying with upcast eyes, old Ireland's hearts and hands. (6.928)

This does not mean that we are to call him simply 'the narrator', since he exists side by side with a colourless primary narrator who sees to the thousand little bits of novelistic housekeeping no one is meant to notice: the cames and wents, saids and askeds, stoods and sats, without which nothing could get done at all. Lounging in this drudge's shadow, the Arranger may now and then show his hand when Bloom is *observed*: when, by a principle we have already dwelt on, the narrative sequence is being responsive to what the character is conscious of:

The mourners knelt here and there in prayingdesks. Mr Bloom stood behind near the font and, when all had knelt, dropped carefully his unfolded newspaper from his pocket and knelt his right knee upon it. He fitted his black hat gently on his left knee and, holding its brim, bent over piously. (6.584)

These are the closely noted actions of a non-Catholic[11] at a Catholic service: aware of kneeling, aware of the danger dust poses to his dark suit, aware of his hat, aware of the need to bend 'piously'. The Arranger, we may guess, arranged those sentences, snatching the pen from his anonymous colleague to achieve not neologistic vividness but a *seriatim* accuracy of observation that hovers just this side of being malicious.

Here we need to confront a more general topic, the fluctuating boundary between character and language, since it matters how much 'bent over piously' comes from Bloom, how much from the narrative voice. If the former, Bloom is feeling or is trying to feel pious; if the latter, indifference or malice may be remarking that a show of piety is incumbent. The line between such options is often impossible to draw: here even to have asked the question is to have shared a little the Arranger's scepticism, and very often small questions of tone and motive in *Ulysses* turn out to pertain to the ascription of forms of words.*

Yet words, especially in the domain of the initial style, are normally ascribable; thus, whereas in 'Calypso' Bloom surely does not spell the

---

*And when mimicry goes on for several pages the effect can be most unsettling, as in the 'Wandering Rocks' account (10.1–205) of Father Conmee's walk. 'It was idyllic: and Father Conmee reflected on the providence of the Creator who had made turf to be in bogs where men might dit it out and bring it to town and hamlet to make fires in the houses of poor people': so for page after page, and some readers find Father Conmee's naïveté endearing while others think the portrait savage. If we could see the Arranger's face, we might be able to tell.

catspeech, Stephen in 'Proteus' just a few pages previously *may* spell (or imagine spelled) the wavespeech: 'seesoo, hrss, rsseeiss, ooos'. As a words-on-paper man, he may well be fancying principles of transcription. Or perhaps not: he may only be listening, and whatever hand writes the pages on which he exists may be supplying the transcription from over his shoulder.

That Stephen both exists on printed pages and fancies himself writing at least some of the sentences we read is an old theme for any reader of the *Portrait*, where in letting the style grow as Stephen grew Joyce lets us perceive in style a system of limits within which Stephen is somewhere to be found: verbal limits to locate the expanding limits of an immature but developing character who increasingly likes the thought of being a writer. Thus *chiasmus* and 'lucid supple periodic prose' reflect Stephen's taste toward the end of Chapter IV, where both are prominent, and Stephen may be thought of as framing some of the chiasmic sentences though not all of them. (Once in *Ulysses* Leopold Bloom exists within an episode he actually fancies himself as writing (16.1229) and the result is stylistic disaster; the episode is 'Eumaeus'.)

The essence of limits is that one keeps encountering them, like the walls of a room; as if to emphasise this principle, Joyce characterised the *Portrait* end to end by a habit of repeating words and phrases again and again in brief compass: [12]

And *if* he had judged her harshly? *If her life* were a *simple* rosary of hours, *her life simple* and strange as *a bird's life*, gay in the morning, restless all day, tired at sundown? *Her heart simple* and wilful as *a bird's heart*? (216)

And already two purposes are at work here, Stephen's and Joyce's. Joyce, shaping the book he was writing, anxious to delimit its hero, had uses for a rhetoric of repetition which sometimes serves his purposes a little more nearly than it always describes the movement of Stephen's thought. But Stephen does have a taste for such writing. 'The spell of arms and voices,' he writes in his diary, 'the white arms of roads, their promise of close embraces and the black arms of tall ships that stand against the moon, their tale of distant nations' (252). But other diary entries are free of this tic, the pervasiveness of which in the book's narrative texture we may want to ascribe to the author's expressive purposes. Similarly, though Stephen at 16 has a taste for *chiasmus*, it was not Stephen's but Joyce's arranging hand that made the whole book chiasmic, reshuffling manuscript sheets to make of Chapter I's events a reverse mirroring of those of Chapter V[13]

So Stephen exists, for us readers of words, in a zone of interference between 'his' habits with words and the practices of James Joyce. Joyce, let us make no mistake, is always present in *Ulysses*, and no talk of that dyad of technicians, the self-effacing narrator and the mischievous Arranger, should permit us wholly to forget that fact. 'O Jamesy let me up out of this' cries Molly Bloom from the chamber-pot (18.1128), as if inadvertently calling on her maker.

Early in *Ulysses* Joyce introduced something new, long passages we have learned to call 'interior monologue', which profess to transcribe the actual movement of a character's thought. This, we might think, disposes of the perplexity we sometimes feel in the *Portrait*, trying to feel sure whose words we read, Stephen's or the author's. Not wholly, though. The same hand that arranged the events of the *Portrait* into a *chiasmus* is still writing 'Proteus' through Stephen's illusory presence, perhaps spelling out the wavespeech, certainly seeing to it that a young man who thinks he is enacting Hamlet's part (obstinate mourning, soliloquies, disobligingness) shall actually be playing Telemachus, a role that never crosses his mind. and shall accordingly meet an unwitting Ulysses.

And Bloom's unspoken words, are they Bloom's? Not wholly:

Might meet a robber or two. Well, meet him. Getting on to sundown. The shadows of the mosques along the pillars: priest with a scroll rolled up. A shiver of the trees, signal, the evening wind. I pass on. Fading gold sky. A mother watches me from her doorway. She calls her children home in their dark language. High wall: beyond strings twanged. Night sky, moon, violet, colour of Molly's new garters. Strings. Listen. A girl playing one of those instruments what do you call them: dulcimers. I pass. (4.91)

Bloom's memories of 'The Dance of the Hours' have shaded this, and of such books as *In the Track of the Sun* ('sunburst on the titlepage'; later read so much the titlepage has become detached and vanished: 17.1395). And 'what do you call them: dulcimers' is unmistakably Bloom, no doubt fumbling for a classroom memory of 'Kubla Khan'. The Arranger's merciless eye fastens on 'what do you call them', and we are not allowed to forget it when the voice of Si Dedalus in 'Sirens' comes to Bloom's ear 'like no voice of strings of reeds or whatdoyoucall them dulcimers' (11.675). So much is Bloom. But 'their dark language'? 'She calls her children home in their dark language': no, those are not Bloom's words, they are surely James Joyce's, supplying a phrase that shall bridge the text's continuity across an instant Bloom did not verbalise, merely felt. So, too, in 'Lestrygonians' when Bloom espies Sir Frederick Falkiner, the chief judicial officer of Dublin –

I suppose he'd turn up his nose at that stuff I drank. Vintage wine for them, the year marked on a dusty bottle. (8.1154)

'The year marked on a dusty bottle' seems too many words for Bloom's swift thought; seven words have evidently been supplied for what passed before Bloom as a visual fancy.

So there has been a look of autonomy for the initial style to serve and transcribe, but under close inspection this autonomy is compromised. The initial style creates nearly as much as it records. It creates Stephen, and permits a central ambiguity in all Stephen's speculations on his entoilment in a web of determinism, caught as he is in Joyce's book where Joyce is composing his words though he often thinks (and we think) that he composes them. It creates Bloom, too, and if we think the style simply responds to Bloom as Bloom responds to the sensations of the morning – Bloom's mind an ironic surrogate for objectivity itself – we are mistaken to the extent (we can't calibrate it) that Bloom, too, is a creation of words, which sometimes overlay and amend 'his' words and are also sometimes shut off, as when he came through his front door and later could not remember what the words did not record, what he had done with his hat.

The poet, Aristotle thought, shows men in action, and in Homer a character is a doer of deeds; even a speech is a deed. The men of *Ulysses* are generally dwelt on by the poet when they are between such deeds as the day affords: rather reflecting than acting, and generating spoken or unspoken words which on the book's page are not wholly theirs. A character in *Ulysses* (in a city of talk) is an interference phenomenon between 'his' language and language not his, sometimes other characters', sometimes the author's. The second half of *Ulysses* dissolves into 'styles' the way all events in Dublin dissolve into gossip. From end to end *Finnegans Wake* is a mull of gossip.

Ulysses will also supply, in its second half, innumerable details which supplement, modify, sometimes contradict what we have come to suppose. Only after Bloom has angrily asserted his Jewish identity (12.1804) shall we learn that he is not circumcised (13.979), lacks a Jewish mother (15.281), and has undergone two valid Christian baptisms (17.540). Bloom, seemingly one of fiction's little men, will grow when we are apprised of his stature and his hidden fiscal assets. Stephen, whom we may once have thought was to be the book's hero, at any rate its focal consciousness, will lose his bright subjectivity, will be reduced to grunted replies, will be deprived (in part by drink, in part by narrative method) of his quick-darting faculties, and will eventually walk out of the Joyce universe altogether. Molly, at first a voice that grunted 'Mn' ('no') (4.57), then an impression of lazy sluttishness, then a glimpse of 'a plump bare generous arm' (10.251), will turn into an unexpectedly realised character whose final word is Yes.

And linkage after linkage of plot will be supplied, commanding so much terrain of datable past that what seemed a single day's slice of inconsequence will become the chronicle, generations in extent, of an immigrant family in Ireland, that country whose citizens characteristically emigrate.[14] (The very potato that doomed Ireland in the 1840s will become in this odd family a good-luck charm, preservative against pestilence.)

So as the Arranger takes increasingly prominent charge the ten-episode *Ulysses* of 'objective' irony, the book that terminates with 'Wandering Rocks', will turn into a different sort of book altogether. Still, there is no sharp break. The Arranger was there all the time, and the principles according to which he will now commence to alter *Ulysses* were potential from the start, latent, obeying an aesthetic of delay.

NOTES

1 Joyce wrote to Harriet Weaver of 'the initial style' (*Letters*, I, 129) in a context that makes this phrase include the first ten episodes; he is defending 'Sirens', the first manifest departure. The most wilful disruption of this style, the captions in 'Aeolus', got added as late as August 1921, while the book was in press. (Groden, 105.)

2 See *Letters*, II, 190. Titles in the *Dubliners* mode – e.g. 'Grace' – make simple ironic points. It is hard to see how much more Joyce could have intended in calling a short story 'Ulysses'.

3 Gorman, 224.

4 The famous Budgen anecdote: see Chapter 1, note 10.

5 Groden, 64–114.

6 *Letters*, I, 114, where the main part of the book is to have only eleven episodes. See Groden, 33.

7 David Hayman, *'Ulysses': The Mechanics of Meaning* (Englewood Cliffs, NJ, 1970), 70: 'I use the term "arranger" to designate a figure who can be identified neither with the author nor with his narrators, but who exercises an increasing degree of overt control over his increasingly challenging materials.'

8 Clive Hart, 'Wandering Rocks', in Hart and Hayman, 186.

9 Hart, 190.

10 Conor Cruise O'Brien, *States of Ireland* (Frogmore, Herts, 1974), 160, supplies the biographical information but doesn't notice the Arranger's reticence, and supposes that the date of Bloomsday is idealised. But not in this chapter.

11 Bloom had a Catholic baptism prior to his marriage with Molly, but has apparently never received communion, since he wonders (5.346) if the hosts are in water. 'Non-Catholic' seems appropriate.

12 In 'The text of James Joyce's *A Portrait* . . .', *Neuphilologische Mitteilungen*, 65 (1964), Chester G. Anderson noted the frequency of this device. Since typists' eyes tended to skip from one repetition to another, it was a prime occasion for textual corruption.

13 See Hans Walter Gabler, 'The seven lost years of *A Portrait of the Artist as a Young Man*', in Staley and Benstock, 49–51.

14 In John Henry Raleigh's *A Chronicle of Leopold and Molly Bloom* (1977), the earliest entries date from the eighteenth century.

CHAPTER 8

The Aesthetic of Delay

In a foretime of uncomplicated pleasures, when pocket-watches were ubiquitous, before digital readouts and also before sweep second-hands, the challenge ran, 'Make a "6" like the one on your watch'. This depended on the victim's not having noticed that his watch had no '6', its space being occupied by the little second-dial. And yet he had looked at the watch a thousand times.

This information may help a modern reader with a much-reprinted passage in *Stephen Hero,* where the terminology has attracted more attention than the example:

He told Cranly that the clock of the Ballast Office was capable of an epiphany. Cranly questioned the inscrutable dial of the Ballast Office with his no less inscrutable countenance.

– Yes, said Stephen. I will pass it time after time, allude to it, refer to it, catch a glimpse of it. It is only an item in the catalogue of Dublin's street furniture. Then all at once I see it and I know at once what it is: epiphany.

– What?

– Imagine my glimpses at that clock as the gropings of a spiritual eye which seeks to adjust its vision to an exact focus. The moment the focus is reached the object is epiphanised. It is just in this epiphany that I find the third, the supreme quality of beauty.

– Yes? said Cranly absently.

The Ballast Office clock, an object of no special interest, was perhaps the most looked-at object in all Dublin. It was right at the gullet of the city, where O'Connell Bridge delivers flowing crowds to the south side of the Liffey for shops and offices to absorb. Seamen could set their chronometers by the drop of its time-ball, and in a city of stopped and casual clocks, before homes had wireless or watches were cheap and reliable, the authority of its dial reassured countless glancing eyes daily, or else admonished hurrying feet to hurry harder. Does any of those many thousand pairs of eyes, Stephen is asking, ever *see* that clock? Could anyone, for instance, describe it, let alone contemplate its *quidditas*? One would need to look at it as frequently, as intently, as one looks at, say, a fine statue: in part to kill the habit of merely asking it the time, in part to grow used to it as more than a florid curiosity;

for a while, as precisely 'an item . . . of Dublin's street furniture'; then as itself.

Leopold Bloom does not see it, he who sees so much, when making his way southward through the city toward lunch he looks up at it for distraction from a painful thought.

> Mr Bloom moved forward, raising his troubled eyes. Think no more about that. After one. Timeball on the ballastoffice is down. Dunsink time. Fascinating little book that is of sir Robert Ball's. Parallax. I never exactly understood. There's a priest. Could ask him. Par it's Greek: parallel, parallax. Met him pike hoses she called it till I told her about the transmigration. O rocks! (8.108)

This far into the book, we are meant to have acquired enough experience both of *Ulysses* and of Bloom to negotiate these sixty-four words without trouble. Bloom sees the dropped timeball but not the face of the clock because he is on the same side of the street as the clock is* and has insufficient need of the exact time to crane his neck upward. He remembers that local time (twenty-five minutes later than Greenwich) comes to this timepiece by wire from Dunsink Observatory. 'Observatory' aided by 'time*ball*' reminds him of Sir Robert *Ball,* the Dublin-born Astronomer Royal of England. As for Ball's 'fascinating little book', it is *The Story of the Heavens* (1885), as we shall learn when we eventually find it on Bloom's bookshelf (17.1373). He remembers 'parallax' from Ball's exposition, attributes the word's obduracy to its Greek origin, mistakenly etymologises *par-* instead of *para-*, supplies a related word, 'parallel', the single '*r*' of which had detained his attention an hour earlier (7.165) when thoughts of Martin Cunningham's conundrum set him spelling 'unpar one ar elleled', and elides, via 'Greek', to the Greek word he'd explained to Molly at breakfast-time: 'metempsychosis'. 'O rocks!' was what she said when he told her it meant 'transmigration'; 'Tell us in plain words' (4.343).

So here is the Ballast Office clock of Stephen's example, not manifesting 'the third, the supreme quality of beauty' – it is not even seen – but still embedded in ambiguities of perception ('parallax' – seen from different spots, *Gestalts* alter); associated moreover with explanation, bringing light to another.

---

*How do we know this? We know it because he started his southward walk on the same side – the west side – as Graham Lemon's and Butler's Monument House (8.27) and will only cross to the east side (8.155) a minute or so after his glimpse of the Ballast Office timeball. Joyce assumes that we either know Dublin or have available what Hart and Knuth provided as late as 1975, a set of detailed maps.

A dozen pages later, having walked the length of Westmoreland Street and passed Trinity, Bloom has another encounter with a time-piece, also unseen. Field-glasses in the window of Yeates & Son, opticians and instrument makers, 2 Grafton Street, prompt him to look purposefully upward:

> Goerz lenses six guineas.... There's a little watch up there on the roof of the bank to test those glasses by.
> His lids came down on the lower rims of his irides. Can't see it. If you imagine it's there you can almost see it. Can't see it. (8.554)

This effort to perceive a watch that perhaps isn't there – Bloom groping to adjust not his spiritual but his corporeal eye to a correct focus – corresponds in Joyce's intricate bookkeeping to the earlier failure to so much as glance up at the dial of the blatant Ballast Office clock. And if that clock's exemplary status in a theory of perception is accessible to us only because some pages Joyce discarded from the Ur-*Portrait* chanced not to be lost we need no such happenstance, only an act of attention, to enjoy the fun when Bloom vainly squints his eye moments after an encounter with the incorporeal vision of theosophy. For just before his failure with the watch he had overheard 'the eminent poet Mr Geo Russell' ('AE') discoursing to a lady disciple of 'the twoheaded octopus, one of whose heads is the head upon which the ends of the world have forgotten to come', and his only comment had been 'Something occult. Symbolism' (8.530). Such people he reflects, eat only vegetables, and 'I wouldn't be surprised if it was that kind of food you see produces the like waves of the brain the poetical'. So when he, by choice an eater of 'the inner organs of beasts and fowls', bends his eye toward a sign of the time he can't see it. 'If you imagine it's there you can almost see it. Can't see it.'

Yet another twenty pages and this same AE will be asserting in Stephen Dedalus' hearing that art reveals 'formless spiritual essences', and Stephen will inaudibly rebut him on behalf of what you can see.

> Streams of tendency and eons they worship. . . . Through spaces smaller than red globules of man's blood they creepycrawl after Blake's buttocks into eternity of which this vegetable world is but a shadow. Hold to the now, the here, through which all future plunges to the past. (9.85)

The now, the here. Outside Yeates & Son Bloom's mind, responsive to optical instruments and invisible timepieces, is drawn back half a mile to the Ballast Office timeball.

Now that I come to think of it that ball falls at Greenwich time. It's the clock is worked by an electric wire from Dunsink. (8.571)

He proceeds to query 'parallax' again, and concludes: 'Never know anything about it. Waste of time.'

And yet he has just let slip through his mind unnoticed a homely example of parallax: two standpoints, two different alignments of phenomena. For not only have his thoughts in two different places assessed the dropped ball differently (metaphorical parallax); not only that, but the Ballast Office clock itself presents parallactic readings, two times simultaneously: Greenwich Time by the ball for mariners, Dunsink Time by the dial for pedestrians. And Greenwich Time and Dunsink Time differ by twenty-five minutes because astronomers in those two places observe the sun from stations separated by $6\frac{1}{4}°$ of longitude; this is, precisely and technically, parallax. (And the timeball fell at 12.35 by the dial, so when Bloom deduced 'after one' from the fact that it had already fallen his correct conclusion, as so often, was drawn from false premises and correct by luck.)

Parallax makes possible stereoscopic vision: 'In order to see that basket,' Stephen instructs Lynch in the *Portrait*, 'your mind first of all separates the basket from the rest of the visible universe which is not the basket' (212), something the mind can do more easily since two eyes have presented it with separate versions of the basket's location. Two different versions at least, that is Joyce's normal way; and the uncanny sense of reality that grows in readers of *Ulysses* page after page is fostered by the neatness with which versions of the same event, versions different in wording and often in constituent facts – separated, moreover, by tens or hundreds of pages – reliably render one another substantial. Indeed, the book's first parallax is the double incident of the little cloud which occludes Stephen's sun in 'Telemachus' (1.248) and Bloom's sun in 'Calypso' (4.218), turning both men's thoughts deathward. Since the tower and Eccles Street are seven miles apart these occultations cannot be simultaneous; from the fact that the cloud seems to come later in 'Calypso' we may judge that the winds over Ireland are blowing, as usual, westerly.

The poet Russell, pushing his bicycle along the kerbstone, passed Bloom from behind at the south-east corner of College Green and Nassau Street. That kerb, swerving left, will lead him straight as a tramline to the foot of Kildare Street, two minutes from the National Library. And, when the next episode opens an hour later, there is Russell ensconced in the Library, 'oracling' out of its shadows. This does much to assure us that Bloom did really see Russell, a substantial Russell in motion through Dublin's Newtonian space. It does something, too, since Russell 'existed', to help confirm the reality of Bloom. It is perhaps elementary narrative technique.

The technique of letting Bloom drop a phrase about Sir Robert Ball's 'fascinating little book', to be complemented when Bloom's books are catalogued some 500 pages later, is harder to match in the work of antecedent writers, less scrupulous about trivia (but Joyce is all trivia). Both elements, book and title, are intelligible when we encounter them. The first creates no mystery to whet our alertness for the second; the second, so many pages later, quite likely stirs no memory whatever. Yet the two do something, minute, incremental, to help Bloomsday cohere in any mind that chances to unite them, if only by confirming that as the foxes have their holes and the birds their nests, so each speck in this book has somewhere its complementary speck, in a cosmos we can trust. Einstein thought that God did not play dice with the universe.

A device that can make dustmotes vivid has obvious power over scenes and incidents. Thanks to Bloom's busily associative memory, virtually every scene in *Ulysses* is narrated at least twice, and by varying what he tells and emphasises Joyce ensures that repetition shall not dilute but intensify. 'Now, my miss,' says the pork-butcher Dlugacz to a customer, making 'a red grimace' (4.166). 'Deep voice that fellow Dlugacz has,' Bloom recalls some pages later. 'Now, my miss' (4.492). Bloom's recall omits the red grimace, adds the deep voice; the incident has grown stereoscopic, stereophonic. But when he reappears in the phantasmagoria of 'Circe' Dlugacz (dreams going by contraries) has become 'a ferreteyed albino' who speaks 'hoarsely' (15.987), and the words he speaks are words he never spoke, merely words Bloom read on a handbill in his shop. This is normal operating procedure for Joyce. One effect is to thicken the book's human texture without overpopulating it, another is to turn Moses Dlugacz from a supernumerary into a Theme, and a third is to help us think 'Circe' phantasmal since what is transfigured there is elsewhere substantial, twice testified.

Leopold Bloom is much pressed upon by his past. We must feel with him how substantial is that past. The substantiality of past scenes, though they exist for us only in his recollections, is achieved by comparable means, each scene built up out of numerous partial recalls. There was an evening at Mat Dillon's in Terenure 'fifteen seventeen golden years ago' (6.696),* at which he and Molly first met; they played musical chairs, and the game isolated the two of them (Molly got the last chair). Later she sang; he turned her music. He was 21, she 16. This may have been the same evening the solicitor John Henry Menton felt humiliated because lucky Bloom bested him at bowls and ladies laughed; the same, too, when a boy of five stood on a garden urn, supported by Molly and by three of Mat Dillon's daughters, and declined to shake hands with the 21-year-old Mr Bloom. By outrageous coincidence . . . but we'll come to that.

*Seventeen is correct; it was May 1887.

No single account governs our sense of all this. We cannot even know whether one occasion or several is denoted by the four principal vignettes which Dillon's name and the name of lilacs unify. Mat Dillon's and lilacs come to stand for Eden, a fragrant girl-filled garden; nuance by nuance an alluring past emerges. First the sight of Menton at Paddy Dignam's funeral recalls the bowls and Menton's long-ago choler, and places theme-words parallax will not alter:

> Solicitor, I think. I know his face. Menton, John Henry, solicitor, commissioner for oaths and affidavits. Dignam used to be in his office. Mat Dillon's long ago. Jolly Mat. Convivial evenings. Cold fowl, cigars, the Tantalus glasses. Heart of gold really. Yes, Menton. Got his rag out that evening on the bowlinggreen because I sailed inside him. Pure fluke of mine: the bias. Why he took such a rooted dislike to me. Hate at first sight. Molly and Floey Dillon linked under the lilactree, laughing. Fellow always like that, mortified if women are by. (6.1007)

Dillon and lilac-trees are united, and Molly and Floey (special friends), and Dillon's garden and good times gone. Some four hours later, while Bloom sits in the Ormond in the knowledge that Molly is preparing to cuckold him, words of a tenor song – 'When first I saw . . .' – bring back that time of first sight.

> First night when first I saw her at Mat Dillon's in Terenure. Yellow, black lace she wore. Musical chairs. We two the last. Fate. After her. Fate. . . .
> – *Charmed my eye . . .*
> Singing. *Waiting* she sang. I turned her music. Full voice of perfume of what perfume does your lilactrees. Bosom I saw, both full, throat warbling. First I saw. She thanked me. Why did she me? Fate. Spanishy eyes. Under a peartree alone patio this hour in old Madrid one side in shadow Dolores shedolores. At me. Luring. Ah, alluring. (11.725)

Dillon's, lilac-trees. Bloom, too, is plotting a (minor) infidelity; 'what perfume does your' has strayed into his revery from his lady penpal's letter (5.258), one he's just on the point of answering under his postalbox pseudonym, Henry Flower. Still, the lost time shines in memory. It is clear why Bloom's dream cottage, focus of his habitual bedtime fantasies, will feature among its hundreds of amenities 'a sundial shaded and sheltered by laburnum or lilac trees' (17.1569): lilacs to emblematise a magical evening, shading a sundial on which no minatory shadow will ever move; clear, too, why the mock Wedding of the Trees, in a context mocking Bloom, will cite two girls named 'Lilac' as well as 'Senhor Enrique Flor' (Henry Flower) who 'presided at the organ with his wellknown ability' – here 'organ' is a word that snickers – 'and, in addition to the prescribed numbers of the nuptial mass, played a new and striking arrangement of *Woodman, spare that tree*' (12.1288).

Another seven hours, and a chance word in a bitter harangue of Stephen Dedalus' prompts one more evocation of the lilac-shaded scene. The word – unspecified – may have been 'mother'. Eden this time is distanced by elaborate cadences; a Victorian hand like Pater's is holding the pen, evoking 'a shaven space of lawn one soft May evening, the wellremembered grove of lilacs at Roundtown, purple and white', and amid the lilacs 'another as fragrant sisterhood, Floey, Atty, Tiny and their darker friend . . . Our Lady of the Cherries, a comely brace of them pendant from an ear'. These are Dillon's daughters and Molly.

A lad of four or five in linseywoolsey . . . is standing on the urn secured by that circle of girlish fond hands. He frowns a little just as this young man does now with a perhaps too conscious enjoyment of danger but must needs glance at whiles towards where his mother watches from the *piazzetta* giving upon the flowerclose with a faint shadow of remoteness or of reproach (*alles Vergängliche*) in her glad look. (14.1371)

'*Alles Vergängliche*' bids us see Stephen's mother not as the wraith who haunts his thoughts today but as the Mater Gloriosa who summons Goethe's errant Faust aloft.* (An imitation of the *Faust* Walpurgisnacht will commence in just a few pages.)

Readers skilled in the clichés of Victorian fiction will expect the child in this tableau to have been Stephen; such a style cherishes that order of sentimental coincidence. Sure enough, when the two men are at last installed in Bloom's kitchen drinking cocoa, the catechist of Ithaca asks and is answered:

How many previous encounters proved their preexisting acquaintance?

Two. The first in the lilacgarden of Matthew Dillon's house, Medina Villa, Kimmage road, Roundtown, in 1887, in the company of Stephen's mother, Stephen being then of the age of 5 and reluctant to give his hand in salutation. . . . (17.466)

Faust, 1. 12104–11: 'Alles Vergängliche/Ist nur ein Gleichnis;/Das Unzulängliche,/Hier wird's Ereignis;/Das Unbeschreibliche,/Hier ist's getan;/Das Ewig-Weibliche/Zieht uns hinan.' ('The transitory is but appearance; here the incomplete is actualised, the indescribable is accomplished; Eternal Womanhood draws us upward.') The last clause might have been Ulysses' motto, though in the last words of Joyce's book Molly, 'Ewig-Weibliche', remembers how she drew Bloom 'down'.

They were all there together once in Eden, Bloom and a not yet unfaithful Molly, Stephen and a not yet spectral mother. Ministering to a cosy sense of the fitness of things, this sort of revelation would have served a Victorian novelist for the stuff of a climax. But making things fit together inheres in Joyce's method, and *Ulysses* abounds in coincidental alignments to such an extent that no one is especially crucial. This particular one, emerging slowly as we correlate several passages against the grain of styles that resist correlation, is likely to be missed altogether by the first-time reader. The last two episodes, 'Ithaca' and 'Penelope', supply missing facts for so many suspended patterns, momentous and trivial, that a reader who should work carefully through them sentence by sentence, equipped with perfect knowledge of the rest of the book, would experience bewilderment from the very profusion of small elements dropping into place.

And he would be deceived, this reader, if he supposed the whole book had declared itself to him. There are elements dropping into place among the late pages that effect clarifications only on early pages, and only when on a later reading those pages are revisited.

For consider the potato. Bloom's 'potato I have' (4.73) – as he checks his pockets on first leaving the house – is wholly unintelligible (what on earth does he want with a potato?). Still, the mystery is too slight to detain us; we have much else to attend to. Twice later (8.1189; 15.243) we are assured that 'potato I have' means something: that a potato is indeed in his pocket, from which (15.1309) a harlot's exploring hand can extract it. Later (15.3513) we find him firmly requesting its return: 'It is nothing, but still, a relic of poor mamma.' Here, suddenly, is something new to correlate.

Points of correlation have already appeared: the phantasm of Bloom's mother with 'a shrivelled potato' among her talismans – a phial, an Agnus Dei, a celluloid doll (15.289); Bloom's phrase, 'poor mamma's panacea' (15.201), as he feels his pocket (but does not then name the potato); finally, the disclosure of its principle in one of his hallucinatory speeches: 'the potato . . . a killer of pestilence by absorption' (15.1357).

Sure enough, in the Litany of the Daughters of Erin (15.1952) we hear phantom voices chanting 'Potato Preservative Against Plague and Pestilence, pray for us'. Bloom carries a potato in his trousers pocket, has thought to transfer it to these black trousers from his everyday ones even though he has forgotten to transfer his latchkey, and *touches it as he crosses the threshold when a more orthodox Jew would touch the 'mezuzah'*,* all because his mother told him long ago that it would

---

*A word he can't think of when he's thinking of luck-charms; a rusty Hebraic memory supplies 'tephilim', which is something else: 'And the tephilim no what's this they call it poor papa's father had on his door to touch. That brought us out of the land of Egypt and into the house of bondage. Something

absorb disease from the air. And there is no one place where we are given this information.

Probably most students of *Ulysses* derive the doctrine of the potato from a commentary. Still, its elements are in the text, the most elucidative ones – 'poor mamma's panacea'; 'killer of pestilence by absorption'; 'Potato Preservative Against Plague and Pestilence' – all in one episode and not many pages apart. Attention unassisted by commentary could unriddle the potato as it unriddles so much else. But the equivalence of the potato and the *mezuzah* (a small case containing Deuteronomy, 6:4–9 and 11:13–21, affixed to the right-hand doorpost for the devout to touch or kiss as they cross the threshold) – this, assuming even that we possess the lore and have the luck to make the connection – is not something we might hope to think of when we first read of how Bloom crossed his threshold and said 'Potato I have', because at that time we have some hundreds of pages to traverse before the meaning of 'potato' will have been disclosed. Nor, when we know the meaning, does it work retroactively, since by then we have surely forgotten the doorframe adjacent to the initial 'Potato I have'. The *mezuzah*-epiphany will occur at some future reading, perhaps even never. If it never occurs, still, others will occur.

Joyce's strange book has no stranger aspect than this, that no one comprehensive reading is thinkable. A book – certainly, a novel – normally presupposes that ideal attention will reap it at one traverse; if we need, as we frequently do, repeated readings, that is because our attention is plagued by lapses, or perhaps because the writing is faulty. But *Ulysses* is so designed that new readers, given, even, what cannot be postulated, ideal immunity to attention overload, cannot possibly grasp certain elements because of a warp in the order of presentation, and veteran readers will perceive after twenty years new lights going on as a consequence of a question they have only just thought to ask. Such a question would be: Why is Bloom made to advert to the potato just when he does, on a page where there seems no earthly reason for him to remember the potato or for us to be apprised of it? And when we think to ask something happens.

Clarifying early puzzles with late information, *Ulysses* resembles a detective story, paradigm of the nineteenth-century novel – *Great Expectations*, *The Moonstone* – in which all hinges on postponed revel-

---

in all those superstitions because when you go out never know what dangers' (13.1157). He might have mentioned 'potato' here but didn't: seems not in fact to number it among 'superstitions'. His temperament, we are later told (17.560), is 'scientific', and is not 'absorption' a scientific word? Though he couldn't think of it when he tried to think of what black cloth does to radiation (4.79).

ations. Changing our earlier understanding with late facts, it resembles a plot like that of *Oedipus Rex*, where a terminal revelation alters all. But mutating each time it is reread, altering the very sense of early sentences as the import of later ones chances to come home, it resembles chiefly itself. Its universe is Einsteinian, non-simultaneous, internally consistent but never to be grasped in one act of apprehension: not only because the details are so numerous but also because their pertinent interconnections are more numerous still. Why was young Poldy Bloom, of all people, invited to Mat Dillon's that evening? Why Molly was there we know — she was Floey Dillon's special friend (18.720); but Poldy? Was handsome Poldy perhaps invited as a partner for Molly? (Very likely, daughter of a girl named Lunita Laredo — 18.848 — she looked as exotic as he.)

Some possible interconnections, though mutually exclusive, are not interdicted. Is one of the numerous women whom we see by any chance Bloom's correspondent 'Martha Clifford'? Very possibly. Possibly not. Is Cissey Caffrey, in Nighttown, really Gerty MacDowell's friend of the same name, 'madcap Cis'? Possibly; it was only by unprompted inference that when we were detained with Gerty's friends we assigned them to the middle class. Did Molly Bloom really move all that heavy furniture, including a piano and a sideboard so high it cracked Bloom's temple? Thinkably; though there was also, that afternoon, a strong man on the premises named Boylan.

There are things we shall never know, and we think it meaningful to say we shall never know them, quite as though they were entities on the plane of the potentially knowable, forgetting that nothing exists between these covers after all but marks on paper, in a system very nearly consistent. (The great world offers experiences, too, that are very nearly consistent.) Joyce's aesthetic of delay, producing the simplest facts by parallax, one element now, one later, and leaving large orders of fact to be assembled late or another time or never, in solving the problem of novels that go flat after we know 'how it comes out' also provides what fiction has never before really provided, an experience comparable to that of experiencing the haphazardly evidential quality of life; and, moreover, what art is supposed to offer that life can not, a permanence to be revisited at will but not exhausted.

There is sometimes a Heisenbergian trouble with the evidence itself. What did Molly say when she asked about 'metempsychosis'? We are to believe that she found that word in a book called *Ruby, Pride of the Ring*. (Is that, by the way, believable?) The narrative runs:

> She swallowed a draught of tea from her cup held by nothandle and, having wiped her fingertips smartly on the blanket, began to search the text with the hairpin till she reached the word.

– Met him what? he asked.
– Here, she said. What does that mean?
He leaned downward and read near her polished thumbnail. . . .
– Metempsychosis, he said, frowning. It's Greek: from the Greek.
That means the transmigration of souls.
– O, rocks! she said. Tell us in plain words. (4.333)

'Met him what? he asked.' What does *that* respond to? A murmur the
narrator has not transcribed? Or a no-murmur? (When a cup can be
held by a nothandle, may an answer also be given to a no-question?)
Or did he spot the word on the page, misread it, before her hairpin
found it? No knowing. We do know, though, from that scene by the
Ballast Office clock, that Bloom, remembering 'Greek', says 'Met him
pike hoses she called it till I told her about the transmigration. O rocks!'
It is right that Ulysses should explain a Greek word to Penelope (one
more thing to be lost on a first-time reader). Is it not also conceivable
that Ulysses master of lies – you could not believe him, Homer avers
repeatedly – should say to himself 'Met him pike hoses she called it' if
she called it nothing of the kind? (He has a stake in thinking Molly
less astute than she is.) And the grotesque phrase comes up again and
again and again, seven more times in all,* till we're quite sure we heard
her say it though we never did. Her own recall (18.565) runs 'that
word met something with hoses in it and he came out with some jaw-
breakers about the incarnation'. But that's seventeen hours after she'd
heard him pronounce the word three times.
Parallax falsifies. But maybe she did say it, while Homer was nodding.
It would be like Joyce, to insert an equivalent for that famous nod.

*8.1148; 11.500; 11.1062; 11.1188; 13.1280; 16.1473; 17.686. To compound the
mystery there's 'metamspychosis' (4.351), which survived through the first two editions
and (Gabler remarks) is either a double misprint or is what Joyce wrote. If the latter, it
may record Molly's mispronunciation on its first passage through Bloom's mind, before
it had stabilized to 'met him pike hoses'.

CHAPTER 9

Oceansong

Ulysses the naturalistic novel ends with 'Wandering Rocks', and with it ends, for the present, the role of the book's first Homer, a naturalist who had been added to Europe's inventory of Homers during Joyce's early lifetime. This is the Homer Samuel Butler extrapolated from the archaeological discoveries that had begun as late as 1870 at Hissarlik, Mycenae, Tiryns: a Homer who 'did not like inventing', based characters on people he knew, projected (Butler thought) the whole world of the *Odyssey* from experience of a single city (Trapani, in Sicily: like Dublin, a seaport on an island), and set down words locked to things, places, physical actualities: Greek words that in Joyce's time were getting reclaimed one by one from vague poetry as the soil yielded up corresponding artefacts.[1]

Confronting περόναι ... κλεῖσιν ἐϋγνάμπτοις (*Odyssey*, XVIII, 293–4) with only etymology to guide them, Butcher and Lang had written in 1879 that a robe for Penelope had 'golden brooches fitted with well-bent clasps' which neither they nor their readers could see clearly. In a post-Schliemann world where museums have examples of the *peronè* on display to show us what is bent and what fits into it, Robert Fitzgerald (1961) can render the same words 'pins pressed into sheathing tubes of gold'. Like a thousand other Homeric words, *peronè*, a fastener, has come to denote something definite as all words did for Joyce, who in his counterpart to the same passage displays Penelope/Molly's outsize drawers 'containing a long bright steel safety pin' (17.2095).

If that was perhaps a lucky coincidence, still Joyce, whose first Homer had been Charles Lamb's taleteller, read in school, felt comfortable with this new Homer defined by Butler, from whose translation (1900) he apparently derived the idea that Telemachus might sleep in a tower: * a Homer who observed exactly, meant exactly, whose Greek words were

---

*Butler made his translation not by replacing Homer's words with plain English ones, but by imagining what Homer must have been talking about and putting *that* in plain English. This method seems never to have been tried before, and was apparently unthinkable until archaeology conferred assurance that Homer was indeed talking about something real. Butler placed Telemachus' bedroom 'in a lofty tower', and marked 'the tower where Telemachus used to sleep' on a floorplan in *The Authoress of the 'Odyssey'* (1897, p. 16), as a consequence of pondering one adjective, ὑψηλός, 'lofty' (*Odyssey*, I, 426).

as specifying as Joyce's preferred English ones, 'felly', 'hank', 'bronze-foil', 'dung'.

But there had been other Homers; and with 'Sirens', an episode of song and piano-playing, an earlier Homer disconcerts us by striding onstage: the Homer of onomatopoeic mastery who 'of all poets', thought Dionysius of Halicarnassus, 'exhibited the greatest variety of sound', achieving 'innumerable passages in which length of time, bulk of body, extremity of passion, and stillness of repose; or in which, on the contrary, brevity, speed and eagerness are evidently marked out by the sound of the syllables'. Samuel Johnson, who worded this summary,[2] was sceptical about most of Dionysius' examples ('either he was fanciful, or we have lost the genuine pronunciation') and rejected with special vigour the assertion 'that the sound of Homer's verses sometimes exhibits the idea of corporeal bulk'.

Johnson's readers were familiar with Pope's claim that

> When Ajax strives some rock's vast weight to throw
> The line too labours, and the words move slow.

and many may have reflected that what Johnson could not hear in Pope ('In these lines, which mention the effort of Ajax, there is no particular heaviness, obstruction, or delay') it was unsurprising that he should have been deaf to in Homer also. Homer's acoustic finesse has never been easy to discredit, especially when vernacular poets are making a virtue of sound's support to sense.

In English poetry the second half of the nineteenth century was a great time for autonomous sound. In 1847 Tennyson published *The Princess*, with its 'moan of doves in immemorial elms', one symptom of a renewed poetic of sound-painting, and by 1858 Mr Gladstone (soon to be Parnell's adversary, hence of interest to Joyce) was hearing the sound of hammering in six spondees of Homer's that pertain to armour, of galloping horses in a horsy sequence of dactyls, of pathos in the very cadences to which Odysseus' old dog Argos is made to die:

> The words too are so calm and still, they seem to grow fainter and fainter, each foot of the verse seems to fall as if it were counting out the last respirations, and, in effect, we witness that last slight and scarcely fluttering breath, with which life is yielded up.[3]

Before long the tune the old dog died to was to seem rudimentary indeed; by 1886 George Lansing Raymond, the Professor of Aesthetics at Princeton University, was devoting whole chapters of his *Poetry as a Representative Art* to such matters as 'The imitative effects of letter-sounds', and inviting us to 'hear the knife *carving* the ivory in this:

> Ancient rosaries,
> Laborious orient ivory, sphere in sphere.'[4]

(The example is from *The Princess*.) By 1918 it was possible to read lines Gerard Manley Hopkins had written at about the time Joyce was born:

> . . . like each tucked string tells, each hung bell's
> Bow swung finds tongue to swing out broad its name.

And soon after 'Sirens' was written Abbé Henri Brémond would be finding in French bells' telling of names –

> Orléans, Beaugency . . . Vendôme, Vendôme

– something to be preferred to a hundred volumes of 'vers raisonnables'.[5]

As aesthetic intuitions converged on *la poésie pure* it even began to be claimed that Homeric surge and thunder could thrill hearers with no Greek at all, as in the famous παρὰ θῖνα πολυφλοίσβοιο θαλάσσης, 'By the shore of the many-noised sea'.* William Empson thought Pure Sound worth refuting as late as 1930; he was reminded of 'Darwin playing the trombone to his French beans',[6] and on this wholly acoustic Homer Joyce, too, casts a notably cold eye, as much in according the many-voiced sea four words

> seesoo, hrss, rsseiss, ooos (3.457)

that look grotesque on the printed page as in taking off *polyphloisboio thalasses* in *Finnegans Wake* as 'polyfizzyboisterous seas' (547).

But how cold an eye is that? Pure Sound aside, *Ulysses* prior to 'Sirens' has displayed much deftness of rhythmic imitation, from Davy Byrne's memorable yawn, 'Iiiiiichaaaaaaach!' (8.970) to small narrative links: 'The felly harshed against the curbstone: stopped' (6.490). 'Harshed' mimes the sound, an abrupt 'stopped', an abrupt syntax, mimes the stopping. Embedded in the *Iliad*, such a line would have compelled Dionysius and Gladstone. Corporeal bulk and the expiration

---

*Where poets and lexicographers tacitly disagree about what we are supposed to hear. Poets seem to perceive a quiet sea; Pope in a footnote to *Iliad*, I, 34 mentioned 'the melancholy Flowing of the Verse', Tennyson's sea 'moans round with many voices', Fitzgerald has 'the tumbling clamorous whispering sea', and for another occurrence of the word (*Odyssey*, XIII, 220) 'the endless wash of the wide, wide sea'. But Liddell and Scott, than whose nineteenth-century fictions none have been more influential, instruct us that *polyphloisbos* means 'loud-roaring', the sea's many voices therefore mighty ones, and the Loeb translator and much casual comment obey them.

of dogs aside, the sound of words can surely at the very least put us in mind of other sounds and often movements, especially when assisted by their sense; here Joyce and the Arranger concur.

Assistance from the sense, that is what is crucial. 'The mysterious glory which seems to inhere in the sound of certain lines is a projection of the thought and emotion they invoke,' wrote I. A. Richards roundly in 1929, 'and the peculiar satisfaction they seem to give *to the ear* is a reflection of the adjustment *of our feelings* which has been momentarily achieved.' Richards even supplies a toothsome chunk of Pure Sound:

> J. Drootan-Sussting Benn
> Mill-down Leduren N.
>   Telamba-taras oderwainto weiring
> Awersey zet bidreen
> Ownd istellester sween
>   Lithabian tweet ablissood owdswown stiering
> Apleven aswetsen sestinal
> Yintomen I adaits afurf I gallas Ball.[7]

– with which compare:

> Yea, Truth and Justice then
> Will down return to men,
>   Th'enamel'd *Arras* of the Rainbow wearing,
> And Mercy set between,
> Thron'd in Celestial sheen,
>   With radiant feet the tissued clouds down steering,
> And Heav'n as at some festival,
> Will open wide the Gates of her high Palace Hall.[8]

Clearly, Sense tells us what to ascribe to Sound.

The sense, though, can subvert; it is surely a disproportion between 'fizzy' and the voice of Poseidon that undermines the security of 'polyfizzyboisterous' in its own accomplishment. In 'Sirens', accordingly, where every resource of onomatopoeia is bent upon musical effects and musicians' procedures, the balance between sound and sense is kept uneasy. Yes, it can be done, it can be done: words can render at least short phrases of mock-music:

Pwee! A wee little wind piped eeee. In Bloom's little wee. (11.1203)

Or with more majesty:

Boylan impatience, ardentbold. Horn. Have you the? Horn. Have you the? Haw haw horn. (11.526)

Or in lyrical intimacy with what is attempted:

A duodene of birdnotes chirruped bright treble answer under sensitive hands. Brightly the keys, all twinkling, linked, all harpsichording, called to a voice to sing the strain of dewy morn, of youth, of love's leavetaking, life's, love's morn. (11.323)

Or with resolved pathos, even:

By rose, by satiny bosom, by the fondling hand, by slops, by empties, by popped corks, greeting in going, past eyes and maidenhair, bronze and faint gold in deepseashadow, went Bloom, soft Bloom, I feel so lonely Bloom. (11.1134)

Yet a sceptical impatience breaks through such effects, especially through that trio of sonorous Blooms, three left-hand chords barrumed by a barroom pianist:

> went
> BLOOM
> soft
> BLOOM
> I feel so lonely
> BLOOM

It is to the barroom order of virtuosity that the episode repeatedly reverts, fingers vamping the easy trill and boom, untrained voices treating themselves to the fellowship of close harmony, comfortable standby words and tunes, the worn fragments of familiar acoustic junk. Correspondingly, Joyce has set the episode on the north bank of the Liffey, a place of junkshops and pawnshops prating of 'antiques', stagnant rooms to which have drifted brass bedsteads, fenders, framed patriotic pictures, caskets, broken cornets, lamps with statuette bases – cast-off splendours; Dublin's Sargasso Sea. We encounter Bloom adrift toward the Ormond Hotel, eyeing in successive windows bright exotica: pipes, jewellery, icons of the Virgin. We take leave of him outside an antique dealer's, contemplating candlesticks, a battered melodeon and a picture of Robert Emmet addressing his judges – communing with which ornate disjecta he sounds his anal windnote ('Pprrpffrrppffff') in counterpoint to a tram's big percussion ('Kran kran kran. Krandlkran kran'), while iconic Emmet utters silent words: '. . . then and not till then let my epitaph be written. . . .' 'Eppripfftaph,' runs a fused version, 'Be pfrwritt'; and 'Rrrpr. Kraa. Kraandl' (11.1289).

'Pprrpffrrppfff' would not be the sound the cheeky devil made, which put Dante in mind of a trumpet: 'Ed egli avea del cul fatto trombetta' (*Inferno*, XXI, 139), remembered by Stephen in the Library (9.34). No, Mr Bloom's posterior trumpet is muted: to Boylan is assigned the loud 'Horn. Hawhorn', and Boylan is a shabby devil at that.

Shabbiness everywhere in 'Sirens' aspires to elegance. A barmaid whose unguarded idiom has it that 'He sang that song lovely' (11.1175) achieves phrases like 'exquisite contrast' (11.68) when her taste is on display. Lenehan, 'the essence of vulgarity' in the other barmaid's judgement (11.418), uses some of the fanciest words spoken by anybody in the book ('I quaffed the nectarbowl with him this very day, said Lenehan.... The *élite* of Erin hung upon his lips': 11.263). Si Dedalus' glorious voice is not what it was; the other singer, Ben Dollard, has gone a bit soft in the head; the pianist who can move into any key with facility is a spoiled priest with bad breath; Bloom indites the formulaic phrases of his letter to Martha Clifford ('Accept my poor little present enclosed. . . . Why do you call me naughty? . . . How will you punish me? Tell me, I want to know': 11.865) on newly purchased 'reserve' cream vellum, and when with Bloom's letter-writing under his eye the Arranger interpolates his Shakespearean 'Do. But do' (11.908) we are to reflect that heroic doing is not here in question, nor yet a writing energised by the will to do or by the done – only a sham-genteel epistolary teasing. What has been held elegant and is now dusty, compromised, is called 'antique' if you are selling it but 'junk' if we look dispassionately; and the melodeon in the antique-shop window is 'oozing maggoty blowbags' (11.1263).

Accordingly the episode is filled with onomatopoeic junk, and introduced by a selection of this junk arranged in a thematic catalogue, as it might be by some enthusiast of Homer collecting beauties; for instance,

> Jingle. Bloo.
> Boomed crashing chords. When love absorbs. War! War! The
>   tympanum.
> A sail! A veil awave upon the waves.
> Lost. Throstle fluted. All is lost now.
> Horn. Hawhorn. (11.19)

We may also think of this list as the orchestra tuning, or as an overture, the kind a composer hurries together the night before the first night out of his opera's tunes in order of occurrence. Or better still, imagine the music they played with silent films: how would it sound in the absence of the film? When *Ulysses* was newer responses were more solemn; Ernest Robert Curtius in 1929 discerned 'an exact transposition of the musical treatment of the *leitmotif*, the Wagnerian method', but found the experiment 'of questionable value': as it would be did it reflect quite so unquestioning a submission to Wagner's spirit as Curtius supposed.* The achievement of 'Sirens' is both unique and a little absurd, and we had best acknowledge the text's many acknowledgements of its own absurdity. When Walt Disney in *Fantasia* made elephants, hippos and ostriches dance Bloom's favourite ballet, *The Dance of the Hours*, the film analyst Parker Tyler remarked acutely that while satire was clearly intended another art cannot satirise music; what was being satirised, he thought, was *the music appreciation of the audience.*[9] So in 'Sirens' what is being elaborately imitated is the musical taste of the Dubliners present; also the literary taste that, detained with one set of characters, enjoys portentous reminders of an absentee:

But Bloom? (11.133)

– another of those left-hand chords (how Joyce exploits, in this episode, the resounding bathos of his hero's surname!), and a rhetorical figure once beloved by writers of newspaper serials.

That is no way to tell a story, nor is this:

From the saloon a call came, long in dying. That was a tuningfork the tuner had that he forgot that he now struck. A call again. That he now poised that it now throbbed. You hear? It throbbed, pure, purer, softly and softlier, its buzzing prongs. Longer in dying call. (11.313)

'That he forgot that he now struck' is good bad writing, abrogating syntactic canons in adhering to imitative ones. Later (11.674) the Arranger raises his eyebrows both at an hours-ago fumble of Bloom's and at the pedantry of his own expressiveness:

Through the hush of air a voice sang to them, low, not rain, not leaves in murmur, like no voice of strings or reeds or whatdoyoucallthem dulcimers. . . .

No writer wholeheartedly committed to the miracles his language was performing would compromise their fine moments in this way, and

---

*Wagner was an enthusiasm of Joyce's late adolescence, his *Lohengrin* a touchstone in the 1900 'Drama and Life', his book of libretti a necessity to be sent posthaste to Paris (*Letters*, II, 25). But by 1906 self-mockery is detectable: '. . . Wagner and the Ring and Bayreuth, (memories of my youth!)' (*Letters*, II, 154); and by the mid-*Ulysses* years Joyce could be brusque with Wagnerians (Ellmann, 393, 473). Though see William Blisset, 'James Joyce in the smithy of his soul', in Thomas F. Staley (ed.), *James Joyce Today* (1966), 96–134, to which I'll add that you'd never guess from it that Joyce was funny.

though Joyce seemed annoyed when in 1919 Ottocaro Weiss declined
to think the musical effects of 'Sirens' superior to Wagner's[10] his text
guards their frequently remarkable achievement ('A low incipient note
sweet banshee murmured: all': 11.630) against seeming to claim that
word-sound welded to sound can simultaneously pursue sense without
strain. We are permitted to discern a certain mad literalness procuring
the casual presence of musical terms – a tea-tray that is *transposed*,
tenors who get women by the *score*, a barmaid who *taps* a *measure* of
whiskey – and much imputation of portent collapses once we spot the
governing pun by which these musical virtuosities are confined to a *bar*.
In *Finnegans Wake* a seaborne sentence can assign itself to horn, oboe,
flute, and even ocarina –

> And all the way (a horn!) from fjord to fjell his baywinds' oboboes
> shall wail him rockbound (hoahoahoah!) in swimswamswum and all
> the livvylong night, the delldale dalppling night, the night of bluery-
> bells, her flittaflute in tricky trochees (O carina! O carina!) wake
> him. (6–7)

– but *Finnegans Wake*, referring always to itself, has no obligations to
sequential obduracies.

These beset Bloom, for whom the clock moves irreversibly toward
his day's nadir, the hour of the assignation, now for the first time
specified: 'At four, she said' (11.188). He and Molly have agreed to
pretend that the business of the starred hour will be with vocal music,
'La ci darem' and 'Love's Old Sweet Song', Mozart's great duet of
seduction and every Irish tenor's favourite encore. In accordance with
Joyce's policy of keeping strong scenes offstage – this book is no *Sweets
of Sin* – we wait with Bloom while Boylan's car jogs northward,
bewildered as we wait by immensely complicated pages that give off
rich wisps of feeling, even as Bloom is bemused by an ill-arranged
programme for piano and voice: 'Goodbye, Sweetheart, Goodbye', a
keyboard solo by the widowed Si Dedalus; 'When Love Absorbs my
Ardent Soul', sung by Ben Dollard in the wrong register; 'All Is Lost
Now', whistled by Richie Goulding; 'When First I Saw that Form
Endearing', the featured rendition in Si Dedalus' faded but still glorious
tenor, Bob Cowley, piano, contrapuntal elastic-band twiddling by L.
Bloom; Minuet from *Don Giovanni*, played by Bob Cowley; 'The
Croppy Boy' (innocence betrayed) sung by Ben Dollard.

It is after Bloom has gone that the company sings 'True men like
you men/Will lift your glass with us', since as the next episode will
emphasise hearty Irishmen will never deem Bloom a glass-lifting true
man. Not that their song is meant for him. They have been all the time
in the bar, he and Richie in the dining-room, and they do not know

he was ever there till someone unnamed says so ('– Was he? Mr Dedalus said': 11.1204). As so often, coincidence simulates intention. Had this programme been assembled for the occasion we should have to regard it as tactlessly chosen ('All Is Lost Now'), but it was chance that was tactless.

Chance's dispositions fall under the tireless eye of the Arranger, who in music's fusion of time commands all space and misses no facile irony. The sauntering gold-haired barmaid says of men, 'It's them has the fine times,' and presto, we are shown a man whose lot is far from fine:

> – It's them has the fine times, sadly then she said.
> A man.
> Bloowho went by by Moulang's pipes bearing in his breast the sweets of sin, by Wine's antiques, in memory bearing sweet sinful words, by Carroll's dusky battered plate, for Raoul. (11.84)

Boylan's progress toward Eccles Street ('Jingle jaunty') is reported at helpful intervals; he sets foot on its dirt just when Bloom is thinking men 'Want a woman who can deliver the goods', and raps out ('Cock-cock') the announcement of his presence just when Bloom's thoughts depict Molly on the chamber-pot: 'Chamber music. Could make a kind of pun on that. It is a kind of music I often thought when she' (11.979). We may want to speculate that the imitative form of this episode grew out of Joyce's decision to cut to and fro in this way between Bloom at the Ormond and Boylan's progress, extending a trick the Arranger had begun to play in 'Wandering Rocks', but doing it so frequently the effect resembles not interpolation but counterpoint. And if Bloom/Boylan, why not barmaids/Bloom, why not tram against Emmet and posterior trumpet, song against song, Bloom against Shakespeare, words here against words from earlier in *Ulysses*? And why not orchestrate these schemes, fill them out with arpeggios and trills, and in this hour of unheroic evasion let clarity go hang?

So frequent and so intricate is the crosscutting in fact, the voices sounding from so many parts of the city and from so many moments of the past, that *Ulysses'* normal spatial clarity is blurred. Often we are unsure for an instant where we are, and the inexperienced reader is unlikely ever to be quite sure: may not really grasp, for instance, that Bloom is never in the same room with the music, is listening from the dining-room to sounds from the saloon, removed from that scene as he is removed from the passion in Eccles Street. What cannot be missed is his agitation, his busy mind, his self-pity, and the curve of his passion as he undergoes rape by voice.

'Tenderness it welled: slow, swelling, full it throbbed.' That is Si Dedalus' voice, but the words take on other connotations: 'Throb, a throb, a pulsing proud erect' (11.701). Achieving climax, the voice of Si invades him, anticipating by perhaps half an hour the counter-climax at 7 Eccles Street: 'Bloom. Flood of warm jimjam lickitup secretness flowed to flow in music out, in desire, dark to lick flow, invading. . . . To pour o'er sluices pouring gushes. Flood, gush, flow, joygush, tupthrop. Now! Language of love.' And:

> – *To me!*
> Siopold!
> Consumed. (11.751)

Consummatum est; and Leopold for an instant rapt from his misery fuses with Simon the father of Stephen Dedalus, also with Lionel whose part Si sings in this book of roles. Music, which can pour many notes into a chord, can fuse souls, fuse identities, while it is in progress: by relaxing the alert faculties can permit Bloom simultaneously Molly's satisfactions, receiving, Boylan's, aggressing, Si's, performing, Henry Flower's, deceiving, in a rite of enraptured slosh. When he leaves the Ormond on a new errand his agitation of 4 p.m. is strangely composed, the chief among his problems now nothing more than a flatulent urgency which benign coincidence masks with the sounding wheels of a mighty tram.

NOTES

1 For more detail, see Hugh Kenner, *The Pound Era* (London, 1971), 42–9.
2 *Rambler*, no. 92, with further comments in no. 94. Dionysius' remarks are in his ΠΕΡΙ ΣΥΝΘΕΣΕΩΣ ΟΝΟΜΑΤΩΝ ('On literary composition'), XVI.
3 The Rt Hon. W. E. Gladstone, DCL, *Studies on Homer and the Homeric Age* (Oxford, 1858), III, 528, 412, 410.
4 George Lansing Raymond, *Poetry as a Representative Art* (New York, 1886; revised edn, 1889), 145.
5 The Hopkins is from the sonnet 'As kingfishers catch fire . . .'. For the Frenchman, see Henri Brémond, *La Poésie pure avec un débat sur la poésie par Robert de Souza* (Paris, 1926), 20.
6 William Empson, *Seven Types of Ambiguity* (London, 1930; revised edn, 1949), 8. (It was Erasmus Darwin, not Charles.)
7 I. A. Richards, *Practical Criticism* (London, 1929), 229, 232.
8 John Milton, 'On the Morning of Christ's Nativity', XV.
9 Parker Tyler, *The Hollywood Hallucination* (New York, 1970), 153.
10 Ellmann, 473.

CHAPTER 10

Maelstrom, Reflux

'Done', the last word of 'Sirens', completes a massy resolved chord – tram and Bloom's wind and what is done at last at 7 Eccles Street, and Robert Emmet's words, memorised by every Irish schoolchild: 'When my country takes her place among the nations of the earth, then and not till then let my epitaph be written. I have done.'

Having said that, Emmet was taken out and hanged; within fifteen pages the longest single set piece in *Ulysses* (12.525–678) will be describing the immense gratification of an estimated 500,000 persons at a composite of all the Irish scaffold dramas the grimly cherished memory of which still fuels sullen patriotic rage. By the time Joyce wrote 'Cyclops', events had occurred of which the characters in *Ulysses* could have no knowledge: the 1916 rebellion, Pearse's proclamation of a republic from the steps of the Post Office, British gunboats in the Liffey shelling central Dublin to bits, the execution by bullet of yet another sixteen martyrs, the birth (W. B. Yeats announced) of 'a terrible beauty'.*

Joyce's own sense of such events seems closer to that of Yeats's father, who thought the English would have done better to keep the rebels alive in jail. Then 'Ireland would have pitied and loved and smiled at these men, knowing them to be mad fools. In the end they would have come to see that fools are the worst criminals.'[1] A dark tavern dominated by a mad fool is Joyce's synecdoche for the state of Irish patriotism twelve years before the rebellion. The folly, moreover, is contagious; Bloom only excepted, everyone present chimes in. His fools exult in their own fermenting hatreds, quick with a hostile word for every passer-by, spraying with impartial contempt the French ('set of dancing masters'), 'the Prooshians and the Hanoverians' ('sausageeating bastards'), the late Queen Victoria ('blind drunk in her palace every night of God, old Vic . . . and her coachman carting her up body and bones to roll into bed and she pulling him by the whiskers and singing him old bits of songs about *Ehren on the Rhine* and come where the boose is cheaper'), her son the recently crowned Edward VII ('a bloody sight more pox than

---

*Most of *Ulysses* in fact was written in the knowledge that all the cityscapes of 'Aeolus' and of parts of 'Hades', 'Lestrygonians', 'Wandering Rocks', would never be seen again as they had been; hence Joyce's reflections on the possible disappearance of the city and his hope that it could be 'reconstructed out of my book' (Budgen, 69).

pax about that boyo'), the priests and bishops of Ireland, its moulders of opinion, the spokesmen of its patriotism, even and especially one another. The very barman whose ministrations guarantee the free flow of talk is savaged for 'hanging over the bloody paper with Alf looking for spicy bits instead of attending to the general public', and the words 'All wind and piss like a tanyard cat' are aimed not at any outsider but at the ostensible hero of the episode, 'the citizen', incarnation of truculent love of the land, whose talk in the talkative narrator's judgement is nevertheless only talk. 'As much as his bloody life is worth to go down and address his tall talk to the assembled multitude in Shanagolden where he daren't show his nose with the Molly Maguires looking for him to let daylight through him for grabbing the holding of an evicted tenant' (12.1312).

These are the Irish Joyce once complimented for not throwing the fallen Parnell to the English wolves ('They tore him to pieces themselves').[2] Their eponymous spokesman, the 'I' of the episode, voices the city's only ascertainable public opinion, barroom opinion, which draws no distinction between public and private concerns, claims access to every order of hidden fact, and mistrusting every informant cites all with equal freedom, the most discreditable account being likely the truest and certainly the most gratifying.

His talk, in the book's first sustained solo performance, pours out as copious as a heroic *emesis*, its gobbets of spite for one whole paragraph inextricable from the pangs of a difficult urination –

> . . . (ow!) all a plan so he could vamoose with the pool if he won or (Jesus, full up I was) trading without a license (ow!) Ireland my nation says he (hoik! phthook!) never be up to those bloody (there's the last of it) Jerusalem (ah!) cuckoos. (12.1569)

It is illustrated, like a lantern lecture, by set pieces which display his subject of the moment dressed up in some more magniloquent costume. There are thirty-two of these, and they interrupt his sour garrulousness the way the captions in 'Aeolus' interrupt that episode's cinematographic unrolling, with this difference, that they take a good deal longer to read.

> So we turned into Barney Kiernan's and there, sure enough, was the citizen up in the corner having a great confab with himself and that bloody mangy mongrel, Garryowen, and he waiting for what the sky would drop in the way of drink. (12.118)

– which is followed by:

> The figure seated on a large boulder at the foot of a round tower was that of a broadshouldered deepchested stronglimbed frankeyed red-

haired freelyfreckled shaggybearded widemouthed largenosed long-
headed deepvoiced barekneed brawnyhanded hairylegged ruddyfaced
sinewyarmed hero. From shoulder to shoulder he measured several
ells and . . . [some six hundred more words]. (12.151)

These are versions of the same scene, the second as obviously *written*
as the first is audibly spoken. *Verba volant, litterae manent,* and the
written word accepts responsibilities inherent in its not passing away.
These, though, typify fugitive words, tumbled together at an early stage
of the Irish Revival by someone with no ear at all, as the total absence
of a speakable rhythm indicates. By such means were the heroes cobbled
in translatorese that Ireland was exhorted to thrill to.

The translator of Irish sagas was reclaiming for the laity matter
thought to rival Homer, who was after all alien whereas this stuff was
Erin's very own. Analogously, nineteenth-century translators of Homer
into English were supplying a people who commenced to have doubts
about the Bible with new paradigms of nobility. (Homer is *noble,*
Matthew Arnold affirmed.) Whether from the Irish or from the Greek,
such translations had many awkward features in common, since prose has
fewer ways of concealing unassimilable mannerisms than verse, and also
fewer excuses for eliding them. Its norms are bedevilled, moreover, by
dictionary 'fidelity', and get entangled in devices for inserting loftiness.
(Thus, for all that we hear of Augustan couplet artifice, Pope's language
is more natural than that of Lang, Leaf and Myers.) In so far as the
'Cyclops' episode has a Homer, he is the Homer who forces translators
to write dreadful prose, the Homer of epithets and catalogues, of ap-
positive syntax and dangling honorifics:

> And lo, as they quaffed their cup of joy, a godlike messenger came
> swiftly in, radiant as the eye of heaven, a comely youth and behind
> him there passed an elder of noble gait and countenance, bearing the
> sacred scrolls of law and with him his lady wife a dame of peerless
> lineage, fairest of her race. (12.244)

The latter part of this transposes 'And begob what was it only that
bloody old pantaloon Denis Breen in his bath slippers with two bloody
big books tucked under his oxter and the wife hotfoot after him, unfor-
tunate wretched woman trotting like a poodle', which is quite as mannered
but noticeably more fluent.

Politics, though, binds these interpolations together; David Hayman
has noted acutely[3] that most of them 'parody nineteenth-century adapta-
tions of earlier styles', and the direction of the parodies is toward
newsprint.

A most interesting discussion took place in the ancient hall of *Brian O'Ciarnain's* in *Sraid na Bretaine Bheag* [i.e. Barney Kiernan's in Little Britain Street], under the auspices of *Sluagh na h-Eireann* [a patriotic society], on the revival of ancient Gaelic sports and the importance of physical culture, as understood in ancient Greece and ancient Rome and ancient Ireland, for the development of the race. ... (12.897)

That resembles a report of the doings of the Gaelic Athletic Association, founded in 1884 to infuse national consciousness into sport (cricket and polo were *English* games). Likewise the coy author of the report on the talking dog –

We subjoin a specimen which has been rendered into English by an eminent scholar whose name for the moment we are not at liberty to disclose. . . . The metrical system of the canine original, which recalls the intricate alliterative and isosyllabic rules of the Welsh englyn, is infinitely more complicated but we believe our readers will agree that the spirit has been well caught. (12.730)

– has been intoxicated by the cause of the Gaelic League, founded in 1893 to promote the ancient language. Of such currents, swirling round in journalism's cracked bowl, was the vortex made that drew sane men screaming into civil war. Joyce drafted 'Cyclops' in the third quarter of 1919, the year in which Yeats wrote of 'the weasel's twist, the weasel's tooth',[4] and his beplumed set piece, elaborated to enormous length through revision after revision, is the execution scene, in which the condemned man 'evinced the keenest interest in the proceedings from beginning to end', the executioner gets cheered to the echo, and tasteful souvenirs are distributed to every lady in the audience. It has been, the voice of reportorial silliness keeps assuring us through every headlong adjectival plunge, an unutterably perfect day.

Though our first sense may be that these parodies are interruptions, Joyce had carried many of them to a first degree of finish before he was clear what he meant them to interrupt. The curious fact that in his early stages of thinking about 'Cyclops' he had supposed that one of the drinkers in Barney Kiernan's might be Stephen Dedalus may remind us of a precedent for interruptions in the very first pages of the book, pages written long before the captions in 'Aeolus' were thought of. The precedent is Stephen's habit of framing unspoken asides, which recast what is going on according to impudent analogies, stylistic, historical, or both.

The first of these, on the first page of *Ulysses*, is the single word 'Chrysostomos', which reframes Mulligan's golden grin as emblem of a golden-tongued prelatic persuader. Soon afterward we encounter a set piece longer than some of those in 'Cyclops', its relation to what it interrupts far from unambiguous. What does Stephen mean by serving two masters? Haines has just asked.

– The imperial British state, Stephen answered, his colour rising, and the holy Roman catholic and apostolic church.

Haines detached from his underlip some fibres of tobacco before he spoke.

– I can quite understand that, he said calmly. An Irishman must think like that, I daresay. We feel in England that we have treated you rather unfairly. It seems history is to blame.

The proud potent titles clanged over Stephen's memory the triumph of their brazen bells: *et unam sanctam catholicam et apostolicam ecclesiam*: the slow growth and change of rite and dogma like his own rare thoughts, a chemistry of stars. Symbol of the apostles in the mass for pope Marcellus, the voices blended, singing alone loud in affirmation: and behind their chant the vigilant angel of the church militant disarmed and menaced her heresiarchs. A horde of heresies fleeing with mitres awry: Photius and the brood of mockers of whom Mulligan was one, and Arius, warring his life long upon the consubstantiality of the Son with the Father, and Valentine, spurning Christ's terrene body, and the subtle African heresiarch Sabellius who held that the Father was Himself His own Son. Words Mulligan had spoken a moment since in mockery to the stranger. Idle mockery. The void awaits surely all them that weave the wind: a menace, a disarming and a worsting from those embattled angels of the church, Michael's host, who defend her ever in the hour of conflict with their lances and their shields.

Hear, hear. Prolonged applause. *Zut! Nom de Dieu!*

– Of course I'm a Britisher, Haines' voice said, and I feel as one. I don't want to see my country fall into the hands of German jews either. That's our national problem, I'm afraid, just now. (1.643)

Stephen's rising colour marks his complex embarrassment, more stirred by the proud words of ecclesiastic majesty than his role should allow. The words he has just spoken reappear in Latin as Haines talks, still words only but now with a sound like 'brazen bells'. If the interpolation stopped with 'chemistry of stars', it would be like so many other early interpolations, notation for a brief movement of Stephen's psyche. But it goes on for 150 more words, an emblematic picture of Stephen's own composing, by the Michelangelesque sweep of which he is once more embarrassed ('Hear, hear. Prolonged applause'). When this is over Haines is still talking; it is uncertain whether we have missed some of his discourse or not, though if Stephen actually spoke this paragraph to himself we were detained by it for at least sixty seconds, longer than Haines seems likely to have chattered on.

What has happened, as repeatedly in 'Cyclops', is that a once-potent phrase – 'the holy Roman catholic and apostolic church' – has been snatched up from the plane of banality where it made its entry divested even of honorific capitals, and installed in a pocket of time outside the scene's clock-time, to generate a highly styled interpolation which ('*Zut! Nom de Dieu!*') is also parodic high style. And we have been charmed by the convention of the opening pages into supposing that this interruption is like 'Chrysostomos', a flick of the chameleon Stephen's tongue, though it can't have been. It exists *alongside* the narrative, with Stephen's presence to excuse it.

As so often, the analogy of later episodes permits us to see that earlier ones didn't work quite as we may have thought, responsive (we naïvely supposed) to psychic continuities, taking note of sequential happening in the way of all narrative and novel only in attending to inner happenings as well. Conversely, we may conclude that the break-up of a seamless book after 'Wandering Rocks' is apparent merely. It was fissured already, and the microplanes of its surfaces minutely canted.

When he thought of bringing Stephen into 'Cyclops' Joyce was also thinking that the episode might revert to the book's initial style, interior monologue and neutral narrative.[5] He even drafted passages in this manner, and may have been thinking to use Stephen in the old way as occasion for the parodies he had in mind. They could have furthered the motif of Stephen's self-laceration, being many of them pertinent to two temptations he has undergone: the old Fenian Kevin Egan's effort 'to yoke me as his yokefellow, our crimes our common cause' (3.228) and the editor Myles Crawford's 'I want you to write something for me' (7.616). In deciding not to justify the parodies by the presence of someone to whose mental workings they are congruent, Joyce confirmed the convention that *Ulysses* is from now on at the disposal of the Arranger, who is free to interpolate what he likes without a by-your-leave.

If he was uncertain for a while about how to start writing 'Cyclops', its thematic outlines at any rate were firm in his mind. Bloom would enter a pub where the atmosphere of gaga patriotism was defined by passages of parody, and would be assaulted by a wheezing patriot: an incident obviously prompted by the need for an encounter between the book's Ulysses and some counterpart of Homer's Cyclops.

This is the first time the existence of an entire episode has been obligated by the parallel, as though to acknowledge that you could not write a book called *Ulysses* and leave out the Cyclops. Paddy Dignam's funeral had been a normal event of a normal June morning, and a natural thing for Bloom to have gone to (he likes funerals, Molly says: 'hed go into mourning for the cat': 18.1310). The analogies with *Odyssey*, XI, 'Hades', settle quietly into place around it. In 'Cyclops', though, the analogy takes priority. Our question is apt to be: What is Bloom doing *here*?

Most of us learned the answer from commentaries, the authors of which learned from Stuart Gilbert, whom Joyce prompted. Not that the text is empty of the information, but it is oddly buried. Thus we learn in 'Wandering Rocks' (10.974) that some time after Paddy was interred – presumably on the carriage-ride back from the cemetery which occurred between 'Hades' and 'Aeolus' – Bloom had subscribed five shillings to the fund for Dignam's children. Martin Cunningham was keeping the list, and Jack Power was there, too, to testify that not only the pledge but also the money was forthcoming 'without a second word either'. There will have been more talk on that journey, touched on in slight phrases in 'Sirens': 'Barney Kiernan's I promised to meet them. Dislike that job. House of mourning' (11.910), and 'Wish I hadn't promised to meet' (11.1181). In the intricate chords of 'Sirens' these are elements easy to miss and opaque even if we notice them; not till mid-'Cyclops' do we learn that the people he promised to meet included Cunningham (12.410), or that the errand has to do with Dignam's mortgaged insurance:

> As a matter of fact I just wanted to meet Martin Cunningham, don't you see, about this insurance of poor Dignam's. Martin asked me to go to the house. You see, he, Dignam I mean, didn't serve any notice of the assignment on the company at the time and nominally under the act the mortgagee can't recover on the policy. (12.760)

So this rendezvous has lain ahead since noontime, the duration of five episodes; yet not until a few minutes beforehand do we mark it passing through Bloom's mind, not even in the Bloom-centred 'Lestrygonians' where at several points it might have come in patly.

Has Joyce commenced to improvise links and incidents just a few pages before they are needed? One might guess so on the strength of manuscript evidence that he commenced 'Cyclops' in a state of surprising uncertainty. But manuscripts also show that he was taking a deliberate risk of being thought to improvise, since in 1920–1 the first half of the book underwent extensive multi-levelled revision during which he could have planted many forward links if he had wanted to. So we had better ask what their absence means.

It means, first, that the book's look of discontinuity from 'Sirens' through 'Oxen of the Sun' did not displease him since he did nothing to repair it by inserting further preparations. These episodes stand conspicuously separated, disjunct in space and in time and in narrative method, new beginnings repeatedly made. It is as though the spatial disjunctions of 'Wandering Rocks', the verbal disjunctions of 'Sirens', were reproducing themselves on a very large scale. These episodes, moreover, derive further isolation from their unique way of twinning with earlier episodes. The first three episodes of the book contain links with the next three, but that is natural since their timing is synchronised. But for 'Cyclops' to contain numerous analogies with 'Aeolus', 'Nausicaa' with 'Proteus', 'Oxen of the Sun' with 'Scylla and Charybdis', that is something else. And the resemblances are not at all casual.

Thus not only do the interpolations in 'Cyclops' resemble the captions in 'Aeolus', they are journalistic in thrust as 'Aeolus' is journalistic in locale, and they vulgarise themes the *bricoleurs* of 'Aeolus'* had imagined themselves to be treating with suave detachment: the Irish language, English *maladdresse*, eloquence, Ireland's great days gone but recoverable. 'Aeolus', we may remember, was itself interrupted with set pieces: three specimens of rhetoric (two nationalist in thrust) and Stephen's 'parable' in which plumstones drop as later a biscuit-tin flies. There is even Cyclopean rhetoric which one might mistake for excerpts from Professor MacHugh's effusions: 'the winebark on the winedark waterway', or 'the oldest flag afloat, the flag of the province of Desmond and Thomond, three crowns on a blue field, the three sons of Milesius' (12.1308). But that is not the Professor talking; that is the troglodytic Citizen.

Though widely separated in *Ulysses*, these two episodes are adjacent adventures in the *Odyssey* (IX, X). So are 'Oxen of the Sun' and 'Scylla and Charybdis' (XII), which as we shall be seeing also make twin episodes for Joyce: almost as though he were repaying in ingenuity a debt incurred by his free rearrangement of Homer. 'Nausicaa' and 'Proteus', however, his third pair, have no special connection for Homer, but could hardly not have been twins for Joyce, involving as they do his two heroes separately, each alone, each on Sandymount Strand, each at a node of uncertainty what to do next; one early in the day, one late; one at high tide, one at low. This parallel is relatively easy to discern and Joyce may have hoped it would prompt us to look for the others, since the more our discernment of such matters progresses the more we shall understand why the formalisms of the book itself have commenced to supplant its narrative continuity.

*Many of whom he at one time planned to have present in the 'Cyclops' pub, notably Stephen, Prof. MacHugh, O'Madden Burke; and Joyce did carry over from the one episode to the other Lenehan, J. J. O'Molloy, and Ned Lambert. So the twinning was no afterthought. A 'Cyclops' list even contains the name of Seymour Bushe, whose sentence on the Michelangelo 'Moses' (7.768) is an 'Aeolus' showpiece. See Michael Groden, *'Ulysses' in Progress*, 133–4.

Stephen and Bloom, by now densely established as characters, are commencing their metamorphosis into types and portents. By the time they take cocoa in Bloom's kitchen ('Ithaca') and part in his back garden, it will be hard to say whether we are more conscious of their human substantiality or of their symbolic grandeur: 'wanderers', Joyce said, 'like the stars at which they gaze'.[6]

In withdrawing emphasis from their idiosyncratic humanity – chiefly by suppressing the tang of their familiar voices, audible or silent – Joyce courted the danger that many pages of indirect discourse would drain the blood out of his book. He compensated with styles. The characterisation withdrawn from Bloom and Stephen is lavished on the episodes themselves, each of which (Joyce wrote to Carlo Linati in 1920) 'is so to say one person although it is composed of persons – as Aquinas relates of the Angelic hosts'.[7] 'Cyclops', the overt transition to this principle, is a person because narrated by a person, the only speaking narrator in Joyce's canon, whose performance is so engaging we hardly notice that, though Bloom is present, we are no longer hearing Bloom, only the narrator's paraphrases and imitations of him. Subsequently half of 'Nausicaa' is narrated by the Arranger imitating a Victorian lady novelist, and most of 'Oxen of the Sun' by a gallery of voices that do not even pretend to report words spoken in 1904 Dublin.

As they assume individuality, the episodes draw apart from one another not only in character but in narrative time. Whole hours are commencing to drop out of a narrative the motion of which had once seemed as continuous as an electric tram's. After the end of 'Cyclops' (say, 5.45 p.m.) occurs a gap of over two hours, and when we pick up Bloom's thoughts again on the beach (8.30, perhaps) he has almost nothing to say to himself about it. 'A blank period of time,' says the 'Ithaca' catechist pointedly, 'including a cardrive, a visit to a house of mourning, a leavetaking (wilderness)' (17.2051). We shall lose Bloom again at 9.00 and pick him up once more after 10.00, at the lying-in hospital. Only after the birth of Mrs Purefoy's child is the old tight-packed narrative resumed.

And now we are in a position to understand that Joyce has not forgotten his former criterion of fidelity to the rhythm of his characters' thoughts. For, if the book seems for some hours temporarily adrift, that reflects Bloom's state, adrift, too, putting in time, neither free to go home nor sure how long to stay away. ('Go home,' he tells himself on the beach; then, 'No. Might be still up': 13.1212.) The new stylistic complications, too, which tend rather to screen than to clarify the chain of events, correspond to a span of time he won't want to discuss with Molly when she catechises him about his wanderings, a habit she formed about the time of Milly's puberty (17.2285). During 'Sirens' he wrote a clandestine letter; at the end of 'Cyclops' he is engaged in an uncharacteristic 'public altercation'; in 'Nausicaa' he does more than ogle Gerty. We are explicitly told (17.2250) that these doings were edited out of the version Molly heard just before 2 a.m., and we do not need to be told that all mention of the visit to Bella Cohen's whorehouse was omitted also.

The triumph of the day, though, cannot be omitted: his feat in bringing home, however briefly, 'Stephen Dedalus, professor and author'. So he improvises a visit to the Gaiety, where Mrs Bandman Palmer played *Leah*, a play he knows well enough to answer any awkward questions; also an after-theatre supper with Stephen at Wynn's and – fine zany stroke – 'a postcenal gymnastic display' in the course of which Stephen concussed himself.* This serves to account for the time from 'Nausicaa' through 'Circe', also for the injuries which had justified Stephen's being brought home for cocoa. Analogously, the primary narrative of these events is screened off by only partly penetrable styles, a continuous rhetoric of evasion, as though Bloom were permitting himself only oblique awareness of what Molly can't be permitted to hear about.

As for the visit to the Dignams' about the insurance, though there he has nothing to hide, has in fact performed an act of conspicuously disinterested charity on which we might expect him to draw heavily when Molly puts him to accounting for his time, we are allowed to surmise only that he didn't leave it out. But it is strangely absent from his fifteen pages of unbroken rumination on the beach, apart from a few words about how depressing it was. 'Houses of mourning so depressing because you never know' (13.1226): the Bloom we know is not that easily depressed.

By featuring this errand a little more, both before and after it happened, Joyce could have made easier not only the reader's lot but also his own; he wouldn't have had to contrive subsidiary links – Joe Hynes's money, Nannetti's errand to London – to give 'Cyclops' some look of entrainment with the rest of the book. Yet the psychology of this willed omission proves expressive once we ask why Bloom, whose Irish acquaintances routinely overlook his presence, has been bidden on this particular errand. Joe Hynes, who found him convenient to borrow money from, doesn't even know his first name ('your christian name', he tactlessly calls it: 6.880). But here are three men of position, Martin Cunningham, Jack Power and Crofton, keeping a rendezvous to pick Bloom up at Kiernan's and take him in an official car clear over to the Dignams' as though his presence there were indispensable.

---

*What can he have said Stephen was up to? And was he inspired to this flight of invention by the dance he saw Stephen execute in the whorehouse? 'Stephen with hat ashplant frogsplits in middle highkicks with skykicking mouth shut hand clasp part under thigh. With clang tinkle boomhammer tallyho hornblower blue green yellow flashes' (15.4123).

As it is, in Martin Cunningham's mind. For what they are about amounts to defrauding a moneylender named Bridgeman on a technicality. Dignam had assigned his insurance as security for a loan and, now that he can never repay, the lender would seem entitled to the insurance. But Dignam failed to complete the process of assignment by informing the company, so 'nominally under the act' the company may be constrained to pay the original beneficiary, the widow Dignam. Though everybody would want her to inherit what there may be, the situation is sticky. It will need, so Cunningham seems to have concluded, a technician of hereditary skills – a Jew, in fact. That is to be Bloom's role, and Bloom surely knows it.

Martin Cunningham's resemblance to Shakespeare, remarked on periodically, belongs to an order of coincidence which for Joyce is never aimless. He resembles Shakespeare, we may note, in three particulars. He has a face like Shakespeare's (6.345). He has a wife who in pawning the furniture on him condemns him repeatedly to a second-best bed. And he has devised for Bloom a role modelled on Shylock's. Being cast in the stereotype of Semitic fiscal cunning, *that* seems to be what Bloom senses and resents; that is why he pushes the rendezvous out of his mind for nearly five hours after it is made, and why he does not dwell on it with any satisfaction after it is consummated. And we may note the congruence between this mission and the episode in which it receives what explication it does, 'Cyclops', the episode that culminates in the Citizen's anti-Semitic outburst.

Though 'anti-Semitic' must be qualified, implying as it now does a biological mystique of which the 1904 Irish cynophiles are innocent. They reject outsiders of any category. (Thirty years later De Valera's Spanish strain was said to unfit him for the office of Taoiseach.) An instructive anomaly in the Joseph Strick film of *Ulysses*, which in postulating for budgetary reasons the 'timelessness' of the book settled for a visual Dublin of sports cars and TV aerials, was the sight of Bloom expounding anti-Semitism to a gathering whom we had to perceive as living in a post-Nazi world. But the Bloom of the book and his tormentors pre-date racial purity and death-camps, and they victimise him chiefly out of xenophobic passions, which Joyce represents as pervasive and unquestioning. Mulligan has already proposed treating the Englishman Haines to an English ritual, debagging (the face smeared with marmalade, the braces snipped with tailor's shears, the spectators whooping), on the assumption apparently that insufferable Englishmen understand no other language (1.162). The Citizen proposes treating the pseudo-Irishman, Bloom, to a crack on the head with an Irish biscuit-tin trademarked 'Jacobs' because that is the way to serve someone whose effrontery in using the holy name ('Your God was a jew. Christ was a jew like me': 12.1808) merely caps the unpardonable offence of trying to leave without treating when his pockets (supposedly) are filled with Gold Cup winnings: five quid, the narrator calculates – as much money as some of those present can hope to see in a month. 'And they beheld Him even Him ben Bloom Elijah, amid clouds of angels ascend to the glory of the brightness at an angle of fortyfive degrees over Donohoe's in Little Green Street like a shot off a shovel' (12.1915). At the end of this episode's twin episode, 'Aeolus', Professor MacHugh, following the example of the two old women in Stephen's parable, looked up at a similar angle and saw only Horatio Nelson in stone minus an arm.

'Nausicaa', too, is a twin episode, twin to the morning's 'Proteus' but a malformed twin. Like 'Proteus', though more overtly, it has two parts (Stephen walking, Stephen on a rock; the girls on their outing, Bloom leaning against a rock). Like 'Proteus', it catches the protagonist at a moment of indecision about going home. Stephen won't be returning to the tower, and came to the beach half-intending to seek refuge at Aunt Sara's nearby; he realises, without quite making the decision, that he won't be doing that either and heads into town to call on *Evening Telegraph* and *Homestead* editors. Bloom won't be going home yet (Molly 'might still be up') and came to the beach for a breather half-intending to go to the theatre; he realises it's too late (13.1212) and heads into town to ask after Mrs Purefoy, who will bring forth more than the *Evening Telegraph* will. Both episodes mix approximately equal parts of literature and meditation, though in 'Proteus' the two co-exist in Stephen's mind while in 'Nausicaa' they are divided as though by a dyke. The meditative parts of both turn much toward the past, Stephen's because paternity and the Paris fiasco oppress him, Bloom's out of post-orgasmic melancholy and because darkness is obliterating the stimuli to which his quick mind normally responds. Both culminate in writing: Stephen's quatrain, Bloom's 'I AM A . . .' on the sand. There are lesser convergences, as when 'O those transparent!' (13.1261) – said of Gerty's stockings – translates Stephen's learned 'Diaphane' (3.7). Both contain a masturbation.[8]

So the sunlit early hour of one man's day is rhymed with the crepuscular later hour of the other's, just when the two are on the threshold of their portentous meeting. The tide was nearing full when Stephen walked; he climbed on the rocks to escape it. It is just past the ebb as Bloom muses, the wide flat beach exposed, the wavespeech hushed and remote. Bloom's spirits, too, have been at low tide, at Mrs Dignam's. English narrative skills, too, are in conspicuous ebb: 'Chalk-scrawled backdoors and on the higher beach a dryingline with two crucified shirts' banished by the appetite for unreality: 'No prince charming is her beau ideal to lay a rare and wondrous love at her feet . . .' (13.209). This episode's Homer is the one excogitated by

Samuel Butler, 'The Authoress of the Odyssey', the island girl who managed man–woman dialogue quite well but had to guess about ships and on one occasion put the rudder at the front.

Studied in part from 'that book *The Lamplighter* by Miss Cummins' (13.633), this style creates a new Bloom: 'Passionate nature though he was Gerty could see that he had enormous control over himself' (13.539). He has just taken his hand from his pocket because someone is approaching, and we are later made sure what his hand was doing in his pocket. It was the style, only the style, that obligated that Bloom of enormous control. 'His voice had a cultured ring in it and though he spoke in measured accents there was a suspicion of a quiver in the mellow tones.' (He is saying that his watch has stopped.)

It is the style, too, that stops his watch, at 4.30, just when (he thinks) Molly and Boylan would have been sending out shock waves; the stopped watch is the sort of event that happens in such novels as such a style shapes, and elsewhere in *Ulysses* Joyce wouldn't ask us to credit it. And Bloom isn't a watch-consulter, not like Father Conmee whose watch is 'smooth' from much sliding in and out of pockets. Long ago schooled in impecunious habits, he relies on bells and public timepieces, and not even the parallax of the 1 p.m. timeball – Dunsink time or Greenwich? – impels him to verify either that his interpretation is right or that his watch is. He consults it twice that we know of, in Davy Byrne's before deciding on the burgundy (8.735), and in Pill Lane on his way to his appointment at Kiernan's (13.986); the latter would have been just after it stopped. Joyce conjures it out of Bloom's pocket on the strand by having Cissy Caffrey go and ask him the time, thus deftly prising to the surface a long-suppressed misery:

> Funny my watch stopped at half past four. . . . Was that just when he, she?
> O, he did. Into her. She did. Done. (13.846)

Was it indeed? We don't know, though the time could fit. Boylan left the Ormond shortly after four o'clock, could have arrived in Eccles Street by 4.15, and was moreover 'Boylan with impatience'. Yet time was passed in the music room. The music he brought is left open on the piano (17.1306), and Molly attests that he was 'in great singing voice' (18.149). After 5 p.m. seems a better guess, though it is a general truth that on Bloomsday things tend to happen faster than we'd have thought possible.

For Leopold Bloom, 'Nausicaa' kills an hour, also a sexual edginess. For the purposes of the book it has several uses. It prepares for Bloom's unresponsiveness in the quarter of the whores. It accelerates his convergence with Stephen Dedalus, not only supplying parallels with the morning's 'Proteus' but also granting Bloom a vision of a girl on a beach for off-rhyme with the vision Stephen had been granted on a different beach in the *Portrait*. (Stephen's bird-girl is dressed in Mary's colour, and snatches of the litany of Our Lady of Loreto transpierce repeatedly Gerty's ruminations.) Withdrawing all human jostle like the tide, it shows us a Bloom utterly alone, in a rest between two crowded episodes, 'Cyclops' where drinkers throng, 'Oxen of the Sun' where noisy students drink. And, being half of it written (like the parodies of 'Cyclops') in a notably degenerate nineteenth-century idiom, it prepares us to entertain a parallax of styles.

Bloom seen through Victorian novelese is a different Bloom; in 'Oxen of the Sun' we shall be seeing him through many verbal systems, and shall see him reborn repeatedly. Was Odysseus perhaps a Bloom perceived through Ionic hexameters? Are a time's historical givens as inessential, as ascribable to the plane of costume and metaphor, as its idioms? A Ulysses who travels by tram instead of swift ship, has received on a solemn occasion a moustache cup (17.361) instead of a gold-wrought beaker (*Odyssey*, VIII, 430–1), wears a bowler hat – Plasto's, high-grade – instead of a helmet – bronze, horse-plumed, well-fitted (*Odyssey*, XXII, 102, 111) – says 'Bad . . . to sit on that stone. . . . Might get piles' (13.1081) instead of

μή μ' ἄμυδις στίβη τε κακὴ καὶ θῆλυς ἐέρση
ἐξ ὀλιγηπελίης δαμάσῃ κεκαφηότα θυμόν (*Odyssey* v, 467–8)

as it were,

Lest the bitter frost and the copious dew overcome me,
Weak and worn as I am, and I breathe forth breath for the last time

– is this 1904 Ulysses perhaps the same man, reclad in circumstance as also in headgear and idiom? In Homer he seems different, very; may we say, though, thanks only to parallax?

NOTES

For details of the way Irish politics looked and felt in 1904, see F. L. Radford, 'King, Pope, and Hero-Martyr: *Ulysses* and the nightmare of Irish history', *James Joyce Quarterly*, XV, IV (Summer 1978), 275–323.

1 William M. Murphy, *Prodigal Father: The Life of John Butler Yeats* (Ithaca/London, 1978), 453.
2 Joyce, *Critical Writings*, ed. Mason and Ellmann (New York, 1959), 228.
3 Hart and Hayman, 274.
4 W. B. Yeats, *Nineteen Hundred and Nineteen*, section IV.
5 Groden, 125–6.
6 *Letters*, I, 160.
7 ibid., I, 147.
8 See Chapter 6, note on page 57.

CHAPTER 11

Metempsychoses

So we enter a chapter of stylistic parallax, in which the Bloom whom young Dr Dixon treated for a bee-sting on 23 May 1904 looks different screened through a fourteenth-century idiom.

> And the traveller Leopold was couth to him sithen it had happened that they had had ado each with other in the house of misericord where this learningknight lay by cause the traveller Leopold came there to be healed for he was sore wounded in his breast by a spear wherewith a horrible and dreadful dragon was smitten him for which he did do make a salve of volatile salt and chrism as much as he might suffice. (14.126)

So do sardines in tins:

> And there was a vat of silver that was moved by craft to open in the which lay strange fishes withouten heads though misbelieving men nie that this be possible thing without they see it natheless they are so. (14.149)

These sardines are as miraculous as they would have seemed to Sir John Mandeville, and the traveller as unremarkable in an idiom where spears and dragons abounded like our pencils and puppies. Similarly a medical student named Crotthers, demanding that the bottle be passed, is prevented by the idiom of Sterne from saying a single word that we might expect:

> ... having desired his visavis with a polite beck to have the obligingness to pass him a flagon of cordial waters at the same time by a questioning poise of the head (a whole century of polite breeding had not achieved so nice a gesture) to which was united an equivalent but contrary balance of the bottle asked the narrator as plainly as was ever done in words if he might treat him with a cup of it. (14.741)

We do not see him move a hand at all, nor hear him say a word; thirty-five pages, for that matter, of loud and bawdy talk are so muted by indirect discourse in 'Oxen of the Sun' that we would be hard put to reconstruct convincingly a sentence of it. The language mutates, mutates, manners shift, conventions shift; the very personnel, listed time after time, seem each time reconstituted by metempsychosis. In a chapter of birth they are repeatedly reborn. A voice like Bunyan's lists them

> all in their blind fancy, Mr Cavil and Mr Sometimes Godly, Mr Ape Swillale, Mr False Franklin, Mr Dainty Dixon, Young Boasthard and Mr Cautious Calmer. (14.467)

An eye like Pepys's thereupon discerns not this group at all but

> Leop. Bloom of Crawford's journal sitting snug with a covey of wags, likely brangling fellows, Dixon jun., scholar of my lady of Mercy's, Vin. Lynch, a Scots fellow, Will. Madden, T. Lenehan, very sad about a racer he fancied and Stephen D. (14.504)

A pen like Burke's is grave in summary:

> The young sparks, it is true, were as full of extravagancies as over-grown children: the words of their tumultuary discussions were difficultly understood and not often nice: their testiness and out-rageous *mots* were such that his [Bloom's] intellects resiled from: nor were they scrupulously sensible of the proprieties though their fund of strong animal spirits spoke in their behalf. (14.848)

This last is explicit: the company brangle, wrangle, whoop, carouse; we cannot hear a sound. (And in the *Odyssey* do we sense the *haeccitas* of Odysseus' voice, since he never speaks save in hexameters?)

Nor do we really hear, either, the voices of the authors Joyce is parodying, in part because he punctuates so lightly we must often try sentences over to pick up their construction, hence their cadence. A 'style', for the purposes of this episode, is not the man nor the voice nor even the age, but an agglomeration of habits of diction: rare words (*tumultuary, difficultly, resiled*) that link arms in a visual field decreed by paragraphing. The considerable mimetic powers of James Joyce are not at work here, not ventriloquising. We do not travel in time; we are locked in the early twentieth century where the past exists in museums and past writing in word-museums; and Joyce would not have been affronted at all by J. S. Atherton's discovery that his chief sources for the episode were Saintsbury's *History of English Prose Rhythm* (1912), Peacock's *English Prose: Mandeville to Ruskin* (1903), and as much of the *Oxford English Dictionary* as was then available, A–T.[1]

So this noisiest scene in all of *Ulysses* seems as noiseless as the interior of a library. Then, like an emerging newborn, the company pops

(14.1398) out of the hospital doors toward a pub, and for ten paragraphs we can hear nothing but the noise of their voices and can barely understand the import of a word. Like the afterbirth? Like the impenetrable wail in the nursery? Like pentecostal tongues? We had best look back.

Joyce seems to have had several things in mind at once, and they have to be thought of separately since they won't lie on parallel planes. There are, to begin with, *two* Homeric parallels. In their light talk of sterilising the act of coition, Odysseus' crewmen are slaying the Oxen of the Sun-god; and all the cattle that have walked through the book since Deasy ranted in mid-morning of foot and mouth disease (2.331) and a whole lowing herd in the street delayed Dignam's funeral procession (6.385) join a zodiac of beasts in a dream-procession toward the Dead Sea, 'horned and capricorned, the trumpeted with the tusked, the lionmaned, the giantantlered, snouter and crawler, rodent, ruminant and pachyderm, all their moving moaning multitude, murderers of the sun' (14.1093). For from animal intestines the contraceptives were once made that are still illegal in Ireland lest they conduce to animal lust.

But the carousing suitors of the Ithacan court are surely present also, eating, drinking, roistering (cf. *Odyssey*, XVII, 532–7); this makes Mina Purefoy, in labour, whose travail is blasphemed by their wassail, a sort of displaced Penelope; her husband, like Penelope's, is absent at the moment. These suitors, of whom Mulligan is chief, trifle with truth and jeer. They drink up at Burke's tavern the substance of Stephen/ Telemachus, under the eye of his symbolic father whom neither he nor they can recognise in that role. At the end of the episode most of them run off after fire-engines and are never seen again.

There is a parallel with embryonic development, a good joke when we chance to notice it, not worth the digging out if we don't. Thus Bloom (Joyce said) is the spermatozoon, and the virginal Nurse Callan opens the hospital door 'that he would rathe infare under her thatch': at this instant lightning flashes in the west (14.81), and she sensibly crosses herself. Eleven paragraphs – Joyce's number of regeneration is always eleven – bring Bloom inside, holding his hat; eleven more, at the end of the episode, conduct the noisy crew out of the hospital and into and out of the pub. Between the elevens stand just forty paragraphs, one for each week of gestation, in the first of which Bloom hears Nurse Callan tell of the death of a mutual friend, and in the last of which he greets her again in going: 'Madam, when comes the storkbird for thee?' (14.1405). What anyone really says in these paragraphs 'style' keeps us from discerning, and Bloom's tact would have kept him from saying anything like that; Joyce risked an improbability for the sake of bracketing his forty-part *tour de force*, in which something other than Mina Purefoy's infant – who arrives as early as paragraph twenty-seven (14.945) – is surely getting born.

Partly, it is the speech of 1904 that is born, emerging into the air after a long travail that has spanned the centuries from Roman and Anglo-Saxon times. Spoken by a dozen voices simultaneously and picked up as if by an unseeing microphone, it is inelegant and nearly unintelligible:

> Your attention! We're nae tha fou. The Leith police dismisseth us. The least tholice. Ware hawks for the chap puking. Unwell in his abominable regions. Yooka. Night. Mona, my thrue love. Yook. Mona, my own love. Ook.
> Hark! Shut your obstropolos. Pflaap! Pflaap! Blaze on. There she goes. Brigade! Bout ship. Mount street way. Cut up! Pflaap! Tally ho. You not come? Run, skelter, race. Pflaaaap! (14.1565)*

If 'style' has previously been an irritant, we should be grateful for some now; the mike held up to nature, like the mirror, records chaos.

And the bond of 'fatherhood' between Bloom and Stephen is also born, though it would not do to say that Stephen is reborn as Bloom's son. Which brings us to the 'story', notably their portentous meeting toward which so much has been straining. To narrate it plainly: after his brief doze on Nausicaa's rocks Bloom has come by tram in from Sandymount Strand, reversing his morning route from the baths out to Dignam's. Still putting in time, he has stopped off at Holles Street Maternity Hospital to inquire about Mrs Purefoy. The minor problem of getting him into the common room where the students are carousing Joyce solved by letting him encounter Dr Dixon, who had dressed his bee-sting at the Mater on Eccles Street and now urges him to join the company. Bloom, who 'never drank no manner of mead', pours most of the drink Dixon provides 'privily' into someone else's glass, and takes a seat 'for to rest him there awhile' (14.163).

How Stephen came to be there we aren't told. A medical student – possibly his old friend Lynch – perhaps found him in a pub and brought him along. He is much the most drunken of the crowd, having done nothing but drink since we last saw him six hours ago. His talk is expansive, his manner prodigal; there is no reason for the company to know what we know, that he is excessively fatigued and resorting to self-quotation, even Mulligan-quotation. His talk is ecclesiastical-bawdy; others' is simply bawdy.

---

*'We're nae tha fou' is Crotthers singing a chorus from Burns's 'Willie brewed a peck of maut'. The 'Leith police' line is a sobriety test which somebody here passes, somebody else doesn't. 'Yooka' and 'Ook' are sounds of vomiting. 'Mona' is from another song. 'Pflaap' is the fire-engine's siren. 'Mount street way' is south-east, and 'Bout ship' urges the company to swing round and chase the engines. 'You not come?' is shouted after Stephen and Lynch, who are setting out north-west towards the brothels.

Mulligan enters, bringing in tow, as we know but Bloom does not, the same Bannon whom Milly mentioned in her morning letter (4.406), the one who sings Boylan-songs, and Bannon describes to the nearest listener (14.752–778) his *amour* with a girl who we know (but Bloom doesn't know) was Milly. The photo-girl has given him a photo, and he boasts that he would have scored had he only had a contraceptive handy. (Could there have been a means to murder the oxen, there would have been coition.)

Mulligan has been at the *littérateur* George Moore's, 4 Upper Ely Place, a few blocks away. We have seen him walk in on Stephen's discourse before this, in the library of 'Scylla and Charybdis'. That was where we first heard of the *soirée* at Moore's, to which Mulligan was even told to bring Haines whereas Stephen was never invited (9.306), confirmation of Stephen's exclusion from the one *milieu* to which he makes some claim to belong, the small shifting circle of talkers who were fostering the not unfounded illusion that a Literary Revival was astir in the drab capital. To harangue drunken medicos while wine and wit are flowing in Upper Ely Place is Stephen's shabby fate, and the knowledge that he is *here* while primrose-vested Buck is majestically *there* no doubt helps impel his reckless drinking, his flights of erudite nonsense, his late-night descent upon the brothels. He is, moreover, talking in a hospital where one might rather expect to find Mulligan: keeping Mulligan's chair warm while the sleek usurper occupies a place at Moore's.

Not, we must reflect, that Stephen had seemed any more at ease in the Library. We are encouraged to this reflection by the pairing of the two episodes, 'Scylla and Charybdis', 'Oxen of the Sun', successive happenings in the *Odyssey* (XII), twin episodes in *Ulysses*. Joyce took evident pains to pair them, only most conspicuously by the entrance, each time, of Mulligan to break the stride of Stephen's discourse. 'Scylla' commences about 2.15 in what would have seemed Stephen's likely terrain, the National Library on Kildare Street; 'Oxen' at about 10.00 in what may pass for Mulligan's terrain, the maternity hospital on Holles Street. (So the poet who spends his day not writing and the doctor who spends his not doctoring has each a place appointed as though by Aristotle, in which conspicuously not to fulfil his function.) There is, in each episode, a certain decentring; we are neither in the reading-room of the Library nor in the wards of the hospital, but in an office of the one and a common room of the other: convivial enclaves for the staff and their guests. (This resembles, to invoke a persistent analogy, being taken by time-machine to the Globe Theatre and then being confined to its greenroom.) In each we confront a bookish verbal surface which tends to repel our penetration: in 'Scylla' a mosaic of Shakespearean phrases, attributable to the presiding consciousness of Stephen, in 'Oxen' a chronological anthology of prose manners, attributable to 'the mind of the text'.[2] (The stylistics of 'Aeolus' and 'Cyclops', also twin episodes, were discriminated on a similar principle. And we may note that 'the mind of the text' grows increasingly diffuse, since in 'Cyclops', though he had no name, he was clearly a speaking person, abetted by the hidden hand that supplied the parodies; this hand has wholly taken over the writing of 'Oxen'.) And there are numerous minor links: Stephen's telegram, 'cribbed out of Meredith' (9.546; 14.1486); the evocation, early in 'Scylla', of Stephen dictating a new *Paradise Lost* to 'six brave medicals' (9.18), represented in 'Oxen' by Dixon, Lynch, Madden, Crotthers, Costello, Mulligan; the George Moore *soirée* (9.1098; 14.495); Haines's repeated failure to keep a rendezvous with the Buck (9.513; 14.1026); Bloom's silent proximity. And Stephen's talk.

In the Library Stephen talks, having drunk three whiskeys; it is his speaking episode, in a book where he mostly talks to himself or gives other men short answers, and his intricate talk is of paternity: the father a playwright, the offspring a brainchild. In the hospital he talks also, quite as volubly, though the narrative manner wholly screens off his voice. He has drunk much more whiskey, is still drinking malt, and his talk is now of maternity, which he mocks.

Paternity, maternity; Shakespeare, Anne Hathaway: in 1904, the tercentenary of the 'good' Second Quarto of *Hamlet*, these analogies rise out of natural literary talk, which Shakespeare had been dominating for at least fifty years. It is hard to think of another age when a single writer could have been so sure to materialise wherever two or more bookish folk were gathered together. In Ireland as in Germany, England, America, professionals, amateurs and cranks alike were engaged on a Shakespearean quest of which by 1874 the formidable Frederick James Furnivall – first editor of the *Oxford English Dictionary* (and founder of the Early English Text Society, one of whose publications, known to Stephen by title at least,[3] was *Agenbite of Inwit*) – had stated the collective business: (1) 'By a very close study of the metrical and phraseological peculiarities of Shakespere, to get his plays as nearly as possible into the order in which he wrote them'; (2) 'To use that revised order for the purpose of studying the progress and meaning of Shakespere's mind, the passage of it from . . . the Comedies of Youth, through . . . the Histories of Middle Age, to the great Tragedies dealing with the deepest questions of man in Later Life; and then at last to the poet's peaceful and quiet home-life again in Stratford.'

This states what T. S. Eliot was to restate, that all Shakespeare's work is one work: a statement sufficiently self-evident in a time obsessed by metaphors of evolution to have occurred independently to several workers, notably to Dublin's own Shakespearean Edward Dowden (1843–1913), since 1867 Professor of English Literature at Trinity,

whose *Shakespere: A Critical Study of His Mind and Art* (1875) postulated Four Periods and did much to make them seem axiomatic.

Dowden, on whose serenity in Highfield House, Rathgar, the threadbare Stephen would have hesitated to intrude, once answered a question
of Mulligan's, who quotes him in mockery:

> – Lovely! Buck Mulligan suspired amorously. I asked him what he
> thought of the charge of pederasty brought against the bard. He lifted
> his hands and said: *All we can say is that life ran very high in those
> days.* Lovely! (9.731)

Joyce's eye was on the first sentence of a *Shakespere* Dowden published
in 1877 for the use of schoolchildren: 'In the closing years of the
sixteenth century the life of England ran high.'[4] As for the charge of
pederasty, it was first brought against the bard by Dublin's Oscar Wilde
in 1889; in those days life ran moderately high in Dublin, as in the
London of 1899, where another bisexual critic, Samuel Butler, found
pederasty in *Shakespeare's Sonnets.*

So it was normal to speculate on the presumed time of darkness in
Shakespeare's life, to which the Third Period responded; normal also to
create a Shakespeare in one's own image. In these respects Stephen's
Bloomsday performance in the Library is perfectly conventional. His
Shakespeare in middle life is wounded, driven; moreover, his plight
rhymes with Stephen's own. This Shakespeare has been radically
crippled by the seductive dominance of Anne Hathaway ever since the
night he yielded to her in a ryefield, and Stephen has been pursued by
the ghost of his mother May Dedalus ever since she forced him with a
request he could only refuse: to pray for her. *Hamlet,* he even says, is
a ghost-story, the ghost being Shakespeare himself, Hamlet the son of
his soul, and the guilty Gertrude the guilty Anne who 'overbore' him
once and cuckolds him now with his brothers Edmund and Richard.
Part of Stephen's desire is to astonish, part of it to parade his knowledge
of how genius works, knowledge those present – Dublin's senior *litterati* –
are to understand he has by birthright. It is soon clear that he isn't
magnetising them at all ('Yes, indeed, the quaker librarian said. A most
instructive discussion. Mr Mulligan, I'll be bound, has his theory too of
the play and of Shakespeare. All sides of life should be represented':
9.503). Their casualness and Mulligan's heckling drive him into
reckless postulations, notably when his father crosses his mind, and
'battling against hopelessness' he cries, 'Who is the father of any son
that any son should love him or he any son? (9.844) ('What the hell
are you driving at?' he asks himself in dismay; and 'I know. Shut up.
Blast you! I have reasons.' And 'Are you condemned to do this?' It
becomes a Pyrrhic victory of discourse.)

Still, if we hold on despite countless interruptions as trying surely for Stephen as for us, and keep in mind his need to devise out of his own situation, at whatever cost to Shakespearean fact, a paradigm for the poetic process, we can extract useful themes from his farrago.

Thus we cannot fail to notice how Bloom-like a Shakespeare Stephen succeeds in imagining: a restless man with a lively daughter and a dead son, uneasily yoked to a wife who 'overbore' him once and cuckolds him now, rearranging all this difficult experience in a steady flow of words. And, finding 'in the world without as actual what was in his world within as possible' (9.1041), Stephen is to encounter Bloom but will not know that he has met his Shakespeare's personification.

His mind is still where it was on the beach in 'Proteus', revolving enigmas of paternity, of his subservience to his 'consubstantial father' the drunken bankrupt whose feckless ways he feels astir within himself. Shakespeare, he must establish, sundered such bonds: Shakespeare was Hamlet *père* and Hamlet *fils*; 'not the father of his own son merely, but, being no more a son, he was and felt himself the father of all his race, the father of his own grandfather, the father of his unborn grandson . . .' (9.867); locked no more amid genealogical necessities but free in a realler world of his own creation. Thus in the hospital Stephen brushes aside Punch Costello's questions about former schoolfellows:

> You have spoken of the past and its phantoms, Stephen said. Why think of them? If I call them into life across the waters of Lethe will not the poor ghosts troop to my call? Who supposes it? I, Bous Stephanoumenos, bullockbefriending bard, am lord and giver of their life. (14.1112)

Mere fact is for the artist to subsume, that he may be free from its claims.

Stephen by now is flying very high, playing at being not merely a second Shakespeare but a veritable God-man presiding over his Last Supper:

> Now drink we, quod he, of this mazer and quaff ye this mead which is not indeed parcel of my body but my soul's bodiment. Leave ye fraction of bread to them that live by bread alone. . . . Mark me now. In woman's womb word is made flesh but in the spirit of the maker all flesh that passes becomes the word that shall not pass away. This is the postcreation. *Omnis caro ad te veniet*. . . . (14.281)

In the pub late in the episode he is intoning Prayers After Mass:

> Thrust syphilis down to hell and with him those other licensed spirits . . . who wander through the world. . . . (14.1543)

The role continues, and will continue into 'Circe': Shakespearean Maker become not only a priest of the eternal imagination but a second God. When he and Lynch head for the brothels, he can feel that he is fulfilling his remark in the Library, that 'A man of genius makes no mistakes. His errors are volitional and are the portals of discovery' (9.228). But he does so under the eye of a new, self-appointed father.

> . . . and now sir Leopold that had of his body no manchild for an heir looked upon him his friend's son and was shut up in sorrow for his forepassed happiness and as sad as he was that him failed a son of such gentle courage (for all accounted him of real parts) so grieved he also in no less measure for young Stephen for that he lived riotously with those wastrels and murdered his goods with whores. (14.271)

This repeats a moment in the Dignam funeral carriage:

> Noisy selfwilled man. Full of his son. He is right. Something to hand on. If little Rudy had lived. See him grow up. Hear his voice in the house. Walking beside Molly in an Eton suit. My son. Me in his eyes. (6.74)

(Not many minutes later on the beach Stephen had thought bitterly of 'the man with my voice and my eyes and a ghostwoman with ashes on her breath': 3.46.)

So when the crowd separates after closing-time at Burke's – Mulligan, who's slipped out early, back to the tower, the students after the engines, Stephen and Lynch for Nighttown – 'The johnny in the black duds' (14.1575) follows Stephen and Lynch: an act unplanned, almost un-willed, like so many acts in this book.

As the end of 'Oxen' plunged through rhetorical chaos, the narrative line of the book now passes through a blank during which something of considerable import happens, an event at whose nature we must guess from later and meagre clues. It is after 11 p.m., the hour at which Dublin public transport still shuts down, and the last trains are leaving for the suburbs. Mulligan and Haines have an 11.10 rendezvous at Westland Row Station,* to catch the last train back to Sandycove and the tower. What could not have been anticipated was the nearly simultaneous appearance of Stephen and Lynch at the same station; for

---

*Haines had put in a brief appearance at Moore's to establish this, as Mulligan narrates in the hospital (14.1026). Some readers have supposed that Haines comes to the hospital, but 'the dissipated host', 'the seer' and 'the sage' of Mulligan's narrative are clearly Moore, AE and Eglinton. So Haines missed the evening at Moore's, as in the twin episode, 'Scylla', he missed Mulligan at the Library. How he spent the evening is unspecified, though the 'phial marked *Poison*' of Mulligan's Gothic account is possibly a bottle of Irish.

them to set out for Nighttown by train – a mere half-mile to Amiens Street Station north of the river – is a grand gesture comparable to the morning's telegram. There ensued a 'very unpleasant scene' (16.263) in which 'it was perfectly evident' to Bloom – who arrived at it late – 'that the other two, Mulligan, that is, and that English tourist friend of his, who eventually euchred their third companion, were patently trying as if the whole bally station belonged to them to give Stephen the slip in the confusion'. This makes little sense, since even supposing they hoped not to travel to Sandycove in Stephen's company they could hardly have prevented his getting on the train.

Anyhow, whatever is 'perfectly evident' in the episode ('Eumaeus') where we find this account was almost certainly not in reality what it looked like. We may guess that when Bloom came upon the scene Mulligan and Haines were not trying to 'give Stephen the slip' but were running away from him. Why? An hour or so later Stephen's hand is hurting (15.3720); such pain is often perceptible some time after the trauma. More pertinently, he marches into Nighttown, perhaps ten minutes after the scene at Westland Row, in a state of high elation; he has promoted himself from priest to bishop, the ashplant his crozier, and chants of a flow from the temple on the right side (*'Vidi aquam egredientem de templo a latere dextro'*), which may well conscript the Paschal Antiphon to describe a satisfying gush from Mulligan's head (15.77). If, fortified by many ounces of alcohol, he took a swing at Mulligan, whose mockery has plagued him all day, that would be understandable; it would also explain, what a mere attempt to 'give the slip' would not, why, as Bloom says, if he goes to the tower now he 'won't get in after what occurred at Westland Row station' (16.250). And, so foreign is such violence to his nature, it's unsurprising that after perhaps an hour he can't remember committing it ('Hand hurts me slightly': 15.4414).

Joyce thinks it worth while to remind us of the hurt hand yet again many pages later (16.1296), and again (16.1608). If indeed such an act of aggression did occur, it is consonant with his normal practice that he should move it off-stage; consonant, too, since Stephen is befuddled and Bloom bewildered, that we should receive so fragmentary an account. Finally, since emulating Shakespeare has been an unspecified but apprehensible ambition of this strange book – which ends with the most memorable soliloquy since Hamlet's – it is fitting, after an episode twinned with a Shakespeare episode, that we shall now be offered a play.

NOTES

1 See Atherton's essay on this episode in Hart and Hayman, 313–39.
2 This phrase is Mr Bruce Kawin's, at a Faulkner symposium, 1978.

3 Skeat cites the title in his *Etymological Dictionary,* which both Joyce and Stephen read 'by the hour'.

4 Cited by Aron Y. Stavisky, *Shakespeare and the Victorians* (Norman, Okla., 1969). Don Gifford with Robert J. Seidman, *Notes for Joyce* (New York, 1974), 189, cite Dowden's sentence about pederasty in the Sonnets: 'In the Renascence epoch, among natural products of a time when life ran swift and free, touching with its current high and difficult places, the ardent friendship of man with man was one.' Though clearly Dowden thought more than once of Life as a flooding Liffey, Stavisky's discovery is the closer to Mulligan's report. I am indebted to Stavisky's book also for the quotation from Furnivall and the remark about Dowden's work in reinforcing the Four Periods.

CHAPTER 12

Death and Resurrection

Why 'Circe' is needed at all is, on the mere narrative plane, not evident. Though the plot requires that Odysseus and Telemachus shall meet and come home, it would have been easy to have Bloom take Stephen in charge at Westland Row and bring him straight back to Eccles Street.* We should have missed the most dazzling episode in the book, and not have known we missed it. What need does 'Circe', apart from dazzlement, serve?

Notably, cathartic needs. Bloom has murdered (on the beach, in Gerty's presence) the Oxen of the Sun – indeed, as we shall learn (17.2282), has routinely murdered them ever since Rudy died more than ten years before, to the detriment of his marriage with Molly and in defiance of the injunction laid on his people to be fruitful and multiply. 'Has he not nearer home a seedfield that lies fallow for the want of the ploughshare?' the voice of Junius has asked. 'A habit reprehensible at puberty is second nature and an opprobrium in middle life' (14.929). He needs to undergo purgation by pity and terror, defined (P 204) as the union of whatever is grave and constant in human sufferings with, respectively, the human sufferer and the secret cause. Otherwise the day will have been for nothing. As for Stephen, he must exorcise the ghost of his mother. And both must exorcise the nightmare of history: Hebraic, Irish, human. To this end we need a play, Aristotle's prescription – and a ghost-play.

We need a play, too, because no book concerned with the Dublin of 1904 – the year the Abbey Theatre opened – would be complete without a play: a play, moreover, sufficiently outrageous to exceed the offence Revival dramaturgy had offered repeatedly to the nostrils of bourgeois Dublin. In 1899 *The Countess Cathleen* – an alleged offence to piety – was played under police protection. In 1903 Synge's *In the Shadow of*

---

*A more severe injury, for instance, would have been plausible to arrange. As it is, there are signs that Stephen was sick in Bloom's sight. How else account for Bloom's 'It wouldn't occasion me the least surprise to learn that a pinch of tobacco or some narcotic was put in your drink for some ulterior object' (16.284)? Ingested tobacco is an emetic. The *emesis* probably occurred at the station. It's unlikely that it was Stephen who vomited outside Burke's (14.1566), so alert and vigorous is he moments later.

the Glen drew hisses, boos, and press execrations for its traduction of Irish womanhood; moreover, for passing off as Irish what was in fact a Greek legend. Foreignness was next to ungodliness. And everyone remembers the week of rioting that greeted *The Playboy of the Western World* in January 1907. To outdo Yeats in offensiveness to orthodoxy, Synge in his insults to Irishwomen and in his foreignness, a less resourceful antinomian than James Joyce would have been hard put. Joyce set the play-scene of *Ulysses* in the Dublin red-light district, peopled it with Irish prostitutes, brought bishops and cardinals on stage, and made the foreign origin of his fable detectable by arranging that we should learn to call the episode 'Circe'.

Joyce's evident models for this longest of the episodes included the Walpurgisnacht of *Faust*, Flaubert's *Tentation*, the Dublin Christmas pantomime, and – naturally – Shakespeare, all of whose faults, as noted by all of his critics, he seems to have heaped together for imitation: the word-play, the cavalier disregard of unities, the motivation turning on trivia, the tickles for the groundlings, the offhand mechanics ('Exit, pursued by a bear'), the topicalities, the flagrant mixing of genres, the bawdry. How better epitomise the essential Shakespeare than by seizing on all that distinguishes him from normative dramatists? He made the play illustrate Stephen's Shakespearean discourse, too – 'We walk through ourselves, meeting robbers, ghosts, giants, old men, young men, wives, widows, brothers-in-love, but always meeting ourselves' (9.1044). And for its rationale he turned to contemporary consensus concerning the Shakespearean ghost.

At the turn of the century it was a familiar annotator's theme that Shakespeare's ghosts were of two sorts, the objective, the subjective: those everyone could see, those only one person could see. Thus Hamlet's father appears on the battlements (I, i; I, iv) to everyone present – Francisco, Bernardo, Horatio, Marcellus, Hamlet – but in the Queen's boudoir (III, iv) only to Hamlet, who cries 'Look you how pale he glares!' to a Queen who sees 'Nothing at all'. The former is 'real' because public; the latter 'imaginary' because private (though according to the stage-direction the audience sees it).

We may surmise that such distinctions mattered less to the Elizabethans, for whom ghosts were certainly real and might regulate their manner of appearing, than they did to the Victorians with the essentially novelistic criteria of empirical and phantasmal, outer and inner. Joyce, post-Victorian enough to believe that all in a novel has the reality of text and no other reality, rethought the boundary for his own purposes but kept two kinds between which the boundary lay. Joyce's 'real' ghost is subjective, appearing to Stephen's mind, hence also to the reader; his others are phantasmagoric, visible to the reader of the text alone.

In a scene (15.4156–4240) modelled after the closet-scene in
Hamlet, Stephen – dizzy with dancing and drink and lack of food –
really does see the apparition of his mother. He turns white, Bloom
opens a window, a whore dashes out for water; he swings a stick at his
vision but it is as the air invulnerable and instead he hits the brothel
chandelier. The lampshade really is dented and the chimney broken: a
real shillingworth of damages, paid for in coin by Bloom. The numerous
other so-called hallucinations appear, we must say, primarily to the
mind of the text, since no one's observable behaviour is altered by them
in the slightest. It is not clear that Bloom at any time sees anything
unusual when the text puts him through extravagant masquerades. In
the twenty pages (15.1354–1956) during which he goes from Lord
Mayorhood to Martyrdom no one observes anything amiss; in fact a
girl named Zoe keeps right on talking, and the 'hallucination' fits neatly
between two of her sentences, 'Go on. Make a stump speech of it'
(15.1353) and 'Talk away till you're black in the face' (15.1958). This
busy sequence articulates and extends a transient Bloomish feeling of
which his observable behaviour displays no trace, and there is no later
sign that he remembers it or has even been aware of it. If when 'Circe'
is over he seems a new Bloom, courageous and composed, we must refer
this change to the chemistry of the unconscious, where words have no
purchase; if the hallucination has any relationship to this change, it is
that of a dumbshow to the hidden reality it mimes.

Nor is our first impression correct, that the vision is arranged out of
the contents of Bloom's memory, conscious and unconscious. True, there
are familiar elements like 'U.P.: Up' and '32 feet per second'; but there
are also sometimes elements drawn from scenes at which Bloom was not
present – for instance 'pensive bosom' (7.246) and 'soultransfigured
. . . soultransfiguring' (7.771), which reappear conjoined in a 'Bloom'
hallucination (15.1002) – and also learned matters of which he would
be ignorant, such as the Latin for 'executioner'.

MICHAEL, ARCHBISHOP OF ARMAGH

(*pours a cruse of hairoil over Bloom's head*) *Gaudium magnum annuntio
vobis. Habemus carneficem.* Leopold, Patrick, Andrew, David, George,
be thou anointed! (15.1486)

Bloom might remember the Ireland–Scotland–Wales–England sequence
of names from newspaper accounts of the coronation of Edward VII in
1902, and could even conceivably dredge out of his unconscious the
formula '*Habemus pontificem*' from the announcement of the election
of Pope Pius X in 1903, but Joyce's learned substitution of 'carneficem'
(executioner) for 'pontificem' (pontiff) is as far beyond Bloom's powers
as it is essential to the book's vision of history's nightmare. Emmet was

executed, the Croppy Boy was executed, in 'Cyclops' an eponymous Irish Patriot took up fully 2000 words being executed, and by the time 'Circe' was written the Easter Martyrs were long since executed and apotheosised. That, in *Ulysses*, is what power rests on, a stout executioner. In 'Circe' (15.1177) as in 'Cyclops' (12.430; 12.592) H. Rumbold plays the part; Joyce gave him the name of the British Minister to Bern, to whom he had unsuccessfully appealed a squabble over a pair of trousers.*

We enjoy over Bloom the advantage of existing outside the book, within reach of such aids as biographies of Joyce, Latin dictionaries, and a text in which we can turn to and fro. The 'hallucinations' exist almost wholly for us. We, if not Bloom, see many many strange things in this long episode, though it is not always clear what we may be seeing because the style is misleadingly homogenous. As recently as 'Cyclops' we could make a sure distinction between 'real' events and 'fantastic' interpolations; the 'real' events, whether or not accurately reported, were referable to a consistent narrative voice, the interruption of which by 'fantasy' was signalled by a marked stylistic break.

By 'Oxen of the Sun' the 'real' events were growing difficult to recover from the text, but we were encouraged to feel sure they were going on, and that their substance remained accessible. In 'Oxen' each of the successive styles might plausibly be considered a code, which lost much information – what words are the roisterers actually uttering? – but retained a gist. We persuaded ourselves (with considerable effort) that we could 'read through' each style: could deduce, for instance, from Mulligan's 'Gothic' tale that Haines, to everyone's consternation, had put in a brief and incoherent appearance at George Moore's. The paragraph begins:

> But Malachias' tale began to freeze them with horror. He conjured up the scene before them. The secret panel beside the chimney slid back and in the recess appeared – Haines! Which of us did not feel his flesh creep? He had a portfolio full of Celtic literature in one hand, in the other a phial marked *Poison*. Surprise, horror, loathing were depicted on all faces while he eyed them with a ghostly grin. I anticipated some such reception, he began with an eldritch laugh, for which, it seems, history is to blame.... (14.1010)

*Richard Ellmann, *James Joyce*, 461. And 'Rumbold' is an unbelievably apt name; as is 'Bertha Supple' (15.88) for a whore. One would think 'Supple' had been invented on the model of Doll Tearsheet, but there are currently seven Supples in the Dublin telephone book, and the family came over from France with Strongbow. The universe, Guy Davenport has remarked, often seems to have been designed for Joyce's convenience.

The secret panel, the phial, the ghostly grin, the eldritch laugh, these we incline to assign to the 'style'. In reality he came in, we surmise, by the door; if he was clutching anything it was likely a whiskey-bottle, and if he acted strangely he had no doubt been sipping from it. We note, too – have noted many times in the episode – the book's newly acquired trick of quoting from itself. 'It seems history is to blame' is something Haines said to Stephen in the early morning, when the 'initial' style rendered his words as follows:

> Haines detached from his underlip some fibres of tobacco before he spoke.
> – I can quite understand that, he said calmly. An Irishman must think like that, I daresay. We feel in England that we have treated you rather unfairly. It seems history is to blame. (1.645)

In the Gothic version, 'We feel in England that we have treated you rather unfairly' is what becomes 'Yes, it is true. I am the murderer of Samuel Childs. And how I am punished! . . . My hell, and Ireland's, is in this life.' This, too, however startling, remains within the closed system of the book; the Childs fratricide case, with its inconclusive outcome, has been mentioned already three times,* so to have murdered [Thomas] Childs is to have performed a crime for which there has been no conviction – a crime, moreover, against a brother. We have no difficulty fitting this preposterous confession into a metaphorical scheme: England's treatment of Ireland.

Still, it seems a pity to obliterate by paraphrase the moment when Haines, of all people, confesses to the most celebrated unsolved crime of the day, even though he names the wrong victim, and this is not the only sign that decoding a paragraph from 'Oxen' may not be the most rewarding way to read it: that to strip away the language in quest of some onion's core may be to discard pungent satisfactions for a vestigial reward. For we obtain, at the end of some ideal decoding, a short flat paragraph worded by ourselves,† and we lose a catena of zany serendipities, such as the punning coincidence between contraception and murdering someone named Childs, or such as this:

> The mystery was unveiled. Haines was the third brother. His real name was Childs. The black panther was himself the ghost of his own father. He drank drugs to obliterate. For this relief much thanks.

* 6.469; 7.748; 14.958. It happened in 1899. Seymour Bushe secured Samuel Childs's acquittal for the murder of his 76-year-old brother Thomas on the ground that the evidence was purely circumstantial. Haines in his incoherence has transposed the brothers: no one murdered Samuel.

† Or by Mr Blamires, from whose version – *The Bloomsday Book*, 160 – we'd not even guess that the apparition occurred at Moore's.

Here we may discern, candied, the hurried wind-up of a thriller, Stephen's shocking account of the three Shakespeare brothers (9.973), the black panther of Haines's nightmare (1.57), Mulligan's mocking jumble of Stephen-on-Hamlet (1.555), and a tag from *Hamlet* already (13.939) invoked by Bloom in the afterglow of Gerty MacDowell: 'For this relief much thanks. In *Hamlet,* that is.' It capers like a demented Chaplin, is rich and funny, and would be foolishly thrown away for a pennyworth of paraphrase.

To throw such benisons away may well be what Joyce finally meant by the crime of slaying the Oxen of the Sun: ceaselessly to unwrite the episode as we read it, and to read with a drear eye lighted by no more than a minimal need to find out what is happening, on the unsurprising plane of bodily happenings; merely the entrances, gorgings, departures. This is like sex undertaken that the predictable may happen: what Alex in *A Clockwork Orange* calls the old in-and-out.

And we have all sinned, reading 'Oxen'; and our hell, like Ireland's, is in this life, reading 'Circe'.

Nothing, in 'Circe', distinguishes 'real' from 'hallucinatory', nor any part of the episode from any other. Format and idiom are homogenous throughout: speakers' names in CAPITALS, spoken words in Roman type, narration and description in the *italics* of stage-directions (of Shavian amplitude, not Shakespearean sparseness). Though this seems admirably businesslike, neither notation nor idiom nor voice will acknowledge a difference between

Tommy Caffrey scrambles to a gaslamp and, clasping, climbs in spasms. From the top spur he slides down. Jacky Caffrey clasps to climb. The navvy lurches against the lamp.

and

Shouldering the lamp he staggers away through the crowd with his flaring cresset (15.131)

And this is before what we take for hallucinations have started: casual scene-setting merely.

As for the so-called hallucinations, they obey an elusive variety of principles. All we can safely say of their detail is that it tends to come from earlier in the book, a sort of collective vocabulary out of which, it seems, anything at all can now be composed. As in the kind of course Joyce gave for years at the Trieste Berlitz, the earlier episodes have confined themselves to rather formal conversations and to objects actually present:

– Yes, sir, the chemist said. That was two and nine. Have you brought a bottle?

– No, Mr Bloom said. Make it up, please. I'll call later in the day and I'll take one of those soaps. How much are they?

– Fourpence, sir.

Mr Bloom raised a cake to his nostrils. Sweet lemony wax.

– I'll take this one, he said. That makes three and a penny.

– Yes, sir, the chemist said. You can pay all together, sir, when you come back.

– Good, Mr Bloom said. (5.507)

But as sessions proceed the vocabulary of incidents, images, phrases, words expands, until eventually a fine freedom is available:

MARION

So you notice some change? (*her hands passing slowly over her trinketed stomacher, a slow friendly mockery in her eyes*) O Poldy, Poldy, you are a poor old stick in the mud! Go and see life. See the wide world.

BLOOM

I was just going back for that lotion whitewax, orangeflower water. Shop closes early on Thursday. But the first thing in the morning. (*he pats divers pockets*) This moving kidney. Ah!

(*He points to the south, then to the east. A cake of new clean lemon soap arises, diffusing light and perfume.*)

THE SOAP

We're a capital couple are Bloom and I.

He brightens the earth. I polish the sky.

(*The freckled face of Sweny, the druggist, appears in the disc of the soapsun.*)

SWENY

Three and a penny, please.

BLOOM

Yes. For my wife. Mrs Marion. Special recipe.

MARION

(*softly*) Poldy!

BLOOM

Yes, ma'am?

MARION

Ti trema un poco il cuore?

(*In disdain she saunters away, humming the duet from* Don Giovanni, *plump as a pouter pigeon.*) (15.327–353)

This draws on numerous arrays in the book's memory-bank. 'Stick in the mud' is from the end of 'Nausicaa', where the stick Bloom threw stuck in silted sand ('Now if you were trying to do that for a week on end you couldn't': 13.1271). 'This moving kidney' combines Bloom's burned breakfast (4.380), Mrs Purefoy's 'floating kidney' (14.1426), and one of the amusing minor motifs of *Ulysses*, the mini-Odyssey of the soap, pocket to pocket, daylong. Molly is 'Marion' because Boylan's letter was so addressed (4.244), and her Italian, from the seduction duet she was to rehearse with her visitor, has been on Bloom's mind before:

> *Mi trema un poco il.* Beautiful on that *tre* her voice is: weeping tone. A thrush. A throstle. There is a word throstle that expresses that. (6.239)

As for Sweny the chemist, he peers out of the 'soapsun' like an oleograph of the Divine Face on a consecrated wafer to emblematise one more small guilt of Bloom's, who far from striding into his home with an outraged husband's 'Aha!' will be admitting to Molly that he didn't pick up her lotion after all: 'Never went back and the soap not paid' (13.1045).* Not that Bloom, here in 'Circe', need be entertaining any thought of the soap, which exists on the page as an emblem of something far less specific, his guilt about being in Nighttown, something he'll want to keep from Molly. Nor in general is there any reason to suppose that the things and people, let alone words and images, of the various visions actually cross his mind: that he thinks, for instance, of his parents after buying and discarding the pig's foot (15.248–290). They put in their pantomime appearance – stage Jew, stage Irishwoman – partly for our entertainment, partly for our instruction (since we learn here the capital fact that Bloom's mother wasn't Jewish), partly to apprise us that Bloom, who is also turning into a stage Jew, feels guilt over wasting money (much more remotely, over buying pork, which he screens from his father's gaze) as well as over being in this part of town at night. For that was a syndrome of guilts he learned in juvenile confrontations with them, and their interrogation and lamentation bring it to life on the page, in a book we are still learning to read, learning that 'outer' and 'inner' alike are neither reportage nor science, but ways of rehandling the conventions of writing a novel: good sturdy conventions.

For in 'Circe' all comes to phantasmagoric life, including much that in normal narration would be represented by an adverb or two. Thus, when Zoe mocks his reluctance to enter a whorehouse Bloom feels a childish mixture of embarrassment and security. This becomes:

*In fact it never got mentioned. 'I told him over and over again get that made up in the same place and dont forget it God only knows whether he did after all I said to him' (18.459).

ZOE

Babby!

BLOOM

(*in babylinen and pelisse, bigheaded, with a caul of dark hair, fixes big eyes on her fluid slip and counts its bronze buckles with a chubby finger, his moist tongue lolling and lisping*) One two tlee: tlee tlwo tlone.

THE BUCKLES

Love me. Love me not. Love me. (15.2002)

And if we skip the interpolations we shall not obtain a straightforward narrative, because nothing on which we pause is straightforward. When a major interlude has ended and we hear Zoe saying, 'Suppose you got up the wrong side of the bed or came too quick with your best girl. O, I can read your thoughts' (15.1971), we may think we are back in reality. But the next words are:

BLOOM

(*bitterly*) Man and woman, love, what is it? A cork and bottle. I'm sick of it. Let everything rip.

ZOE

(*in sudden sulks*) I hate a rotter that's insincere. Give a bleeding whore a chance.

BLOOM

(*repentantly*) I am very disagreeable. You are a necessary evil. Where are you from? London?

ZOE

(*glibly*) Hog's Norton where the pigs plays the organs. I'm Yorkshire born. (*she holds his hand which is feeling for her nipple*) I say, Tommy Tittlemouse. Stop that and begin worse. Have you cash for a short time? Ten shillings?

BLOOM

(*smiles, nods slowly*) More, houri, more.

It is hard to say whether or not Zoe's speech is 'realistic'; it's in any case consistent within itself and with her role in the book, a stock figure of street toughness. As for Bloom, if his 'More, houri, more' touches on an oriental fantasy, his 'You are a necessary evil' isn't by contrast a real voice; by now we know Bloom well enough not to imagine him saying it to a woman. (And if 'Circe' were the only episode to have survived some Alexandrian fire we'd not be sure of that; Bloom might be a callous man, or Joyce an incompetent writer.)

Deprived of reliable criteria for 'reality', we have no recourse save to read the text as though everything in it were equally real: the phantasmagoric street, the crowds, the lists, the processions, the instantaneous costume-changes, even Bloom's change of sex (15.2846–3216). Common sense will abstract from this reading certain things it is confident must have 'really happened'. Common sense may point to certain later verifications. As in Borges' story, 'Tlön, Uqbar, Orbis Tertius', an encyclopedia article about a fey planet seems confirmed by the subsequent appearance of unearthly artefacts, so the bewildering scene (15.3530–3617) during which Bloom takes charge of Stephen's money is validated (17.956) when, in another place and two episodes away from 'Circe' 's phantasmagoria, Bloom returns it.* Nothing is more real than money. And the trouser-button that went 'Bip!' (15.3441) amid a delirium of nymphs and waterfalls is, yes, missing (16.35) in a later chapter of indubitable sobriety: a chapter that opens with Bloom picking up Stephen from the street to which he had fallen in the concluding pages of 'Circe'. Otherwise 'Circe' passes as though it had never been, no more than an immense bad dream. Neither Bloom nor Stephen will allude to anything that happened or seemed to happen during that frenzied hour, and the very Budget for the Day (17.1455), though it does not omit penny expenditures (newspaper, tramfare, Banbury cakes for seagulls) is purged of all reference to expenditures at Bella Cohen's, where Bloom left behind eleven shillings, nearly half of his outlay for 16 June. The 'objectivity' of 'Ithaca' is as fraudulent as the 'depth psychology' of 'Circe'.

Yet Bloom at the end of 'Circe' seems a changed Bloom, courageous, ready of mind. Like a psychoanalysis without an analyst – apparently what Joyce understood by 'catharsis' – 'Circe' 's rummaging amid the roots of his secret fears and desires has brought forth a new self-possession, and the man who lost his head at the Citizen's taunts and had to be whisked off amid jeers, pursued by a mangy dog and a flying biscuit-box, has managed Stephen's assailants with aplomb.

Stephen for his part has struck out at the spectre of his mother, much as, an hour earlier, he apparently struck at Mulligan. For Hamlet to become a man of action may be reckoned an achievement of sorts. After that he falls into incoherence. Down in the street a troublemaking Cissy Caffrey ('A woman too brought Parnell low': 2.394) has embroiled him with two drunken soldiers of whom one, Private Carr, elaborates a single idea much as James Joyce elaborated *Ulysses*, by reworking, by accretion. Carr is the sole artist of the obscene in a book that was once thought to contain little save obscenity, and his *chef d'œuvre* in its culminated form runs, 'I'll wring the neck of any fucking bastard says

---

*He returns £1 7s 0d, having taken £1 6s 11d, which at the time he called 'One pound seven, say'. The extra penny a bookkeeper might denominate Usury, paid by the Jew to the Gentile: one more sly Joycean reversal of stereotypes. Bloom keeps the money about an hour and a half; the rate is about four per cent per week.

a word against my bleeding fucking king' (15.4644).* Private Carr chooses epithets with inspired precision: Edward VII was the first womaniser in Europe, also a member of a family that carried haemophilia, and Stephen incurs an adjective by his presence in Nighttown and a noun by his imperfect sonship to Dedalus of Athens. As befits a loyal soldier of the Crown, Private Carr has also the talents of a low-grade Executioner. '*He rushes towards Stephen, fist outstretched, and strikes him in the face. Stephen totters, collapses, falls, stunned. He lies prone, his face to the sky, his hat rolling to the wall. Bloom follows and picks it up*' (15.4747).

Bloom does that; also hinders the police from taking Stephen's name until he has secured the intervention of Corny Kelleher, who we have learned to guess can influence policemen. But for Bloom, Stephen's night would have ended in a cell, and his next day begun before a magistrate, 'fined ten bob for a drunk and disorderly and refusing to go with the constable' (16.209). And when the crowd has dispersed, it is Bloom who stands guard over the prostrate Stephen, alone.

There follows what ought to have been Stephen's most awful moment.

(... *Bloom, holding in his hand Stephen's hat, festooned with shavings, and ashplant, stands irresolute. Then he bends to him and shakes him by the shoulder.*)

BLOOM

Eh! Ho! (*There is no answer. He bends again.*) Mr Dedalus! (*there is no answer*) The name if you call. Somnambulist. (*he bends again and, hesitating, brings his mouth near the face of the prostrate form*) Stephen! (*There is no answer. He calls again.*) Stephen!

STEPHEN

(*frowns*) Who? Black panther. Vampire. (*he sighs and stretches himself, then murmurs thickly with prolonged vowels*)

Who ... drive ... Fergus now

And pierce ... wood's woven shade ...?

(*He turns on his left side, sighing, doubling himself together.*) (15.4920)

Responding to his Christian name (who else calls him that?) he has opened his eyes and seen bending over him, mouth near his face, a black figure: the deathly vampire ('mouth to my mouth') of his morning's meditations; the panther of Haines's nightmare. It has come. And in what he must imagine to be his moment of death he consoles himself

---

*Compare the Citizen's 'By Jesus, I'll brain that bloody jewman for using the holy name. By Jesus, I'll crucify him so I will' (12.1811). Such flights are asymptotic to a canonical form.

not with Christian prayer but by murmuring Yeats's evocation of a
redeemed time:

> For Fergus rules the brazen cars,
> And rules the shadows of the wood,
> And the white breast of the dim sea
> And all dishevelled wandering stars.

He had sung that when his mother lay dying; it is an 'Irish', an
'aesthetic' counterpart to the finale of 'Lycidas' he had listened to a
schoolboy mouth at Deasy's:

> There entertain him all the saints above
> In solemn troops and sweet societies
> That sing, and singing in their glory move,
> And wipe the tears forever from his eyes.

In his own way, he had prayed for his dying mother after all. Now he
is repeating the rite as he shares her descent into blackness. In his
brief sleep, as though accepting death, he dies: dies in (drunken) peace:

> For Poldy rules the brazen cars . . . .

*   *   *

When he is resurrected it is into a domain created by Poldy, shaped,
sustained, bounded by a perfectly awful prose style.

Style, we learned as long ago as the latter chapters of the *Portrait*,
is Stephen's sustaining element, air to his bird. Once *chiasmus* sustained
him, and the rhythms of his being were those of 'a lucid supple periodic
prose' (P 167). 'Her bosom was as a bird's soft and slight, slight and
soft as the breast of some darkplumaged dove' (P 171). 'To live, to err,
to fall, to triumph, to recreate life out of life! A wild angel had appeared
to him . . .' (P 172).

And now the 'black panther monster' has appeared to him. He has
fallen and re-arisen: into this:

> Mr Bloom who at all events was in complete possession of his
> faculties, never more so, in fact disgustingly sober, spoke a word of
> caution *re* the dangers of nighttown, women of ill fame and swell
> mobsmen, which, barely permissible once in a while though not as a
> habitual practice, was of the nature of a regular deathtrap. . . . You
> frittered away your time, he very sensibly maintained, and health and
> also character besides which, the squandermania of the thing, fast
> women of the *demimonde* ran away with a lot of £. s. d. into the

bargain and the greatest danger of all was who you got drunk with though, touching the much vexed question of stimulants, he relished a glass of choice old wine in season as both nourishing and blood-making and possessing aperient virtues (notably a good burgundy which he was a staunch believer in) still never beyond a certain point where he invariably drew the line as it simply led to trouble all round to say nothing of your being at the tender mercy of others practically. (16.61–95)

This is to be entrapped inside a novel with Leopold Bloom in possession of the pen. It is Hamlet taken in hand by Polonius.

By an old custom this style gets called 'tired' – imitative form, appropriate to tired men. And the episode ('Eumaeus') is little regarded because it is 'boring'. Tired it is not: Joyce was never more awake than when he misaligned all those thousands of clichés. As for 'boring', not a word of it would bore Bloom, who even fancies himself writing all of it (16.1229). He deserves the privilege. This is his finest hour. From the wreck of a long dismal day he has salvaged a genuine poet-professor whom he is about to take home; no more for him the snubs he fancied would attend a drop-in call on the Astronomer Royal to ask about parallax (8.573). Now Leopold Bloom can offer advice and be heard out, he who formerly could not so much as venture a funny story without someone else taking over the denouement (6.264–291). Stephen during the long paragraph of practical counsel says 'nothing whatsoever of any kind'. He can advise the poet to write his poetry in Italian; can offer him lodgings, can employ his presence to turn Molly's mind away from thoughts of Boylan; he can even manage him to a lucrative vocal career. (At this climax, as in *Götterdämmerung*, a horse evacuates: 16.1874.)

So completely is the style of 'Eumaeus' Bloom's that when he speaks in the episode he speaks its very idiom; no one else does. The artist may be forgiven if, allowing his own voice and the narrative idiom to coalesce, he awards the elegant lines to himself and permits his supporting cast to grunt barbarisms; *A Portrait of the Artist as a Young Man* was not otherwise configured.* 'Eumaeus' is not in Bloom's speaking style, true, nor even his thinking style to which we are also privy. But no man writes as he speaks or thinks, but more formally, and generally in longer sentences, and with elegant variations. Inexperience, or false models,

---

*And it is a portrait of the artist as a young man, incidentally, that is tattooed on the chest of the lounging sailor in the shelter, the sailor who seems as untrustworthy as Ulysses. 'Fellow, the name of Antonio, done that. There he is himself, a Greek' (16.678). Antonio is as plausible a name for a Greek as Dedalus for an Irishman. Antonio, moreover, went into the sea like Icarus. 'He's gone too. Ate by sharks after. Ay, ay.' Mr Brook Thomas pointed this out.

may set his system of written discourse to oscillating wildly while he sits calm and satisfied at its centre, capable at need of economical speech.

All the years Joyce was writing *Ulysses* the brothers Fowler were compiling *Modern English Usage*, which protests in vain, on behalf of a genteel consensus, against the barbarisms of the Press; Fowler (published 1926) is a useful guide to the rhetoric of this episode. (I have also been told that the 'Eumaeus' style can be matched in such Irish provincial newspapers as the one Bloom consults in the National Library. I have not been able to verify this, but think it most probable.)

After their rest-stop in the cabmen's shelter, Bloom walks Stephen up the hill to Eccles Street, site of Ulysses' castle, at the summit of Dublin. Straight there from Nighttown would have been a shorter walk, but Stephen was not up to a short steep walk at that time, nor was Bloom ready to abridge his triumph.

When they leave the shelter and its abutting quarter of whores they leave behind also the Nightmare of History, which in 'Circe' was enacted and re-enacted, its mobs, postures, screams, executions, hollow triumphs, all its essential tawdry theatricality, to purgative extremes, and in 'Eumaeus' became superannuated, a poetic of yesterday, of the newspapers; for 'sufficient for the day is the newspaper thereof' (7.736). Joe Hynes has done Milton's and Homer's office for Lycidas/Elpenor/ Dignam, embellishing the account of his obsequies with names of mourners who were never there, and converting the name of one who was there into 'L. Boom' (a noise in the street). And 'One morning you would open the paper, the cabman affirmed, and read: *Return of Parnell*' (16.1297).

If you did, you would presumably know better than to believe it. Still, the longing persisted; Joyce runs through a brief catalogue of what were actual rumours: 'Dead he wasn't. Simply absconded somewhere. The coffin they brought over was full of stones. He changed his name to De Wet, the Boer general. He made a mistake to fight the priests. And so forth and so on' (16.1304). Parnell, a living man once, has been transmuted into myth, and 'Looking back now in a retrospective kind of arrangement all seemed a kind of dream. And then coming back was the worst thing you ever did because it went without saying you would feel out of place as things always moved with the times' (16.1400). So returned Ulysses muses. Myths had best stay mythical.

The example is tricky. Not only have things 'moved with the times' since Homer's bronze age, but also Bloom in 1904 is coming back to a home where he will feel displaced by a new man; is coming back, moreover, not in Parnell's role but in Captain O'Shea's: 'It was simply a case of the husband not being up to the scratch, with nothing in common between them beyond the name, and then a real man arriving on the scene, strong to the verge of weakness, falling a victim to her siren charms and forgetting home ties' (16.1379). Nimble-witted Bloom discerns hope in the parallel. Kitty O'Shea (Bloom supposes, since she lived a year in Madrid) is, like Molly Bloom, part Spanish; and he next shows Stephen his ultimate lure, Molly's photo. For if Stephen enters 7 Eccles Street he may oust the pseudo-Parnell, Blazes Boylan.

May. To what plane of the thinkable does 'may' pertain? The incorruptibly good lies in the past. So in 1904, in his compromised finest hour, Bloom cherishes a former finest hour, 11 December 1890, when at 24 he strode History's very stage. A Parnellite mob – but, no, let Bloom tell it, as he does (16.1495) to Stephen, having first rehearsed it silently (16.1333):

> He, B, enjoyed the distinction of being close to Erin's uncrowned king in the flesh when the thing occurred on the historic *fracas* when the fallen leader's, who notoriously stuck to his guns to the last drop even when clothed in the mantle of adultery, (leader's) trusty henchmen to the number of ten or a dozen or possibly even more than that penetrated into the printing works of the *Insuppressible* or no it was *United Ireland* (a by no means by the by appropriate appellative) and broke up the typecases with hammers or something like that. . . .

Parnell's biographers tell us how on that occasion he appeared to eye-witnesses hatless in the window; and as to how he regained his hat:

> . . . as a matter of strict history, Bloom was the man who picked it up in the crush after witnessing the occurrence meaning to return it to him (and return it to him he did with the utmost celerity) who panting and hatless and whose thoughts were miles away from his hat at the time . . . turned round to the donor and thanked him with perfect *aplomb*, saying: *Thank you, sir.* . . .

'Fabled by the daughters of memory. And yet it was in some way if not as memory fabled it' (2.7). Memory fabled it a little otherwise only a few minutes previously, when the unforgettable words were merely 'Thank you' (16.1336). Bloom for his part is consistent in a hatholder's role, having recently recovered Stephen's hat from the street (15.4748) and in fantasy received the straw boater of Boylan on a peg of his antlered head (15.3763). The men around him dwindle. It is only fourteen years since a leader of men was capable of great courtesy, yet this very day when another hat was in question a Dublin solicitor and commissioner for oaths and affidavits said nothing to cherish at all:

> John Henry Menton jerked his head down in acknowledgment.
> – Thank you, he said shortly. (6.1025)

Parnell's very words, by one account of Parnell's words. But the tone was different, and the snub has rankled all day.

Absent from 'Eumaeus' because it didn't occur was Bloom's other alleged involvement with history: 'John Wyse saying it was Bloom gave the ideas for Sinn Fein to Griffith to put in his paper' (12.1573).

> – Isn't that a fact, says John Wyse, what I was telling the citizen about Bloom and the Sinn Fein? . . .
> – He's a perverted jew, says Martin, from a place in Hungary and it was he drew up all the plans according to the Hungarian system. We know that in the castle. (12.1623)

This has been jeered at (e.g. by Adams, *Surface and Symbol*, 100–1) as grotesque improbability, which it would be if Joyce expected us to believe it. But he doesn't, or it would surely cross Bloom's mind at some time; no, in a chapter of misinformations, it is the sort of thing they believe in the Castle, where they make policy. They believe it because Griffith was persistently rumoured to have a Jewish adviser-ghostwriter.* The men at Barney Kiernan's know this rumour – what Dublin rumour is unknown anywhere in Dublin? – and suppose the Jew is Bloom. (Bloom's father was born in Hungary, and Griffith in 1904 offered his partymen the example of Hungarian passive resistance to Austria; only that much is fact.) Bloom knows the rumour, too; hence his otherwise inexplicable comment on a *mot* attributed to Griffith: 'Ikey touch that' (4.103).

In 1904 the future belonged to Griffith; as for Parnell, the Irish were just beginning to forget that they would never forget him. 'Eumaeus' exhibits the style of a people between heroes. It is about to be supplanted by something less slack.

*I learned this in Dublin from Mr Anthony Cronin, in a conversation that didn't pertain to *Ulysses*.

CHAPTER 13

Lists, Myths

In the latter half of *Ulysses* styles are like places: ports of call, with their special sounds and atmospheres and customs, in which the journeying hero lingers. About 1 a.m. on 17 June he and Telemachus enter a spectral place indeed, the domain of the dark catechism that foreshadows the interrogation Molly will administer when he arrives at her bed: 'reiterated feminine interrogation' (17.2294). Religious truths have long been catechetically framed, and in nineteenth-century textbooks scientific truths were so framed also.

> What are comets?
>
> Luminous and opaque bodies, whose motions are in different directions, and the orbits they describe very extensive; they have long translucent tails of light turned from the sun: the great swiftness of their motion in the neighbourhood of the sun, is the reason they appear to us for such a short time: and the great length of time they are in appearing again is occasioned by the extent and eccentricity of their orbits or paths in the heavens.*

The catechism not only requires that the knower repeat what is known according to set formulas, it confines what he can be expected to know to such formulas. The correct answer to the question 'What are comets?' is not

> Comets, importing change of time and state,
> Brandish [their] crystal tresses in the sky
> And with them scourge the bad revolting stars. . . .
> *1 Henry VI*, I, i

Similarly the Ulyssean question, 'What example did he adduce to induce Stephen to deduce that originality, though producing its own reward, does not invariably conduce to success?' is not answered by

> I suggested to [Hely] about a transparent showcart with two smart girls sitting inside writing letters, copybooks, envelopes, blottingpaper.

---

*Richmal Mangnall, *Historical and Miscellaneous Questions*, cited (Hart and Hayman, *James Joyce's 'Ulysses'*, 394) by A. Walton Litz, who notes that Stephen refers to this book in the *Portrait* (P/53).

I bet that would have caught on. Smart girls writing something catch
the eye at once. Everyone dying to know what she's writing. . . .
Wouldn't have it of course because he didn't think of it himself first.
(8.131)

but rather by

His own ideated and rejected project of an illuminated showcart,
drawn by a beast of burden, in which two smartly dressed girls were
to be seated engaged in writing. (17.608)

Abstraction, concision, itemisation, cadence: such are the norms of
catechetical decorum. It moves what would otherwise be pedantry or
garrulity toward the domain of Miltonic blank verse. There was an
aborted catechism in Dalkey in the morning, in an episode ('Nestor')
placed, like this one, second in a three-episode part:

– You, Cochrane, what city sent for him?
– Tarentum, sir.
– Very good. Well?
– There was a battle, sir.
– Very good. Where?
 The boy's blank face asked the blank window. (2.1)

Here information imparted at a former time is retrieved with difficulty
or not at all. By contrast the information about the girls in the showcart
comes prompted by the merest hint. It returns, moreover, shaped,
marmorealised. There are here and there in 'Ithaca' great feats of mar-
morealisation, notably the sonorous hymn to Water, which it would be a
penance not to copy out in full for reading aloud like something of
Browne's or Donne's.

What in water did Bloom, waterlover, drawer of water, watercarrier,
returning to the range, admire?
 Its universality: its democratic equality and constancy to its nature
in seeking its own level: its vastness in the ocean of Mercator's projection: its unplumbed profundity in the Sundam trench of the
Pacific exceeding 8,000 fathoms: the restlessness of its waves and
surface particles visiting in turn all points of its seaboard: the
independence of its units: the variability of states of sea: its hydro-
static quiescence in calm: its hydrokinetic turgidity in neap and
spring tides: its subsidence after devastation: its sterility in the cir-
cumpolar icecaps, arctic and antarctic: its climatic and commercial
significance: its preponderance of 3 to 1 over the dry land of the

globe : its indisputable hegemony extending in square leagues over all
the region below the subequatorial tropic of Capricorn : the multi-
secular stability of its primeval basin : its luteofulvous bed : its
capacity to dissolve and hold in solution all soluble substances including
millions of tons of the most precious metals : its slow erosions of
peninsulas and islands, its persistent formation of homothetic islands,
peninsulas and downwardtending promontories : its alluvial deposits : its
weight and volume and density : its imperturbability in lagoons, atolls,
highland tarns : its gradation of colours in the torrid and temperate and
frigid zones : its vehicular ramifications in continental lake-contained
streams and confluent oceanflowing rivers with their tributaries and
transoceanic currents, gulfstream, north and south equatorial courses :
its violence in seaquakes, waterspouts, Artesian wells, eruptions, tor-
rents, eddies, freshets, spates, groundswells, watersheds, waterpartings,
geysers, cataracts, whirlpools, maelstroms, inundations, deluges, cloud-
bursts : its vast circumterrestial ahorizontal curve : its secrecy in springs
and latent humidity, revealed by rhabdomantic or hygrometric instruments and exemplified by the well by the hole in the wall at Ashtown
gate, saturation of air, distillation of dew : the simplicity of its composition, two constituent parts of hydrogen with one constituent part of
oxygen : its healing virtues : its buoyancy in the waters of the Dead Sea :
its persevering penetrativeness in runnels, gullies, inadequate dams,
leaks on shipboard : its properties for cleansing, quenching thirst and
fire, nourishing vegetation : its infallibility as paradigm and paragon : its
metamorphoses as vapour, mist, cloud, rain, sleet, snow, hail : its
strength in rigid hydrants : its variety of forms in loughs and bays and
gulfs and bights and guts and lagoons and atolls and archipelagos and
sounds and fjords and minches and tidal estuaries and arms of sea : its
solidity in glaciers, icebergs, icefloes : its docility in working hydraulic
millwheels, turbines, dynamos, electric power stations, bleachworks,
tanneries, scutchmills : its utility in canals, rivers, if navigable, floating
and graving docks : its potentiality derivable from harnessed tides or
watercourses falling from level to level : its submarine fauna and flora
(anacoustic, photophobe), numerically, if not literally, the inhabitants of
the globe : its ubiquity as constituting 90% of the human body : the nox-
iousness of its effluvia in lacustrine marshes, pestilential fens, faded
flowerwater, stagnant pools in the waning moon. (17.183)

Only so, by such decorum, with such gravity, ought sacred truths be
communicated. Let the Maynooth Cathechism mend its ways.
  Homer was the world's first poet of the sea, 'winedark', many-voiced,
alive with great lifting waves. 'Ithaca' achieves on one page the improbable feat of raising to poetry all the clutter of footling information that
has accumulated in schoolbooks since the living sea became but an

instance of water, and water a domestic and domesticated amenity concerning which classroom instruction is imparted.

Not that the episode is all of a piece: nothing in *Ulysses* is. 'Of what did the duumvirate deliberate during their itinerary?' (17.11) is schoolboy big words for 'What did they talk about as they walked?', the testimonial to the Wonderworker (17.1824) veers into zaniness, and on the brink of what offers to be the profound we are not infrequently plunged into sonorous ambiguity.

Still, the liturgical cadences prevail, and can be insidious. In repeatedly exalting arrays of particulate information, subsuming whole orders of experience into the domain of archetype, they work as well on our sense of the two men present, Stephen and Bloom, 'guest' and 'host', who become both more and less than the characters we know so well. As voices vanish features fade, and shortly before Stephen goes off, leaving Bloom to be lonely Everyman, the two of them for several pages find themselves playing racial types – last roles in this book of roles – the Irishman, the Jew.

Far from being a Joycean arbitrariness, the theme of the Two Peoples that pervades *Ulysses* was familiar to anyone who listened to Home Rule exhortations. As the most famously persecuted people in the world – a people, moreover, the tale of whose stubborn persistence amidst Egyptian and Babylonian captivity was familiar to every churchgoer – the Jews could hardly not have been invoked when orators commenced suggesting to the Irish middle classes that it behoved them to start resisting persecution, too. For each people had a racial identity, Semitic, Celtic; each had a minute homeland boasting sacred sanctions, each a history of being overwhelmed but not disappearing. Each was long-memoried, monogamous, intensely God-fearing. An arcane language, too, was part of each heritage; and, as the Jews had never permitted themselves to forget Hebrew, so the Irish were told they should end their long compliance with the conquerors' tongue and commence talking Irish in Dublin and Belfast the way the peasants did in Galway. Rebutting a judgement that the language was not worth reviving, John F. Taylor on 24 October 1901 told the Law Students' Debating Society that an Egyptian intellectual might well have admonished Moses in similar terms to calm himself and make his way in Egyptian administration; and if Moses had heeded that counsel 'He would never have spoken with the Eternal amid lightnings on Sinai's mountaintop nor ever have come down with the light of inspiration shining in his countenance and bearing in his arms the tables of the law, graven in the language of the outlaw' (7.866).*

*Joyce's 1924 recording of the passage containing this speech has been reissued on *James Joyce Spricht* (Rhein-Verlag, Zürich), and is also available on a Caedmon disc. Ellmann (*James Joyce*, 95) cites a contemporary newspaper account of what Taylor said.

When Professor MacHugh re-creates Taylor's speech in the *Freeman's Journal* office about noon on Bloomsday – thirty-two months after it was given – it is the marshalling of tropes that earns admiration. The comparison of the Two Peoples seems commonplace enough to pass without remark.

The Jews of Home Rule oratory, though, are Biblical Jews, Jews at a long safe distance, fervent pious folk who cry in time of persecution 'Introibo ad altare Dei', though of course they cry it in Hebrew. Since these are the first words spoken by anybody in *Ulysses*, Joyce may be said to have planted the Two Peoples theme in the opening sentences of his book, and that we miss remarking it there is part of his point: transposed into liturgical Latin, the Psalms have lost all historical, all Jewish content. Moses is likewise put by, representing as he does the *lex talionis*, eye for eye. The *civilised* Moses, 'that eternal symbol of wisdom and prophecy', is a marble of Michelangelo's, 'in the Vatican', J. J. O'Molloy says. (And there's a 'Ha' from somebody – Stephen? – who knows it's in San Pietro Vincoli.) The horns it wears embody a mistranslation of Exodus, 34: 29, by St Jerome, who misread a verb meaning that the face of Moses shone and apparently did not think it odd for the face of the lawgiver to be horned. So Christendom has dealt with Moses rather casually, though it turns to him for tropes: thus Parnell seemed to many eulogists a Moses in dying on the threshold of the land of promise.

These tropes are the more effective while Moses remains entombed in the Vulgate, and his inconvenient people oblige by staying out of sight. In sight, they invite tropes of a different order. After Dublin patriots had had their consciences exhorted by the Mosaic analogy for perhaps a dozen years, a tavernful of them still has no use for Bloom.

So in comes Martin asking where was Bloom.
– Where is he? says Lenehan. Defrauding widows and orphans. (12.1621)

And

– Those are nice things, says the citizen, coming over here to Ireland filling the country with bugs. (12.1141)

And

Mean bloody scut.... There's a jew for you! All for number one. Cute as a shithouse rat. (12.1760)

And

– Where is he till I murder him? (12.1847)

When the biscuit-tin, by heroic amplification, renders North Central Dublin a mass of ruins we are to remember what patriotic idealism could claim to have accomplished by Easter 1916. Thanks to a knot of hotheads with no prospect whatever of accomplishing what they proposed, Dublin had been the first European capital to undergo the bombardment of modern warfare, and James Joyce had little use for the oratory that fuelled hotheadedness.

Not that the analogy between the Two Peoples is senseless. But its particulars demand examination. So in 'Ithaca' a Jew who has demonstrably not been 'All for number one' and the least bloodthirsty Irishman in Dublin confront one another, aware of a racial difference to which neither alludes (17.525). The meeting is neither a success nor a failure, though the grave catechetical manner suffuses it with the calm of the paradigmatic.

There are tensions the paradigm cannot acknowledge; all liturgy transcends factual inconvenience. We know, and Stephen surely guesses, that Bloom has been hatching designs, in which Stephen will occupy the room the Blooms have for rent, receive singing lessons from Molly, tutor her in Italian pronunciation, distract her from Boylan, pass his evenings in agreeable conversation (with Bloom!), produce literature on the side, perhaps even mount to fiscal triumphs as a concert tenor with Bloom (who else?) to manage him. We may think of the man in the Evelyn Waugh story the price of whose deliverance was to be trapped in the jungle reading Dickens aloud to his deliverer for the rest of his life.

In one of the ways *Ulysses* might have ended – would have ended, had Bloom been the author – Stephen has everything he seemed to lack only that morning: decent quarters, a piano handy, a nubile woman about the place, the prospect of the nubile woman's daughter, time for literary pursuits, an indulgent provident 'father': everything save freedom. Bloom poses a serious danger, the more so in the transparent simplicity of his need to fill little Rudy's place with a grown son in whose accomplishments he can take pride. Bearing the danger in mind, we can understand why Stephen sings the ballad about the imperilled Christian boy in the Jew's habitation, and departs within minutes of singing it. But the catechism doesn't encourage us to bear in mind such realities of situation and character. It does, to be sure, touch once, directly, on future 'advantages' for all parties supposing Stephen takes up lodgings here (17.935), and twice, obliquely, on a possible role for Bloom's women in Stephen's life, when a Molly-theme, 'What to do with our wives' (17.657–708), and a Milly-theme, her progress to maturity (17.864–928), get developed just here, as digressions from the colloquy with Stephen, instead of elsewhere in the episode. But we have to think out the implications for ourselves, against the grain of that lofty measured language.

Likewise, a portentous convergence of the twain seems epitomised by the 'Ithaca' pages on the two tongues, Gaelic and Hebrew. Amid abstract imperturbability of cadence, they and their speakers converge as John F. Taylor might have desired, and a long summary paragraph (17.745) appears to itemise weighty features of resemblance, amid which even the dubious clause about their antiquity, 'both having been taught on the plain of Shinar 242 years after the deluge in the seminary instituted by Fenius Farsaigh, descendant of Noah, progenitor of Israel, and ascendant of Heber and Heremon, progenitors of Ireland' seems an amiable antiquarian self-deceit. In cold fact, this particular pair of dilettante philologists has established only that (1) each can remember a few words of his heritage when there's a tune to help, (2) both tongues sound romantically strange to Anglophone ears, (3) their alphabets contain cognate letters which on paper demonstrate quite dissimilar shapes. Again, it's all just as we might have expected and, again, it's an effort to discern that this is so.

Finally, an event which must have occupied several minutes is disposed of in three lines of 'Ithaca' text: Stephen's recitation in Bloom's kitchen of what he improvised on the street in 'Aeolus', his 'Pisgah Sight of Palestine, or The Parable of the Plums' (17.639). 'Pisgah' (Deuteronomy, 34) invokes the Old Testament, 'Parable' the New. Two old women survey the topography of their city from a great height: a Promised Land now in infidel possession which they will not live to see ended. Parnell, the parable seems to say, is dead, and Ireland's access to milk and honey delayed indefinitely; as for the Dublin Michelangelo, he is the confector of the local 'stony effigy in frozen music', portraying the 'onehandled adulterer' (7.1018) whom Stephen's phrase compares to a vessel of clay* and who put horns on Sir William Hamilton's head. If at the prompting of 'Ithaca' we turn back to this parable in 'Aeolus', we shall be struck by how much it must lose, recapitulated far from the presence of the Nelson Pillar, for a hearer who has not heard the evocation of Michelangelo's Moses (7.768) that helped prompt it. Bloom accepts the 'analogy implied' (17.709) between two peoples striving each for a Zion, and senses commercial possibilities in Stephen's talent – such things could be printed as 'model pedagogic themes . . . for the use of preparatory and junior grade students' (17.647). The cynicism apparently escapes him, the way much anticlimax is apt to escape the first-time reader of 'Ithaca'.

Stephen's parable is one of the episode's rare reversions to information

---

*'I see what you mean,' says MacHugh, meaning apparently that he sees how this phrase was prompted by the shape of the statue. Later (7.1072) he repeats 'onehandled adulterer' as he 'peer[s] aloft at Nelson'. 'That tickles me, I must say.' Dublin's familiar onehandled article would have been a chamberpot. An akimbo arm on the statue prompts the comparison.

imparted earlier. One of the salient features of 'Ithaca' is the amount of novelty it contains. Like Socrates with the slave-boy in *Meno*, the questioner in 'Ithaca' elicits from the mind of the text a good deal more than we'd have supposed was known: not merely lore we don't need, like the hydraulic and fiscal particulars of the Municipal Water Supply (17.163), but much we're glad to have filled in, like the particulars of Rudolph Bloom's suicide (17.621; 17.1887), or confirmed, like the evidence that Boylan indeed showed up (17.1303). We're grateful, too, especially after 'Eumaeus', foi the texture of straightforward factuality. Like the final chapter of a Victorian novel, 'Ithaca' abounds in detailed revelations that refocus what we had thought we knew and substantiate what we only guessed.

In doing this it restresses a governing rhythm of the book, whereby impression in the first half is modified by knowledge in the second, though only after resolute rereading has extracted the knowledge from a stylistic that tends to render it inconspicuous.

Thus Bloom, we know, is a Jew. We know that from his name, know it, too, because Celts treat him with diffidence – borrow money from him without knowing his 'Christian' name, or summon him like a little dog with 'Come along, Bloom'. And we have heard him muse on 'the oldest people . . . captivity to captivity' (4.225), and have seen him finger a Zionist pamphlet: that is surely decisive? And in 'Cyclops', sure enough, he says it himself: 'Christ was a jew like me.'

And immediately after 'Cyclops' the qualifications commence. In 'Nausicaa' he proves not to be circumcised (13.979). In 'Circe' his all-important mother turns up with an Irish name, Higgins. In 'Ithaca' his maternal grandmother, too, was Irish ('Hegarty': 17.537), and he has received two valid Christian baptisms (17.540). No barmitzvah is mentioned anywhere. (And amid the circumlocutions of 'Eumaeus' we may not have caught what he himself said, retracting what he said in 'Cyclops': 'his God, I mean Christ, was a jew too and all his family like me though in reality I'm not': 16.1084). Like Homer's Penelope at her tapestry, *Ulysses* unweaves at night what it wove by day.

It is likewise from the earlier episodes that we derive a sense of Bloom inconspicuous and impoverished. It is in 'Ithaca' that we learn of his stature – more than tall enough to be a policeman, whom ordinary Dubliners regarded as a race of giants – and are made privy to the most remarkable of the 'secrets of [his] bottom drawer' (15.384): the £500 insurance policy, the £18 14*s* 6*d* banked, the £900 in tax-free Canadian four-per-cents (17.1855–1867).* By the standards of the people he has

*Thus substantiating what had seemed a rhetorical flourish of the censorious 'Junius' in 'Oxen of the Sun': 'During the recent [i.e. Boer] war whenever the enemy had a temporary advantage with his granados did this traitor to his kind not seize that moment to discharge his piece against the empire of which

bumped against all day this is wealth. (With even porter only 2*d* the pint it wasn't hard to scrape by on a pound a week.)

Not that the grave concisions of 'Ithaca' have always their face value as facts. Thus Bloom chants

> *Kolod balejwaw pnimah*
> *Nefesch, jehudi, homijah* (17.763)

of which he knows but these two lines, and Stephen is said to hear 'in a profound ancient male melody the accumulation of the past'. Stephen is responding to the glamour of intoned Hebrew. '*Kolod balejwaw . . .*', now the national anthem of Israel, dates only from 1878, the musical setting only from the late 1890s. In 1904 it was about as profound and ancient as 'My Girl's a Yorkshire Girl'.

This is only to confirm what the reader of 'Wandering Rocks' can remember, that the scrupulous accuracy of a statement contains no guarantee of an accurate impression. Stephen did indeed hear what 'Ithaca' says he heard, but in his mind, not in his ear, and 'Ithaca' assumes no responsibility for noting the misconception on which his experience is grounded.

Similarly a list doesn't say what it's a list of, notably the most famous list in *Ulysses*, the 'preceding series' intoned as Bloom enters Molly's bed, which commences with Mulvey, Penrose, Bartell d'Arcy, and closes with 'Dr Francis Brady, Father Sebastian of Mount Argus, a bootblack at the General Post Office, Hugh E. (Blazes) Boylan and so each and so on to no last term' (17.2133).

This is easily taken as a list of Molly's lovers other than Bloom, twenty-five of them in all – confirming, as it seems to, impressions we've picked up earlier in the book 'Ay, ay, Mr Dedalus nodded. Mrs Marion Bloom has left off clothes of all descriptions': 11.496). It was long so taken by critical consensus, and Molly long regarded as a hardened adulteress, a misconception which deprives Bloomsday of its special tang. Its conceptions were nearly forty years being challenged,[1] and Molly's character as long a time being refocused, so impervious do the cadences of 'Ithaca' render lists to the kind of attention that weighs their constituent items, perceiving their incompatibility, one by one, with what we know on other grounds. Thus Penrose was a 'delicate looking student', a 'priestylooking chap was always squinting in when he passed' (8.176); that was 1889 when Molly was nursing Milly, and Penrose nearly caught sight of her breasts; 'that was his studenting' is her tart

---

he is a tenant at will while he trembled for the security of his four per cents?' (14.908) Bloom, in short, made pro-Boer noises while hanging on to his Empire investments.

recall (18.575), and we're safe in concluding she taught him nothing further. Dr Brady (elsewhere described as 'old': 15.4359) attended her in her confinement (18.575); Fr Sebastian may have been the cleric who sat beside her at the Jews' Temples Gardens (18.90) or else someone who once heard her confession; gynaecological examination and examination of conscience are intimacies of a sort, but not the sort that contribute to the tale of a hardened adulteress. And so on. No, this list is a list of past occasions for twinges of Bloomian jealousy, and there is no ground for supposing that the hospitality of Molly's bed has been extended to anyone but her husband and Boylan. No rhetoric affords more pitfalls than that of 'objectivity'.*

In much of 'Ithaca', though, we work through less tricky lists, our immediate pleasures those of some beatified Dr Watson – 'You know my methods, Watson; apply them' – for whom item after item settles luminous into a known *Gestalt*. Not one item in the wonderful catalogue of Bloom's books (17.1361–1407) is either incongruous or redundant. Some, if we were alert, we knew would be there: *In the Track of the Sun* (4.99), Ball's *Story of the Heavens* (8.110), the works of Shakespeare (17.385). Some fluoresce in the light of the past; Denis Florence McCarthy's *Poetical Works* was read outdoors, hence the beechleaf bookmark, and read as far as page 5; whereupon, Molly perhaps present, other pleasures supervened and, like Paolo and Francesca, 'That day they read no further'. We may note that Ulysses owns no version of Homer, though *Three Trips to Madagascar* and *Voyages in China* suggest variations on Odyssean themes. And the creator of our mentor Sherlock Holmes is represented by his *Stark–Munro Letters*, now thirteen days overdue at the Capel Street Library.†

The catalogue of objects in the locked drawer in the sideboard would have much to tell Holmes and tells us quite as much (17.1774–1842). It is like an archaeologist's midden-hoard, and we may remember how characteristic of the nineteenth century was skill at reading mute evidence. Geologists read the testimony of the rocks (and a book of that title [1869] furnished Stephen with a phrase he cherishes – P 166: 'A day of dappled seaborne clouds'). Archaeologists read coins, pins, broken pots. Detectives read cigar-butts, footprints, clay stains. We have no difficulty reading a story in the two chairs in the Bloom parlour (17.1292), the one 'squat, stuffed', with 'amply upholstered seat', the other 'slender, splayfoot . . . of glossy cane curves'. These might be Molly and Boylan; and an ashtray on the piano contains 'four consumed matches, a partly consumed cigarette and two discoloured ends of

*See Hugh Kenner, *Joyce's Voices*, 1978, *passim*.
†And apparently never returned; inquirers from the Sixth James Joyce Symposium, Dublin, 1977, learned that the library had got round to declaring the book 'missing' in 1906.

cigarettes': Molly, an inexpert smoker, has needed two matches to light something she left unfinished.

It was Flaubert who taught readers of fiction to read furniture. Two paragraphs near the beginning of *Un Cœur simple* take us clear through Mme Aubain's house in Pont-l'Évêque without our encountering a single human being, learning as we go of the people, their meagre fortunes, their pretensions, their ways of passing time. 'Against the panels, which were painted white, was a row of eight mahogany chairs. On an old piano under the barometer a heap of wooden and cardboard boxes rose like a pyramid. A stuffed armchair stood on either side of the Louis Quinze chimney-piece, which was in yellow marble with a clock in the middle of it modelled on a temple of Vesta.' These are the sacred objects of a people whose rituals include the time and the weather. The boxes suggest that the piano is never opened, the placement of the chairs that this room does not normally receive the number of people it can seat. And a clock like a temple of Vesta!

The Bloom bedroom marks, by some standards, a descent from this. It has no Temple of Vesta in any form or guise. A print from *Photo Bits* – *The Bath of the Nymph*, 'splendid masterpiece in art colours' (4.370) – suffices to acknowledge the cultural heritage. The sanitary ware, though, is 'orangekeyed', as we were first apprised in the morning when that adjective was applied to Molly's chamber-pot (4.330), and this is a numinous word.

'Orangekeyed' is formed the way Homer formed many epithets, of which the most celebrated is *rhododaktylos*, 'rosyfingered', by joining an attribute of colour or brightness with a name: in this case the colour, orange, with the name of the pattern around the rim of the pot. This is the 'key meander' or 'key pattern'; the citation for the latter term in the *Oxford English Dictionary* (s.v. 'key') is dated 1876, in the first decade of Homeric archaeology. Thus as Ulysses in the fresh of the morning sat upon a 'jakes' (4.494), a word Sir John Harington's 1596 paean united with 'Ajax', so Penelope in the dead of the night will squat on a piece of ware ornamented with the pattern which characterised much Greek pottery of the Geometric Period, the ninth to seventh centuries BC: pottery of the lifetime (if he lived) of Homer.

NOTES

1   Ellmann stated roundly (388) in 1959: 'The two lovers Molly has had since her marriage are Bartell D'Arcy and Boylan.' In 1962 Professor R. M. Adams, *Surface and Symbol: The Consistency of James Joyce's 'Ulysses'* (New York, 1962), 37, is rightly sceptical about D'Arcy: 'A tenor may kiss a girl or even a married woman very vigorously indeed on the choir stairs, and yet not effect formal entry into her bed.' David Hayman ('The empirical Molly', in Staley and Benstock, 113–14) concurs and adduces in support

Stanley Sultan's *Argument of 'Ulysses'* (Columbus, Ohio, 1964). Hayman, though, raises (134) the spectre of Lt Gardner, whom Raleigh (167, 173–4) obligingly brings into Molly's bed midway in her ten-year abstinence. So by post-1959 consensus the number of Molly's lovers other than Boylan swings between 0 and 1.

ADDENDUM

I've discovered since writing this chapter that Joyce had a more immediate model for his form than either the Maynooth Catechism or Richmal Mangnall. Each issue of Bloom's favorite periodical, the weekly *Tit-Bits*, contained a page called 'Tit-Bits Inquiry Column': answers to questions no one would have thought to ask save the office help who had the answers ready. The questions seldom exceed a dozen words: 'Has any man lived long after being deprived of both arms and legs?' 'Has a duel on bicycles ever taken place?' 'What is the horse-power of a 100-ton gun?' The answers by contrast are leisurely, paragraph-long, each item as substantial as any other and the paper's voice implacable in its knowingness. A demotic base for Joyce's most arcane conventions is something we should probably expect.

CHAPTER 14

The Gift of a Book

Ulysses asleep, Penelope is wide awake: 'Yes because he never did a thing like that before as ask to get his breakfast in bed with a couple of eggs ...' (18.1). If he did, it was a major event, since at 8 a.m. we beheld him preparing her breakfast as though it were the most normal of domestic rituals ('and I love to hear him falling up the stairs of a morning with the cups rattling on the tray': 18.933). Is it thinkable that he has decreed a reversal? We had best review the sequence.

He got silently into bed; she woke and questioned him minutely; his responses left things out – Martha's letter, the imbroglio with the Cyclops, the provocations of Nausicaa – and contained inventions. He claimed to have spent the evening at the Gaiety, then supped with Stephen, whom he brought home for cocoa, he said, after an injury. He also boasted of the 'aeronautical feat' – befitting the proximity of a Dedalus – by which he'd effected entry into the house. The stress of the narrative, we're assured, was on Stephen, Poldy's one compensation for a miserable day and a focus of hope though he didn't stay the night.

His response to her sharp questioning is described as 'intermittent and increasingly more laconic narration' (17.2273), an unlikely context for some sudden assertion of the right to breakfast in bed. All that happens afterward is that he falls asleep, and the last semi-articulate answer to a question may be an expressive felicity of the Arranger's, or may be a somnolent mutter:

> Going to dark bed there was a square round Sinbad the Sailor roc's auk's egg in the night of the bed of all the auks of the rocs of Darkinbad the Brightdayler. (17.2328)

'Eggs', 'bed', 'brightday . . .': is that what Molly heard, and heard as a request for eggs in bed in the morning? It seems more probable than that Bloom in his deep fatigue disturbed the universe.

If so, there's a reader-trap at the beginning of 'Penelope', and we ought to expect another at the end. And, yes, another expositor's cliché, that Molly rises to a fervent Affirmation of Life, is equally suspect. James Joyce, yes, he for once is affirming something. ('If *Ulysses* isn't fit to read, life isn't fit to live.'[1]) The last words of his book make an affirmation of that order the way 'Ithaca' affirms its several archetypes, by sheer rhythmic pressure:

Yés ănd his | heárt wás | góïng lĭke | mád ánd || yés Ĭ săid | yés Ĭ wĭll ||
        Yés.

– a Homeric hexameter with one more stressed syllable appended: 'Yes.' But does Molly? At well past 2 a.m. she has made herself sleepy; the silence after that 'Yes' is procured by sleep. 'In *Ulysses*, to depict the babbling of a woman going to sleep, I had sought to end with the least forceful word I could possibly find. I had found the word "yes", which is barely pronounced, which denotes acquiescence, self-abandon, relaxation, the end of all resistance.'[2] Moreover, Irish voices do not rise to climaxes; to Anglo-American ears they throw climaxes away. Most *Ulysses* episodes end *diminuendo*. The bravura ending of 'Cyclops', a memorable exception, is achieved by overlayered planes of diction, Biblical, Topographical, Geometrical. The spoken cadence tugs against this polyphony; in 1977 a consummate Dublin actor, several times exhorted to raise it, still could only let it fall: 'like a shot off a shovel', 'shovel' weaker than 'shot', and the pitch descending.[3] Joyce heard Dublin voices so; his ear was for what dropped, and no one's exceeds his connoisseurship of anticlimax. No, Molly does not lift up her voice in affirmation whatever the unvoiced rhetoric may be doing. *Ulysses* trails off into 'acquiescence, self-abandon, relaxation': supine in old memories on Howth amid the rhododendrons she whispers a soft 'yes' to oblivion.

Or to Bloom, re-enacting a day sixteen long years gone?

Or to Lieutenant Mulvey, his fervour on Gibraltar, though not his first name, remembered for eighteen years?

It skills not which man or either is in her mind. Her blurring of pronouns, of occasions, is incessant. Time and again a 'he' elides from Boylan to Bloom to Boylan, from Bloom to Stephen to Bloom, from any male to any male with Bloom for ground bass.

hes a widower now I wonder what sort is his son he says hes an author and going to be a university professor of Italian and Im to take lessons what is he driving at now (18.1300)

Here the first 'he' is Si Dedalus, the second is Bloom, the third is Stephen, the fourth is Bloom.

Her locutions are artlessly wonderful. She has been to sea with Ulysses, and as she tells it they seem to be riding Stephen's whitewind-bridled steeds of Mananaan:

Id never again in this life get into a boat with him after him at Bray telling the boatman he knew how to row if anyone asked could he ride the steeplechase for the gold cup hed say yes then it came on to get rough the old thing crookeding about and the weight all down my side telling me pull the right reins now pull the left and the tide all swamping in floods in through the bottom and his oar slipping out of the stirrup its a mercy we werent all drowned he can swim of course me no theres no danger whatsoever keep yourself calm in his flannel trousers (18.954)

Neither is she intending these surreal effects ('keep yourself calm in his flannel trousers') nor are they being mocked, and 'crookeding about' is a verb for Homer to envy.

There is no mockery because there is no 'style': for once, no style. A style is a system of constraints; it denotes limits, and implies our sometimes amused complicity with the stylist who knows what those limits are. As style succeeds style in 'Oxen of the Sun', we are kept aware, paragraph by paragraph, of what can not now be said. The illusion created by 'Penelope' is the Shakespearean one, that anything at all can be said, and at any moment: an illusion the more remarkable for its economy of means, a small obsessive vocabulary heavy in monosyllables, a total lack of punctuation, an abrogation of syntactic dykes.

And what gets said is astonishing in its profusion. This episode, a mere six per cent of *Ulysses*, supplied by Professor Raleigh's estimate half the pages of his *Chronicle of Leopold and Molly Bloom*.[4] And, as Penelope weaves and unweaves her web, virtually every judgement in these dense 25,000 words is substantially contradicted by a counter-judgement somewhere else. Boylan was superb, Boylan is merely coarse; Bloom is trivial, perverse and inadequate, Bloom has 'more spunk in him' even than Boylan; the prospect of Stephen excites, Stephen may have long greasy hair hanging into his eyes (she hopes not: 18.1321). She's proud to be a woman, she hates it; she'll bring Poldy his morning breakfast, she won't bother, she'll throw it at him: on and on, like the earthball turning. Boylan (she doesn't say so) is like the locomotive with which she recapitulates their duet:

frseeeeeeeefronnnng train somewhere whistling the strength those engines have in them like big giants and the water rolling all over and out of them all sides like the end of Loves old sweeeetsonnnng (18. 596)

and

Frseeeeeeeeeeeeeeeeeeeeeefrong that train again* weeping tone once in the dear deaead days beyondre call close my eyes breath my lips

*'That strain again! It had a dying fall' *Twelfth Night*, I, i, 4.

forward kiss sad look eyes open piano ere oer the world the mists began
I hate that istsbeg comes loves sweet soooooooooooong Ill let that out full
when I get in front of the footlights again (18.874)

No, Boylan has 'no manners nor no refinement nor no nothing in his
nature slapping us behind like that on my bottom' (18.1368). Her switch
of pronouns is exact: Boylan's swat was directed at womankind, hers
was the bottom that offered. He is mere directed force like a locomotive,
whereas Bloom is omnipresent, omnidirectional, like a gravitational field.
Hers is the very voice of the magnetic ellipsoidal earthball Stephen
heard about in the physics theatre what seems a lifetime ago, in another
book (P 191–3), and by no accident in the grand design of *Ulysses*,
'Penelope', its fluent amoral unsystematised self-cancelling outpouring,
follows hard on 'Ithaca', arcanum of the enchained determinisms in
which Western high thought was immobilising itself at the century's
turn. Joyce worked on the two episodes simultaneously.

By late in the nineteenth century it seemed clear that understanding
of a world constituted by four fundamental realities, space, time, matter,
motion,[5] had been subtilised to a point where there was very little left
for physics to do. It was a replete world, a plenum; the 'omnipresent
luminiferous diathermanous ether' (17.263) pervaded it, a kind of
insubstantial jelly within which light waves occurred as ocean waves in
water. States of the system were finite in number, like arrangements of
cards in a pack. Motion was imparted by impingement, as on a billiard-
table, and from every observed effect a train of impingements could ideally
be traced back to its remote cause: itself caused by some cause still more remote. Laplace had written:

> An intellect which at a given instant knew all the forces acting in
> nature, and the position of all things of which the world consists –
> supposing the said intellect were vast enough to subject these data to
> analysis – would embrace in the same formula the motions of the
> greatest bodies in the universe and those of the slightest atoms;
> nothing would be uncertain for it, and the future like the past would
> be present to its eyes.[6]

That is like the dream of a neophyte reader of *Ulysses*, who perceives,
for instance, the magisterial formulations (17.257) by which solar
heat stored in prehistoric forests is unlocked by combustion of coal and
transferred to Bloom's kettle, and takes this for a paradigm of understanding.

In a closed plenum like Laplace's cosmos – and, we are sometimes
encouraged to think, in this book – all chains of action and reaction are

folded in, coupled end to end, determined. Such a cosmos perpetually trembles in its sleep while undergoing no real events. From where you stand phenomenon may follow phenomenon, novelty novelty, for a very long time, for many more lifetimes than yours, but eventually the system will exhaust its repertoire and assume some state it has been in before; and that state must necessarily be followed by the state that followed it the last time, and the sequence will be launched yet again: the Eternal Return. Like a comet, even Ulysses must come back: 'Somewhere imperceptibly he would hear and somehow reluctantly, suncompelled, obey the summons of recall' (17.2016).

Concurrently Nietzsche and Spengler were articulating visions of cyclical history, and Vico, who had intuited a patterned history, was being rediscovered by Benedetto Croce. Nietzsche, whom Joyce was reading in college days,[7] is quite explicit in *The Will to Power*:

> It follows therefore that the universe must go through a calculable number of combinations in the great game of chance which constitutes its existence. . . . And since every one of these combinations would determine the whole series in the same order . . . the universe is thus shown to be a circular movement which has already repeated itself an infinite number of times, and which plays its game for all eternity.[8]

'Are you condemned to do this?' Stephen Dedalus asks himself (9.849). History is a nightmare from which no awakening is thinkable.

Models of the eternal return were omnipresent: as various as Halley's comet (which returned in 1910, shortly before *Ulysses* was begun) and reincarnation theories (which were sending Dublin intelligentsia to Plato's myth of Er, where they might read of Ulysses returning as a private and obscure man). And fiction, as it became more rigorous, took its notions of rigour from such models. In France a novel became a closed system like a cosmos, and the reader aspired to become the ideal intelligence of Laplace. Society, family, biology, *idées reçues* held characters in their iron grip: Emma Bovary has no real options. Chapters, paragraphs, adjacent words were fitted together by precision technology, to hand on trains of force through the system. Poe even predicted the ending chapters of *Barnaby Rudge* from a careful reading of the opening ones, and Emerson wrote in his journal that Mr Babbage, even then dreaming of the Analytical Engine which should weave wholly determined patterns of numbers, would one day invent a novel-writing machine.[9]

Such a machine would create in its own image, and *Ulysses* in its first nine chapters seems to approximate the novel as machine. There is nothing that can be changed, and if Blazes Boylan by the Tolka under a full moon squeezed Molly's hand –

She was humming. The young May moon she's beaming, love. He
other side of her. Elbow, arm. He. Glowworm's la-amp is gleaming,
love. Touch. Fingers. Asking. Answer. Yes. (8.589)

– then inevitably he will enter Molly's bed. 'Stop. Stop. If it was it was.
Must.' His entry there is as inevitable as the courses of the moon, which
Bloom calculates must be new about now (16 June) because it was full
the evening of that walk, 'Sunday fortnight', 29 May. As, an almanac
will verify, it was. 'Same old dingdong always.'

Parallax modifies such events not at all; modifies only the way different
people perceive them:

> the last time he came on my bottom when was it the night Boylan
> gave my hand a great squeeze going along by the Tolka in my hand
> there steals another I just pressed the back of his like that with my
> thumb to squeeze back singing the young May moon shes beaming
> love because he has an idea about him and me hes not such a fool
> (18.77)

Two viewpoints are the necessary condition for irony, and we have seen
that irony is the presiding mood of a hypothetical *Ulysses* terminated at
the end of 'Wandering Rocks'.

It was just in 'Wandering Rocks', we have also seen, that certainty
began to be undermined as if by auctorial malice. First we had to be
wary of misunderstanding data: 'Mr Bloom's dental windows' trespasses
on an implicit contract that there should be only one Mr Bloom per
novel unless by prior stipulation.

Then time and space began to dilate and contract. It seemed that we
were simultaneously on the quays and in the Ormond bar and in the
dining-room and jogging toward Eccles Street with Boylan, unsure what
we saw and heard. Someone nameless talked much of 'Cyclops' aloud,
we don't know when or where. Styles were like incarnations; in 'Oxen
of the Sun' we saw the *dramatis personae* reborn paragraph after paragraph as shifted decorums moved them down the centuries: 1500 years
without ageing. In 'Circe' we lost hold altogether of the actualities of
matter and motion, that order of reality machines might document (ciné
camera, tape recorder). What to trust to now? In 'Eumaeus' misinformation seemed the norm, as a perfectly localisable voice claimed to have
seen Simon Dedalus 'shoot two eggs off two bottles at fifty yards over
his shoulder', in Stockholm, on tour with Hengler's Circus (16.389).
In 'Ithaca' physical certainty seemed to return, but awry, discredited,
suppressing the voices, transforming the people, without whom there is
no novel, into bodies at the disposal of Newtonian impingements. Bloom
fell into the areaway 'by his body's known weight of eleven stone and

four pounds in avoirdupois measure' and was eventually reduced to 'a parenthesis of infinitesimal brevity'. Nor is this even an assured objectivity, since the identical rhetoric has power to transform Bloom into a celestial myth, 'an estranged avenger, a wreaker of justice on malefactors, a dark crusader, a sleeper awakened, with financial resources (by supposition) surpassing those of Rothschild or of the silver king' (17.2020) or into 'missing gent about 40, answering to the name of Bloom, Leopold' or into 'Everyman or Noman' (17.2001).

Hatted and mufflered against the weather of these disorienting chapters, we are apt to ignore their hail of information (words, more words). Most readers never realise that Bloom by Jewish standards isn't Jewish, that Stephen's mother has been dead for fifty-one weeks (17.951), which makes his mourning, like Hamlet's, a role rather conspicuously protracted, or that he has been all day without his glasses (15.3628). No wonder the blurry forms he saw moving on the beach in 'Proteus' – the two women, the cocklepickers, the dog – put forth such powers of metamorphosis. And what seemed sharp observation of the middle distance – the chalkscrawled backdoors, the maze of nets – was in that case recitation, reminiscence, what he knew must be there from former visits to Aunt Sara's. Reread (rewrite) *Ulysses* in such knowledge and its equilibria alter.

Nor, furthermore, despite (as Professor Raleigh's *Chronicle* demonstrates) the awesome amount of information about the Blooms that can be retrieved and systematised, do we know a fraction of what we may think we know. We do not even know Bloom's birthday,* and it is a mark of the special quality of *Ulysses* that this seems a telling statement. Nor, far from aspiring to the certainties of the Laplacean intellect, do we know what will happen as soon as tomorrow in that special field of information the Bloom household, where we are privy to the contents of the very sideboard drawers. Will Molly bring breakfast? We do not know. Nor does she. Did Bloom ask for it? We may incline to think not. But she says he did.

Take a lesser question: Who was McIntosh? It has been weighed seriously; this spook haunts stairways at the *James Joyce Quarterly*, where he has been identified with one Joyce character or another, e.g. James Duffy in 'A Painful Case'. Never wholly serious, the pursuit of McIntosh illustrates assumptions readers bring to the novel but never quite articulate.

For either it is a historical question, pertaining to a man who exists outside the novel, or it is a puzzle-question about a counter in a Joycean

---

*Professor Raleigh (*Chronicle*, 15–16, 27) suggests 6 May 1866, but his inferences entail explaining away contradictions Joyce may have planted to frustrate just this inquiry. The lives of saints have been similarly written by fiat.

game. Either *Ulysses* is 'about' extra-novelistic reality, or it is a closed system at the author's whimsical disposal. These have been two regnant assumptions of Joyce criticism. The former gains colour from the degree of demonstrable coincidence between *Ulysses* and the Dublin of 1904. The latter can claim biographical support. The same mind can entertain them in alternation, to damn Joyce doubly as both an unreliable reporter and a self-indulgent artificer. Thus Mr Adams late in *Surface and Symbol*, out of patience with many false trails of fact, discerns 'an appetite for self-destruction' in a Joyce who 'breaks the texture of the book which he has taken such pains to establish, for no other evident reason than that he has gotten the reader to trust in it'.[10]

But the alternatives may be false.

For nearly seven years *Ulysses* was more than a project: it was what James Joyce was doing with the one life at his disposal, and he should be credited with some reflection on the import of this. So we may glimpse a Joyce who commenced by flexing the powers of auctorial omniscience, decreeing Bloomsday's very clouds and winds, and came to perceive as he worked the dangers of hermetic closure, of fastening the last rivet in what he seemed to be achieving, the ultimate late-nineteenth-century novel where everything pertinent seems known and accounted for; perceived the exclusion from such an Analytical Engine of any invited response save a Cheshire Cat's irony; glimpsed its truly terrible knowingness, and the reductiveness of that. Temperament would have aided this perception, for though he loved closed systems he was attracted even more – had been at least since *Exiles* – to a mental cosmos founded, as Stephen tells us the church is founded, on mystery, 'and founded irremovably because founded, like the world, macro and microcosm, upon the void. Upon incertitude, upon unlikelihood' (9.841). Micro- and macrocosm, *Ulysses*, the empirical world. That sentence comes not long before the contrived incertitudes of 'Wandering Rocks', where our empiricism receives many checks, and Joyce surely had moods in which he knocked a few holes in his fabric, to promote a little healthy incertitude. About this time he invented the Arranger, whose antics so annoy Professor Adams.

But toward the end, working on 'Penelope' and 'Ithaca' together, James Joyce seems to have gone farther, divining – no, not the cosmos of Picasso, Einstein, Heisenberg and Gödel, his visual taste being banal, his science but a smattering of terms, his very arithmetic deplorable – divining rather something of what they intuited and modelled in their own idiom, their own arts; for that the human experience is homogenous, that innovators in diverse fields are assuredly one another's contemporaries without necessity of interaction, is one of the exhilarating truths of history.

As Newton's cosmos is a special case of Einstein's, reliable when velocities are low, so realism – a book's fidelity to Dublin – is a special case among possible uses of language. But a post-Einstein physicist, even when he uses Newton's methods, does so without subscribing to what was once their premise, a naïve dualism between observer and observed. This is like the naïve dualism between flawed reportage and mocking puzzzlemaster, which, though it survives in English Departments, comports with a world-view elsewhere obsolete.

We may list several paradigms of the obsolescent. Classical physics with its naïve simultaneity, its succession of world-wide instants which were 'really' synchronous despite observational lags, agrees with classical logic, in which a system of premises will account for all the truths they can enumerate; with classical fiction, postulating events we are to imagine as having occurred in independence of the narrative we read; with classical painting, which is 'of' a subject we could see better without the painter's mediation were we privileged to enter his studio.

But Einstein (1905) in effect denied an ideal simultaneity – 'what really happens' – on which we get our imperfect fixes, and Kurt Gödel (1930) proved closure also impossible to deductive thought: always a hole at the bottom of the well-wrought bag. And Picasso (1909 ff.) ended the ideal separation of subject from painting, and Joyce (1922) the ideal separation of story from book of words. All four, and others, terminate a dualism between the art or science and its materials.

This seems most widely understood of painting. We know that a Picasso does not offer news of a subject. In its indifference to such news it is content with a known motif, familiar as the plot of the *Odyssey* – a woman at a mirror, fruit on a table – which it shapes, creates, amid witty meditations on the history of painting, notably on that point of crisis when perspective space was invented with its immobilised point of view. We no longer complain that 'style' interferes with 'subject', as though preserving the appearance of *those* apples *that* morning had been the sum of painterly desire. To recognise the motif, perceive the apples, is part of what we do in exploring the painting, but we lose nearly all if we stop there with an 'Aha!' when we have just become qualified to begin. In its geometry, its juxtapositions of hue and shape, in its scale, in its local quirks, the painting has acknowledged, not represented, the apples; has re-created them; more, has created itself; more, invites our alert scrutiny of its enigmas, its inner life, which is not that of the apples.

Likewise a part of reading *Ulysses* is reading through the language to extract motifs, but only so that once we have perceived them – perceived, for example, the tale of familiar events in 'Sirens' or in 'Oxen of the Sun' – we may at length more fully read the language in which alone they exist.

In which alone they exist: this is often hard to believe, so vivid is our sense of Bloom and Dublin – sights, sounds, spaces, bodies, clocks, voices. Still, by a kind of Heisenbergian either-or, we must acknowledge two ideal extremes, mutually exclusive like an electron's momentum and position. For, if the Blooms exist beyond the book, they have a future but we cannot know what it is, and we may invent what sequels we like, not excluding one in which Molly falls down the stairs tomorrow and breaks her neck: an event not predicted by the book but surely not impossible. Or, if the Blooms are confined to the book, their existence wholly conferred by systems of words, they have no future whatever because the book has a last page: no future, that is, save the eternal return of Bloomsday 1904, wholly or in snatches, as often as we shall revisit the book.

And the sheer demand the book makes on our attention will ensure, abetted by the Aesthetic of Delay, that no two readings will rehearse one another; *Ulysses* will neither hold together in one simultaneous mental grasp, nor repeat itself as we traverse once more its 260,000 words. It may dawn on us that a late sentence of *Finnegans Wake* has more pertinence to the experience of rereading than to the spectacle of history: 'Yet is no body present here which was not there before. Only is order othered. Naught is nulled. *Fuitfiat!*' (613).

Order. We reread in quest of patterns, finding them in plenty, largely created by ourselves from selective observation of cues, often cues planted by Joyce in those final frantic months of revising the whole while composing the last two episodes. Were the book untitled, had we only the assurance that it is organised round a system of allusions to a classic, we should most likely guess *Hamlet* and not guess wrong. In giving the *Odyssey* priority, the title does not tell us how the Odyssey is present: retrieving its marks is our doing.

It is this compliance with our collaboration, this symbiosis of observer with observed, that marks the radiant novelty of *Ulysses*. Whatever tasks we may set ourselves with its aid, we are oddly liberated from an anxious sense of living in the great Taskmaster's eye, confined by the intentions of the author. He kept his intentions, so far as he could, out of sight, suppressing even the Homeric episode-titles, and much, he saw to it, must emerge that he did not intend.

The letters of *Yes*, the last word, run backward through *Stately*, the first. Joyce may never have noticed this, and assuredly did not arrive at the words together; 'Stately' was in print in 1918, 'Yes' decided on only in 1921.[11]

As the *Odyssey*'s twenty-four books are named by the Greek alphabet's twenty-four letters, so, Guy Davenport has noted,[12] the eighteen episodes of *Ulysses* agree in number with the eighteen letters of the Irish alphabet. The names of these name trees, and meditation will disclose the eighteen emblematic trees enlivening with their traditional symbolism Joyce's episodes in order. If Joyce gave thought to this, it was an afterthought, since half the episodes were written before he had settled on their final number.

The Random House designer in 1934 encouraged attention to the initial letters of the book's three parts by making them six inches tall: S, M, P. Stephen, Molly, Poldy? The three members of a syllogism? Maybe Joyce had cared, or hadn't. The designer's interest was in an elegant page. Whether from auctorial causation or no, these patterns exist. By coincidence, then? *Ulysses* welcomes coincidence.

As did Joyce, even coincidences between his books and external events, the validation of a theme in *Finnegans Wake* by the Russian invasion of Finland, or the death by suicide of the original of Lynch, of whom Stephen had said: '*Exit Judas. Et laqueo se suspendit.*'[13] Superstition has been adduced, or even the assumption of prophetic power, but Samuel Beckett came close when he wrote:

> Why, Mr Joyce seems to say, should there be four legs to a table, and four to a horse, and four seasons and four Gospels and four Provinces in Ireland? Why twelve Tables of the Law, and twelve Apostles, and twelve months and twelve Napoleonic marshals and twelve men in Florence called Ottolenghi? Why should the Armistice be celebrated at the eleventh hour of the eleventh day of the eleventh month? . . .[14]

Numbers are definite; whatever is sufficiently definite attracts correspondences; and *Ulysses* with its thousands of clear-cut stipulations, a book in which each separate word seems thrown into relief, attracts them like burrs.*

On nothing is *Ulysses* more insistent than on the fact that there is no Bloom there, no Stephen there, no Molly there, no Dublin there, simply language. To say this is by no means to surrender to the artificer's whimsical virtuosity. We and he are co-creators; characters and city have their existence in our minds. We may later visit the geographic Dublin, and note much coincidence with what our minds contain; even discover that Bloom's library book never came back.

This is not to say, with Barthes in *S/Z*, that our reading of any book is essentially our doing. Words are prior to us, communal, entangled in human experience, registered in other books and in dictionaries. In most

---

*Why, for that matter, should Bloomsday entail Bloom? Yet I can report three uncontrived Bloomsday epiphanies, all for no reason entailing automobiles: Bloomsday 1954, when I noticed I was driving through Bloom, Kansas; Bloomsday 1975, when a taxicab passed with by Baltimore custom its driver's name on the door, 'L. Bloom'; most oddly Bloomsday 1963, switching off the ignition in a nearly new car after a long day's drive, and noting the odometer reading, '1904'. Each of these would have pleased Joyce, and it seems absurd to suggest he'd have thought his book predicted them.

books they are brushed on to the pages, a thin wash. But *Ulysses* is the first book to be a kind of hologram of language, creating a three-dimensional illusion out of the controlled interference between our experience of language and its arrangements of language.

For only the arrangement could the author claim responsibility, as he seems to have realised in Paris in the latter part of 1921, surrounded for the first time since his long Odyssey began by people who wanted his book, were eager for it. The endless work of finishing it he determined to hand to his readers, for their endless pleasure. Working on two episodes simultaneously, he was impersonating turn and turn about the last embodiment of the Arranger, the catechist of 'Ithaca', and the unarrangeable Molly Bloom ('O rocks!') who is determined to tell the story of the Blooms her own way, and even supplies words for a resonant affirmation on the improbable occasion when her consciousness gets extinguished.

He was reading proof, too, all those thousands of words from Trieste and Zürich now at last distinct in uniform blocks of type, eight pages to a sheet. Each *placard* he corrected and also crammed with additions, springing to mind to be planted here and there, to ask, to answer, to amplify, while the catechist gravely asked and answered, asked and answered, and Molly's *copia* rolled on. The final text of *Ulysses*, before it was released for our collaboration, was a three-way collaboration: between Ithacan omniscience, and Molly Bloom, and the author inspecting what he had been writing for seven years, and seeing that it was good.

NOTES

1 His comment when his Aunt Josephine said the book wasn't fit to read; Ellmann, 551.
2 ibid., 725.
3 The passage was being recorded for the National Public Radio programme, 'A Question of Place: James Joyce'.
4 Raleigh, 9.
5 These paragraphs are indebted to Milic Čapek, *The Philosophical Impact of Contemporary Physics* (New York, 1961), especially chapters VIII–IX. For physics having run out of jobs, see A. P. French, *Newtonian Mechanics* (New York, 1971), 7–8.
6 Quoted by Čapek, 122.
7 Ellmann, 147.
8 Quoted by Čapek, 125–6.
9 Emerson's journal for 2 August 1842.
10 Adams, 252–3.
11 Ellmann, 531.
12 Guy Davenport, 'Joyce's Forest of symbols', *The Iowa Review*, VI, 1 (Winter, 1975), 79–91.
13 *Letters*, I, 408; Ellmann, 611.
14 Samuel Beckett, 'Dante . . . Bruno. Vico . . . Joyce', in *Our Exagmination Round his Factification for Incamination of Work in Progress* (Paris, 1929), 21.

APPENDICES

These are specimen notes, offered here as instances of the kind of attention *Ulysses* invites. The book's quantity of interlocked detail is beyond reckoning and, if Joyce's dealings with all of it do not betoken omniscience, still great issues, Sherlock Holmes said, can hang on a bootlace, and we need to earn the certainty that our insight in each instance surpasses our author's, or that we have taken his point.

APPENDIX 1

The Date of Stephen's Flight

James Joyce was born 2 February 1882, went to Clongowes at 'half past six' in September 1888, and stayed there until June 1891. He was at Belvedere College from September 1893 to June 1898 and at University College from September 1898 to June 1902. His degree was conferred on 31 October 1902, and he departed for Paris a month later, 1 December. The telegram 'Nother dying come home father' (3.199) recalled him to Dublin in mid-April 1902; she died on 13 August. His time in Paris, deducting a long Christmas visit to Dublin, totalled about three months.

Stephen Hero (1904–5) may well have followed this chronology, but the five-chapter *A Portrait of the Artist as a Young Man* (1907–14) opts for symbolic dates, enclosing its narrative of Stephen's time in Ireland between a Resurrection and an Ascension: an illness and recovery coincident with the death of Parnell (6 October 1891) and an Eastertide gesture of flight in his final University year. As Arnold Goldman and Hans Walter Gabler have shown,[1] these alignments, apparently determined after much of the final version had been written, make for elusive internal inconsistencies, and especially after he had accepted, late in the game, additional constraints imposed by the planning of *Ulysses*, Joyce was forced to blur or conceal a number of chronological difficulties.

Though *Ulysses* allows us to deduce (17.447) that Stephen was born like Joyce in 1882, the *Portrait* in its final arrangement makes Parnell's death (1891) happen during his first term at Clongowes, when he seems no more mature than Joyce had been during his first term in 1888. (Joyce when Parnell died was nine and between schools.) So two or three years must be inconspicuously made up. One device was to minimise references to datable events, and render them penetrable only to research. Thus the retreat Joyce made in late 1896 is dated forward to December 1898, as we shall only learn if we ask when the feast of St Francis Xavier fell on a Saturday (107), and Stephen (144) gives the confessor his age as Joyce's in that year, 16. When he composed the third section of Chapter V, Joyce seems to have intended Stephen's time at University to synchronise with his own, making Stephen recall (226) the behaviour of his classmates at the tumultuous performance of *The Countess Cathleen* that took place in the spring of Joyce's freshman year (1899). On this schedule, Stephen ought to depart for Paris in 1902, and it seems plausible that a flight near Ascension Day of that year (8 April) was at one time envisaged.

Stephen's flight is placed in the Paschal season to make it his secular Easter. If in 1902, he will depart some seven months before Joyce did. This will involve the minor difficulty that if we recall how young he seemed when Parnell died – in a part of the book designed to parallel and recall the first part – his age will seem implausible, and the major difficulty that between now and his mother's death in the summer of 1903 there will be too much Paris time to account for. Stephen must skim Paris and return in defeat – 'You flew. Whereto? Newhaven–Dieppe, steerage passenger. Paris and back' (9.952) – not settle in for nearly a year. So the date, at the cost of other difficulties, was fixed as 1903.

Joyce seems to have patterned Stephen's terminal invocation, '*April 27. Old father, old artificer . . .*', on the liturgy for the Vigil of Ascension Day, when Christ is quoted verbatim for the last time: 'Et nunc clarifica me tu, Pater . . .' (John, 17:5). In fulfilment of this parallel we may date the departure 28 April 1903, a canonical forty days after the diary excerpts commence. To have taken wing on Ascension Day itself, forty days after Easter, would have been neat and would have been feasible had that day only fallen as early as it did in 1902 (8 April). But the late Easter of 1903 pushed Ascension Day forward to 20 May, leaving Stephen next to no time in Paris before he is recalled by his mother's illness. (In *Ulysses*, 17.951, we learn that May Dedalus was buried on 26 June 1903, six weeks earlier than Joyce's mother. This date – another awkward constraint – was imposed by a pattern of Ulyssean correspondences. To make Stephen's fates balance Bloom's she must die about the same time of year Bloom's father did, and that death had to be set a few days after Bloomsday to procure Bloom's annual absence in Ennis just when Molly is to be in Belfast with Boylan.) So no synchrony of Stephen's flight with Ascension Day was feasible.

Though the year must be 1903 it is never specified. We only know that it cannot be 1902 because that would make the 30 March talk on the Library porch fall on Easter Sunday, when the Library would have been closed. Easter 1903 fell on 12 April, so the 'heavy night' epiphany of the 10 April diary entry seems appropriate in being written on Good Friday. (And Stephen's 24 March discussion with his mother about the BVM occurred on the Vigil of the Feast of the Annunciation, which falls on 25 March whatever the year.)

All of this matters to the reader of *Ulysses* only in determining the length of Stephen's stay in Paris. Between a Paschal departure in 1902 or 1903 and the funeral of May Dedalus in late June 1903 we have a choice of more than a year or else just a few weeks, four or five. The latter is indicated: a shorter time even than James Joyce's three months. Stephen has the glamour of having been to Paris ('O go on!' a whore cries. 'Give us some parleyvoo': 15.3875) and exiguous memories – St Genevieve's Library, Esther Ostvalt's shoe, Kevin Egan. He brings back 'five tattered numbers' of a naughty magazine (3.197), which suggests a mere five-week stay. It has all been anticlimax, one more defeat.

Finally, since a Paschaltide exodus would have predated not only graduation but term-end, Joyce had to blur the question whether Stephen ever took his degree. The one reference in *Ulysses* to 'Stephen Dedalus, B.A.' (16.1259) occurs in an error-ridden newspaper account which locates him at a funeral he didn't attend.

NOTE

1 Arnold Goldman, 'Stephen Dedalus's dream of Parnell', *James Joyce Quarterly*, VI, III (Spring 1969), 262–4, and Hans Walter Gabler in Staley and Benstock, 25–60.

APPENDIX 2

Bloom's Chest

Joyce wrote 'Ithaca', as Jack Dalton has shown,[1] amid appalling distractions presented by the proofsheets of the other episodes, inundating him from a French printing-house where their struggles with his handwritten corrections routinely yielded such botches as 'Wattly Jrceman' for 'Weekly Freeman' and 'Stackney cass' for 'Hackney cars'. 'I write and revise and correct with one or two eyes about twelve hours a day I should say, stopping for intervals of five minutes or so when I can't see any more.'[2] At one point he was so harried that when he tried to write out the alphabet on a note-sheet he got twenty-seven letters.[3]

'Ithaca', not surprisingly, fell short of the steely imperturbability its rhetoric promises. R. M. Adams notes that it ought to be impeccable, to throw any Bloomian blunders into relief.[4] But haste and worry took their toll. Thus Davy Byrne's address got miscopied (17.330, where '14 Duke street' should be '21 Duke Street'), the mock calculations of comparative ages contain several errors (17.446), the Roman-numeral date (17.99), the one detail not copied from *Thom's* in that list of calendrical lore, got printed 'MXMIV'; these and similar things went wrong at Joyce's hands, not at the printer's, and so mechanically that if we want to we can easily correct them.

Something less easily rectified went wrong with Bloom's measurements. At 5 feet 9½ inches he weighs 158 lb – a datum obtained, incidentally, on Ascension Day, when Christ by contrast was weightless (17.91) – but the before-and-after measurements from his days with the Sandow exercises (17.1815) give chest 28 and 29½ inches, biceps 9 and 10, forearm 8½ and 9, thigh 10 and 12, calf 11 and 12, and for a man of Bloom's build that chest dimension, as Adams observes,[5] is impossibly small.

Without venturing to supply authoritative dimensions for Bloom, it is possible to hazard an explanation.

Eugen Sandow's *Strength and How to Obtain It* (London, 1897) stands on Bloom's bookshelf (17.1397) and had apparently passed through the hands of Joyce, who noted the 'red cloth' binding though he didn't amid his Ithacan turmoil get author and title quite right. One wishes he'd had time to linger with it: a book of minor delights for the Bloomophile, it sports photos of the jaunty moustachioed author, who inhabits what would appear to be the glorified body of Leopold P. Bloom, a man a quarter of an inch taller than Sandow and two pounds lighter.[6] On page 28 a sketch of a fig-leafed Sandow shows where to apply the measuring-tape, and on to the chart on page 29 the student is encouraged to inscribe fifteen measurements before commencing the course of exercises and again at its completion. There are even blanks for the signatures of two witnesses ('Medical man preferred').

But Bloom noted only five data, chest, biceps, forearm, thigh, calf, a good sign that Joyce turned for help to the back of the little book, where testimonials from pupils are documented with neatly calligraphed sets of numbers, and Bloom's five are the categories most frequently reported. The very first, Mr Thos. A. Fox of Limehouse, has supplied (pages 40–1) measurements in just the categories we are given for Bloom, in the same order, plus two more, chest (expanded) and waist. Fox's relevant before-and-after data are chest 29 and 32½ inches, biceps 10 and 13, forearm 9½ and 12, thigh 16½ and 20, calf 11 and 13. There is a pattern of correspondence between his and Bloom's measurements, which could have been obtained by paring Fox's down, notably that thigh, and acknowledging Mr Bloom's two months of exercise *versus* Mr Fox's two years by bringing 'before' and 'after' closer together. And if that is how Joyce invented figures for Bloom, he did so without having studied Mr Fox's covering letter on an earlier page, where we read (pages 37–8), in facsimile handwriting, 'I am nineteen years of age and small of stature being only five feet in height and seven stone in weight': the classic ninety-eight-pound weakling, in fact.

An unlikely error even for a distracted half-blind man in a hurry? Not necessarily. Not all men know their own chest measurements nor even what a plausible one would be, as witness the fact that Bloom's twenty-eight-inch chest was forty years striking anyone as unlikely.

NOTES

1   Jack P. Dalton, 'The text of *Ulysses*', in Fritz Senn (ed.), *New Light on Joyce from the Dublin Symposium* (Bloomington, Ind./London, 1972), 108–9, 117.
2   *Letters*, I, 168.
3   P. Herring (ed.), *Joyce's 'Ulysses' Notesheets* (Charlottesville, Va, 1971), 60, 415.
4   Adams, 183–4.
5   ibid., 184.
6   Joyce raised Bloom's height half an inch from 5 feet 9 inches on the page-proofs. Had he by then noticed Sandow's dimensions and decided to give Ulysses the advantage?

The Circle and the Three Nines

Why did he not elaborate these calculations to a more precise result?

Because some years previously in 1886 when occupied with the problem of the quadrature of the circle he had learned of the existence of a number computed to a relative degree of accuracy to be of such magnitude and of so many places, e.g., the 9th power of the 9th power of 9, that, the result having been obtained, 33 closely printed volumes of 1000 pages each of innumerable quires and reams of India paper would have to be requisitioned in order to contain the complete tale of its printed integers .... (17.1070)

Bloom's venture into circle-squaring is one more of his continuities with Greece, where the problem – to construct a square equal in area to a given circle, in a finite number of steps, using ruler and compass only – assisted Pericles' mentor Anaxagoras to kill time in an Athenian jail[1] and occupied no one knows how many subsequent intelligences in full daylight. Though a solution would contain a geometrical construction for π, the famous problem had no practical implication. By the third century BC Archimedes' estimate of π, $3\frac{1}{7}$, gave as good a numerical measure as anyone was likely to need. It is only 0.04 per cent off, or more accurate than the data any Greek engineer was likely to marry to it.

No, the challenge was as purely intellectual as anything on a chessboard. The conditions are unambiguous and elegant, the construction sounds tantalisingly simple, yet neither Anaxagoras nor anyone else performed it. The ruler–compass restriction, by the way, was meant to fit the problem into the logic of what later became Euclidean geometry, the axiom system of which in effect stipulates that lines and circles are the elements you can draw, all subsequent knowledge derived from their simple properties.[2]

Bloom, who inherits this austere tradition and owns a 1711 printing of Pardies' *Short Yet Plain Elements of Geometry*, is also a child of the nineteenth-century circle-squarers, a gaggle of opsimaths united by three premises: that the problem would yield to fresh-eyed determination from which professional mathematicians had sealed themselves off; that it was somehow of great practical import; that the government had ready therefore a monetary reward. Thus Virag sneers in 'Circe' (15.2399) that his grandson 'intended to devote . . . the summer months of 1886 to square the circle and win that million', and we later read (17.1696) of 'the secular problem of the quadrature of the circle, government premium £1,000,000 sterling'.

A million marks a considerable inflation from the mid-nineteenth century, when the British mathematician Augustus De Morgan, for whom these pests had an unexplained affinity, had to deal with an agricultural labourer who 'squared the circle' and 'left his papers with me, one of which was a copy of a letter to the Lord Chancellor, desiring his Lordship to hand over forthwith 100,000 pounds, the amount of the alleged offer of reward'.[3] De Morgan was also pestered in the 1840s by a Jesuit who 'came from South America, with a quadrature, and a cutting from a newspaper, announcing that a reward was ready for the discovery in England. On this evidence he came over.'[4] Since the Government stood to draw no conceivable benefit from a ruler-and-compass exercise, the source of these rumours is baffling; there may be a clue in the prize that was actually offered in the eighteenth century for a method of discerning a ship's longitude.

Had Joyce held to his first plan of having Bloom attempt the quadrature in the summer of 1882 when he was 16 and at the height of his powers, his efforts would have been exactly contemporaneous with those of F. Lindemann, who in that year terminated the question at last[5] with his clean proof that the construction is simply impossible. But Bloom deferred his enterprise till the ripe age of 20, by which time, not being a close reader of the *Berichte der Berliner Akademie* where Lindemann's result had appeared, he was labouring unbeknownst at a question four years closed. It is perhaps fortunate that the number with the three nines intimidated him into inactivity.

He (and Joyce) may very well have encountered that number in *Titbits*, where I have no intention of searching for it. I certainly remember seeing it four decades ago in Ripley's *Believe It Or Not!* It is a hardy perennial of pointless stupefaction, 9^{9^9}, the largest number you can write with three digits. It means $(9)^{9^9}$, nine raised to the power 9^9, and despite Joyce's euphonious but ambiguous wording is not to be confused with $(9^9)^9$, 9^9 multiplied by itself nine times, a mere seventy-eight-digit number of no special interest.

Since 9^9 is the product of nine nines, or 387,420,489, we get the super-number if we multiply *that* many nines together. This would take thirty-seven years of eight-hour days if we could perform a multiplication every second – as we can't, since we should soon be confronting 1000–digit results it would take hours merely to copy down.

Fortunately the size of this huge useless number can be estimated with a good deal less labour. If we multiply 9^9 or 387,420,489 by the logarithm of 9, and part the result left and right at the decimal point like the Red Sea, we shall be looking at two numbers that give us as much information as we really need. The antilogarithm of the portion at the right gives the opening digit of the unimaginable result, and the portion at the left tells us directly how many digits the unimaginable result will consume.

The latter part is easy: 369-plus million digits. To get anything useful at the right of the decimal point we need the logarithm of 9 to an unusual number of places: the common 4 or 6 will not do at all. Here Joyce scholarship is indebted to British pluck, which celebrated the tercentenary of Briggs's *Logarithmall Arithmetike* with an otherwise futile two-volume publication[6] in which we can look up log 9 to 20 places. It is 0.95424 25094 39324 87459, and with its aid we can be sure that the number which stupefied Bloom will commence with 4 and boast 369,693,099 additional digits.

Thus the '33 closely printed volumes of 1000 pages each' would carry some 11,000 characters per page. Since a page of the *Oxford English Dictionary* can hold about 17,000 characters, the ball lands in the park.

A detail by the way: why 33? The number of digits in 9^{9^9} is easy to estimate: anyone with even 4-place logs can put it in the vicinity of 369,000,000. The natural way to build a *Titbits* entry on that information would be to envisage 1000 pages of 100 lines each holding 100 characters, which leads to 37 volumes, not 33. No doubt somebody miscopied at some stage, or else Joyce elected 33 as a good Christian number, and why not? He liked to pattern absurdity: nothing more cries out for pattern. The prospect of printing that number (think of the proof-reading!) is absurd enough to invite subdual by any pattern even superficially determined. And 33 is a stereoscopic Trinity, and the number of Christ's years on earth, and three times that most potent of Joycean numbers, 11. True, 37 would be the eleventh prime if we count 1, but not if we don't, and usage is divided. No, 33 is right, and it's Molly's age, too. Thirty-three closely printed volumes, that has the ring of rightness.

NOTES

1 Plutarch, 'On Exile', in the Loeb edition of his *Moralia*, VII, 571. This seems to be the earliest mention of the famous problem.

2 For a good discussion see Petr Beckmann, *A History of Pi* (New York, 1971), 48–50.

3 Augustus De Morgan, *A Budget of Paradoxes* (1872), 'Introductory'; page 12 of the 1912 Open Court reprint.

4 ibid., 11.

5 Beckmann, *Pi*, 172.

6 Alexander John Thompson, *Logarithmetica Britannica*, issued in nine parts, 1924–52, and finally in two volumes by Cambridge University Press, 1952. Thompson's thirty years' labour had its inception on a holiday in the Lake District in June of that *annus mirabilis*, 1922, the year of *Ulysses* and *The Waste Land*. During days of incessant rain he had nothing to do but sit in his hotel and fiddle with calculations which persuaded him that Britain's homage to Henry Briggs could be performed by one man. His twenty-place logs run integer by integer clear to 100,000, and were finished just as electronic computers were rendering them irrelevant. Publication of the work of Thompson's contemporary, a certain Mansell, was later sponsored by the Royal Society. Mansell dealt only with the first 1000 integers but carried their logarithms, which he computed without mechanical aid, clear to 110 places. As he finished each number, he was accustomed to copy its 110-digit logarithm on a long strip of paper $\frac{1}{4}$ inch wide, which he would then roll up tightly. He deserves notice as the Cashel Boyle O'Connor Fitzmaurice Tisdall Farrell of twentieth-century computation.

CRITICAL SEQUELS

Ezra Pound in old age liked to recall how Joyce had responded to reviews and explications: 'If only someone would say the book was so damn' funny.' Nearly everything else was said. *Ulysses* attracted every wind that blew, benign, malign, and the keepers even of the favouring gales were not agreed on the direction of Ithaca. The initial tempests of abuse, the accusations of foul-mindedness, obscenity, Bolshevik formlessness, had blown themselves out by the mid-1930s, when the book, at last published in the United States and in England, had ceased to be a cult object to smuggle from Paris.

Even by then a number of critical vectors had commenced to define themselves, three of them sponsored by distinguished names. The one intelligent attack, that of Wyndham Lewis in *Time and Western Man* (1927), took *Ulysses* very seriously indeed, as portending something unsatisfactory about the way postwar modernism was shaping up. Lewis perceived a Joyce who was radically unreflective, not a real innovator, very much at the disposal of random influences; for the notation of the interior monologue he had no difficulty finding precedents in Dickens' Alfred Jingle. Programmatic though they were, his conclusions drew on acute local perceptions, and Joyce took them seriously enough to worry responses to them into the texture of *Finnegans Wake*.

Even earlier, two short but intelligent appreciations, by Ezra Pound ('James Joyce et Pécuchet', 1922) and T. S. Eliot ('*Ulysses*, Order and Myth', 1923), had used the book to prescribe a writer's role amid the social and intellectual chaos of those years. Pound perceived in Bloom a bourgeois epitome, and in *Ulysses* the Flaubertian heritage of diagnostic naturalism, displaying vividly the mess quarter-education and trammelled will had got Europe into. Eliot asserted that 'the mythological method' permitted an ordering of an 'immense panorama of futility and anarchy'. It was the myth, he thought, that did what Pound thought was done by style. Pound meant by style the 'initial style' of the first ten episodes. Apart from Pound's allusion to the Flaubert of *La Tentation* neither man confronted the stylistic extravaganzas of the episodes from 'Sirens' on, and beyond mentioning 'a continuous parallel between contemporaneity and antiquity' Eliot did not venture to explain how the mythological method worked.

It is impossible to read with no idea *what* you are reading, and each of these highly innovative men of letters was reading the *Ulysses* he required a major modern work to be: a symptom (Lewis), a mocking mirror (Pound), an exemplary feat of construction (Eliot). Meanwhile that mythical being 'the general reader' was left with no idea what to expect (unless salacity) until Stuart Gilbert came to his aid (*James Joyce's 'Ulysses'*, 1930). Even partial or wrong expectations can help, and Gilbert aided thousands to persevere past the opening pages and in some way experience *Ulysses* for themselves.

This was achieved at some cost. Responding to early accusations of formlessness, Gilbert adduced a schematic formality from which understanding took several decades to recover. Based on the schema Joyce had drawn up for Valery Larbaud, his exposition moved episode by episode through what was offered for admiration as a great feat of planning, full of cunning esoterica: Bloom cannot light a cigar without portending the fiery club with which Ulysses extinguished the Cyclops' eye. That the schema was not Joyce's working blueprint but a *post facto* orthogonality, that many of its details (e.g. club/cigar) are casual and funny, not central and portentous, did not get clarified till Walton Litz (1961) showed how very late Joyce inserted many such touches, and the Ellmann biography (1959) demonstrated that the schema in question was not drawn up till 1921, and had been preceded by a different one. And so elaborately contrived did the Homeric correspondences seem in Gilbert's hands – he made everything depend on them – that they have never regained the centrality they deserve. In seeming to exhaust them, his presentation caused many readers to lose interest in them, and revert to Pound's notion that they are disposable scaffolding.

In 1934 an accurate note was struck: Frank Budgen's *James Joyce and the Making of Ulysses*, a book Clive Hart has rightly called 'the best ever written about Joyce', affirming the centrality of Bloom and the high spirits in which the book of Bloom was executed. A sounder guide than Gilbert's but, making less show of system, far less regarded (promoted, also, by less prominent publishers), it took a long time to have much effect; Mr Kain, the author of the next compendious *Ulysses*-book, mentioned it exactly once.

A few more things happened before James Joyce's death in 1941. Edmund Wilson in *Axel's Castle* (1931) had perceived that *Ulysses* was no isolated freak but part of the great tradition of nineteenth-century European Modernism. Wilson's puzzlement over the aspects of *Ulysses* that will not yield to a naturalist-psychological interpretation constituted an early warning (unheeded) that neither the novelistic approach (Pound) nor the mythic one (Eliot) will account for the whole book; either Joyce had tried to fuse two incompatible genres, or (as we now tend to say) he redefined both. By 1939 there was a biography of Joyce (Herbert Gorman's). Without committing himself on the value of the work – Gorman was himself a minor novelist with no reason to find outrageous books sympathetic – Gorman concentrated on the author's struggles to get them written and published. By 1941 Harry Levin (*James Joyce*) had located *Ulysses* in the arc of Joyce's development, which with the Gorman biography to draw on and the whole of *Finnegans Wake* available he could perceive more comprehensively than could Wilson. Like Wilson, he read a European novel, in which with much whirring of machinery the burgher and the bohemian are brought together to see what they have to say to each other (not much). Bloom, it will be perceived, fared badly in this decade, except at Budgen's hands. In a time of Marxist and quasi-Marxist impatience with urban passivity, he was ill-cast for any typological role save that of goat.

Meanwhile the Miles L. Hanley *Word Index* (1937) afforded radical acknowledgement that if *Ulysses* was a novel it was one of a new kind. It is hard to know what critical purpose a word index to *Nicholas Nickleby* would serve, but in *Ulysses*, as Martin Joos succinctly demonstrated in an appendix to the Hanley volume, one may discern an intricate narrative motif in following the occasions and contexts of one aptly chosen word (his example was 'prize').

It was 1947 before Richard M. Kain's *Fabulous Voyager* introduced a new concern, the empirical Dublin. With the aid of the *Word Index* and *Thom's Directory*, which no one previously had thought to consult, he indicated both the book's density of local fact – streets and stores and houses correctly located – and its consistency in linking minor as well as major events and pursuing the fortunes of minor as well as major characters. But his Bloom is a pathetic little man, and it is still a bleak vision *Ulysses* presents, as it was in Hugh Kenner's 1956 *Dublin's Joyce*, which however expressed grave doubts about something previously taken for granted, the centrality of Stephen Dedalus in Joyce's scheme of values – a contention partly substantiated by Kevin Sullivan's *Joyce Among the Jesuits* (1958) – and also reproved the custom of reading the book by unwriting it, peering down through styles to discern a muddied simplicity.

Then in 1959 everything changed. Richard Ellmann published his massive biography, *James Joyce*, and Joyce's books became episodes in his life.

It is beyond dispute that few writers have been more intensely, intimately autobiographical: *A Portrait of the Artist as a Young Man* exists in part to keep us from overlooking this, the 'Scylla and Charybdis' episode of *Ulysses* likewise. Whatever we may make of Stephen Dedalus, we cannot doubt that the events of his life parallel those of Joyce's Dublin years: raw fact, these, for the *Portrait's* artifact. But a biography longer than any book of Joyce's – 50 per cent more words than *Ulysses*, moreover with some 2,400 citations of sources – had the sudden effect of reversing this proposition. The life became truth, the books fabrications. Ellmann, it was even assumed by hasty reviewers, had finally written what Joyce had been unable to write straightforwardly, freeing us to abandon our struggles with difficult texts and settle down to the definitive Life instead.

No one who remembers struggling to extract even rudimentary chronology from Gorman will underestimate the service Ellmann rendered in establishing the factual grid: the dates, addresses, sequences. And all those letters; and all that inwardness (much of it from Jim's sour brother Stanislaus): it is no wonder the biography overwhelmed. After twenty years it is easier to see that *James Joyce* is by no means what it still tends to get called, definitive; that many of its briskest assertions are undocumented and many more, notably those pertaining to points of tangency between life and work, oversimple; that it would have made less stir than it did if some of its prime sources – the *Dublin Diary* and the memoir *My Brother's Keeper* of Stanislaus Joyce, the second and third volumes of James Joyce's *Letters* – had been published before it was; and that it is nevertheless the most comprehensive biography we are likely to get, so many sources having vanished since Ellmann was making his inquiries. People have died, Dublin and Paris have changed; most subtly, witnesses to events long gone now know, thanks to Ellmann, what it is they remember.

Post-Ellmann in its condescension to Joyce, Robert Martin Adams's *Surface and Symbol: The Consistency of James Joyce's Ulysses* (1962) agitates what later workers have in several instances shown to be non-problems while establishing the useful principle that the fit between Joyce's text and ascertainable facts outside the text is continually worth examining. This proposition contains two elements: (1) that *Ulysses* was after all *written*, and by a fallible mortal, not dropped to earth from aloft, and moreover not written from beginning to end the way we read it; (2) that it continually impinges on facts with their own autonomy, biographical, topographical, chronological, evidential. The first of these insights has sponsored a sequence of valuable genetic studies, which begin with the pioneer essays of Joseph Prescott, collected in 1964 as *Exploring James Joyce*, and now include A. Walton Litz's *The Art of James Joyce* (1961), Michael Groden's *Ulysses in Progress* (1977) and Michael Seidel's *Epic Geography* (1976); this last is especially lively. To the second we owe not only the Hart and Knuth *Topographical Guide* (1975), which pursues with exemplary thoroughness Kain's early discovery that *Thom's* underwrote much of the book's texture, but such quantities of useful annotation as are to be found in the *James Joyce Quarterly* (1963—　　) and *A Wake Newslitter* (1962—　　), in Weldon Thornton's *Allusions in Ulysses* (1968), Gifford and Seidman's *Notes for Joyce* (1974), Zack Bowen's *Musical Allusions in the Work of James Joyce* (1974). Homer, we have learned from Professor Eric Havelock, was the tribal encyclopaedia; analogously, one cannot foresee what stray fact pertaining to *Ulysses* will serve as the spark under what had seemed a heap of shavings. In its context – 'All those who are interested in the spread of human culture among the lower animals' (12.712) – the phrase 'and their name is legion' catches fire when we refer to its Biblical source (Mark 5: 8–13).

It becomes clear, finally, that 'the novel' is a problematic genre, and that Joyce glimpsed this fact before literary theorists began to assimilate it. We can see in retrospect what it was that affronted the earliest reviewers: a discontinuity between *Ulysses* and English story-telling. Later writers have been troubled by its discontinuities with what seems closer to it, the continental tradition of the novel as a socially responsible work of art. What to make of something that begins as 'Telemachus' and ends as 'Penelope', having traversed, *inter alia*, 'Sirens', 'Oxen of the Sun', 'Circe'? David Hayman in *Ulysses: The Mechanics of Meaning* (1970) helped us think how to answer when he designated the figure he calls the Arranger: not the 'impersonal' author called for by Dedalian and Eliotic theory but an active participant in the shaping of the text, as vividly present often as any character but as much (and as little) separable from the author as the major characters are. Hugh Kenner's *Joyce's Voices* (1978) further particularises the Arranger's antics, and suggests that 'objective' narration is not a neutral norm but simply the least conspicuous of the book's many conventions. In Marilyn French (*The*

Book as Word, 1976) and James H. Maddox Jr (*Joyce's 'Ulysses' and the Assault upon Character*) we see postulated the autonomy of the text, an intricacy from which the abstracting of event and person is our perilous responsibility. Earlier than either, Arnold Goldman in *The Joyce Paradox* (1966) perceived, though he did not put it quite this way, that the autonomy of the text is what permits the diversity of critical response no reader can miss and no critic overlook; for the soul, form of forms, is quick to adequate itself to whatever form it can perceive, and *Ulysses* — book of books, Joyce wanted it to be — is proteiform yet bounded.

BIBLIOGRAPHY

I TEXTS OF *ULYSSES*

There is no final holograph of *Ulysses*, and no final typescript. The so-called 'Rosenbach ms.', published in facsimile by the A. W. S. Rosenbach Foundation, Philadelphia, 3 vols, 1975, is essentially a set of fair copies of the successive episodes, representing each at a stage where Joyce was willing to leave it behind and start working on the next. But a text set up from these holographs would be perhaps two-thirds the length of the book that was published by Shakespeare and Company, Paris, in 1922, a substantial portion of the final text having been composed on the margins of successive proofsheets. Joyce's hand at its best is difficult, typists and printers erred repeatedly, and there are some 5,000 demonstrable instances in which the Paris printing differed from the author's intention. These range from lapses of punctuation to the omission of whole sequences of words, and such is Joyce's precision that it is difficult to think of a criterion by which any can be accounted minor.

Substantially all of these errors were perpetuated in all subsequent resettings, and to them many more got added. The establishment of a text hence entails retracing through manuscripts, typescripts, proofsheets and printed versions the credentials of every line. In 1984 this work was completed, with computer assistance, in Munich, under the supervision of Professor Hans Walter Gabler.

Prior to the Munich edition, any working or library copy the student encountered was, or derived from, one of the following typesettings:

(1) Shakespeare and Company, Paris, 1922.
(2) Same, May 1926 to May 1930 (type entirely reset).
(3) Random House, New York, 1934. This was meant to be set from the 9th (1927) printing of (2); it was inadvertently set from an unproofread forgery. Its more egregious errors were caught in subsequent Modern Library reprintings. The pagination of this printing was standard for early commentaries, and especially for the 1937 Hanley *Word-Index*, and is consequently recorded in the margins of later issues of the reset (1961) Random House printing (6 below).
(4) The Bodley Head, London, 1936.
(5) Same, 1960, entirely reset: the most attractive, physically and typographically, of all editions. 'Tis pity she's a whore.
(6) Random House, New York, 1961. Reset and repaginated from (5), with many errors of (3) corrected and more introduced. This became, *faut de mieux*, the standard text for critical citations.
(7) Penguin Books, Harmondsworth, 1968. Set from and reproduces the errors of (5). Cheap and widely available except in the USA.

The student will also encounter references to the 'definitive standard edition' issued in two volumes by the Odyssey Press, Hamburg, in 1932. This has derived a spurious authority from the claim that it was 'specially revised, at the author's request, by Stuart Gilbert', who later told Mr Jack Dalton he had not in fact done all that much (and had certainly made no effort to penetrate, with mss and proofsheets, the several thousand errors carried over from 1–2).

Relevant proofsheets and mss, other than the Rosenbach facsimile, have been reproduced by the Garland Publishing Co., New York, 1978, as Volumes 13–27 of the *James Joyce Archive*.

II OTHER JOYCE TITLES

The dates of first publication are listed below. In all cases current reprints have greater textual authority.

Chamber Music (London: Elkin Mathews, 1907)
Dubliners (London: Grant Richards, 1914)
A Portrait of the Artist as a Young Man (New York: B. W. Huebsch, 1916)
Exiles (London: Grant Richards, 1918)
Ulysses (Paris: Shakespeare, 1922)
Pomes Penyeach (Paris: Shakespeare, 1927)
Finnegans Wake (London: Faber; New York: Viking Press, 1939)
Stephen Hero (New York: New Directions, 1955)
Critical Writings (New York: Viking Press, 1959)
Letters, Vol. 1, ed. Stuart Gilbert (London: Faber; New York: Viking Press, 1957)
    Vols 2–3, ed. Richard Ellmann (London: Faber; New York: Viking Press, 1966)
    Selected Letters, ed. Richard Ellmann (London: Faber; New York: Viking Press, 1975)

The first volume of *Letters* was premature; fewer than one-third of the extant letters had surfaced. The transcriptions are unreliable, the indexing is scant, the annotation sparse. None of these strictures applies to Vols 2–3, which span the same chronology without duplication. The *Selected Letters* contains a few items not in the volumes from which it is selected.

III BIOGRAPHICAL

Anderson, Chester: *James Joyce and his World* (London: Thames & Hudson, 1968). A concise account of Joyce's life in few words and many fine pictures.
Budgen, Frank: *James Joyce and the Making of 'Ulysses'* (London: Grayson, 1934). Reprinted with additional material (London: Oxford University Press, 1972). The Zürich Joyce, in mid-*Ulysses*.
Curran, Constantine: *James Joyce Remembered* (New York and London: Oxford University Press, 1968). The Dublin Joyce of the 'Stephen Dedalus' period.

Davies, Stan Gébler: *James Joyce: A Portrait of the Artist* (London: Davis-Poynter, 1975). Brisk, hearty, superficial.

Ellmann, Richard: *James Joyce* (New York: Oxford University Press, 1959). The standard biography.

Gorman, Herbert: *James Joyce* (New York: Farrer & Rinehart, 1939). Concentrates on the struggles with publishers and reviewers.

Sullivan, Kevin: *Joyce Among the Jesuits* (New York: Columbia University Press, 1958). With Curran, a corrective to aspects of the *Portrait*.

IV STUDIES, NOTES, CRITIQUES

For a narrative survey of Joyce studies to 1976, see Thomas F. Staley in Richard J. Finneran (ed.), *Anglo-Irish Literature: A Review of Research*, 1976, 366–435. For bibliographies of secondary work, see Robert H. Deming, *A Bibliography of James Joyce Studies*, 1964; Beebe, Herring and Litz, 'Criticism of James Joyce: a selected Checklist', in *Modern Fiction Studies*, vol. XV (1969), 105–82; the *MLA International Bibliography* listings; and Alan Cohn's continuing supplements to the latter in *James Joyce Quarterly*.

The following selected list of books and essays concentrates on *Ulysses* and confines itself to books and chapters in books.

Adams, Robert M.: *Surface and Symbol: The Consistency of James Joyce's 'Ulysses'* (New York: Oxford University Press, 1962).

Blamires, Harry: *The Bloomsday Book* (London: Methuen, 1966). A page-by-page narrative paraphrase.

Bowen, Zack: *Musical Allusions in the Works of James Joyce* (Albany: State University of New York Press; Dublin: Gill & Macmillan, 1974).

Burgess, Anthony: *Joysprick: an Introduction to the Language of James Joyce!* (London: André Deutsch; New York, Harcourt, 1973).

Deming, Robert H.: *James Joyce: the Critical Heritage*, 2 vols (New York: Barnes & Noble, 1970). A sampling of what appeared in Joyce's lifetime.

Eliot, T. S.: see Givens.

Ellmann, Richard: *Ulysses on the Liffey* (New York: Oxford University Press, 1972).

French, Marilyn: *The Book as Word: James Joyce's 'Ulysses'* (Cambridge, Mass., and London: Harvard University Press, 1976).

Gabler, Hans Walter: see Staley and Benstock (1976).

Gifford, Don, with Robert J. Seidman: *Notes for Joyce: An Annotation of James Joyce's 'Ulysses'* (New York: Dutton, 1974). By no means impeccable, but a good place to look first.

Gilbert, Stuart: James Joyce's *'Ulysses': A Study* (New York: Knopf, 1930).

Givens, Seon (ed.): *James Joyce: Two Decades of Criticism* (New York: Vanguard Press, 1948). Important articles include T. S. Eliot's 'Ulysses, Order and Myth' (1923), S. Foster Damon's 'The Odyssey in Dublin'

1929) and Philip Toynbee's "A Study of James Joyce's *Ulysses*' (1947).

Glasheen, Adaline: see Magalaner.

Goldberg, S. L.: *The Classical Temper* (London: Chatto & Windus, 1961). How *Ulysses* would read if it were a novel.

Goldman, Arnold: *The Joyce Paradox* (London: Routledge & Kegan Paul, 1966). A subtle treatment of *Ulysses* as artful kaleidoscope.

Groden, Michael: *'Ulysses' in Progress* (Princeton, NJ: Princeton University Press, 1977). How the text developed: a more complex account than that of Litz (q.v.).

Hanley, Miles L.: 'Word Index to James Joyce's *Ulysses* (Madison, Wisconsin: 1937, mimeo.). Though a museum piece in the computer age, this merits a nostalgic salute, if only for the prescience embodied in seeing it was worth doing. In 1986 Garland Publishers, New York, issued a computerized index to the Gabler text.

Hart, Clive: *James Joyce's 'Ulysses'* (Sydney: Sydney University Press, 1968). A good brief survey.

Hart, Clive, and David Hayman (eds): *James Joyce's 'Ulysses'* (Berkeley, Calif., and London: University of California Press, 1974). A chapter by each of eighteen critics, one per episode. At least half are not to be missed.

Hart, Clive, and Leo Knuth: *A Topographical Guide to James Joyce's 'Ulysses'* (Colchester: A Wake Newslitter Press, 1975). A portfolio of maps, and a text itemising places, times and Joyce's dependence on *Thom's*.

Hayman, David: *'Ulysses': The Mechanics of Meaning* (Englewood Cliffs, NJ: Prentice-Hall, 1970). This concise book first introduced the concept of the Arranger.

Herring, Phillip F.: *Joyce's 'Ulysses' Notesheets in the British Museum* (Charlottesville: University Press of Virginia, 1972). Transcribed, annotated, discussed.

Howarth, Herbert: *The Irish Writers, 1880–1940: Literature Under Parnell's Star* (London: Rockcliff, 1958). Authoritative pages on how popular the Irish-Jewish parallel was among patriots of Joyce's generation.

James Joyce Quarterly (Tulsa, Oklahoma): specialised articles, 1963–

Kain, Richard M.: *Fabulous Voyager* (Chicago: University of Chicago Press, 1947), rev. edn 1959. The discoverer of the relevance of *Thom's* and the first systematic user of the *Word-Index*.

Kenner, Hugh: *Dublin's Joyce* (London: Chatto & Windus; Bloomington, Ind.: University of Indiana Press, 1956).

Kenner, Hugh: *Joyce's Voices* (Berkeley, Calif.: University of California Press; London: Faber, 1978). A rationale for the styles.

Levin, Harry: *James Joyce* (Norfolk, Conn.: New Directions, 1941). The first look at Joyce's whole career.

Lewis, Wyndham: *Time and Western Man* (London: Chatto & Windus, 1927). 'An Analysis of the Mind of James Joyce' is on pages 91–130. This chapter prompted not only Joyce's collaboration with Stuart Gilbert, but whole pages of *Finnegans Wake*.

Litz, A. Walton: *The Art of James Joyce: Method and Design in 'Ulysses' and 'Finnegans Wake'* (London: Oxford University Press,

1961). The first systematic effort to show how the books were written.

Litz, A. Walton: *James Joyce* (Boston, Mass.: Twayn, 1966, rev. edn 1972). A short introductory survey.

Maddox, James H., Jr: *Joyce's 'Ulysses' and the Assault Upon Character* (Brunswick, NJ: Rutgers University Press, 1978). The text as a transcension of its 'contents'.

Magalaner, M. (ed.): *A James Joyce Miscellany, Second Series* (Carbondale, Ill.: Southern Illinois University Press, 1959). Contains Adaline Glasheen's 'Joyce and the Three Ages of Charles Stewart Parnell', pp. 151–78.

Peake, C. H.: *James Joyce: The Citizen and the Artist* (London: Edward Arnold, 1977). Excellent on the cohesion of *Ulysses*.

Pound, Ezra: see Read.

Prescott, Joseph: *Exploring James Joyce* (Carbondale, Ill.: Southern Illinois University Press, 1964). Dating from the previous decade, these papers concentrate on Joyce's skill at revision.

Raleigh, John Henry: *The Chronicle of Leopold and Molly Bloom: 'Ulysses' as Narrative* (Berkeley, Calif., and London: University of California Press, 1977). The family facts and dates, chronologically arranged, to outline the chronicle-novel Joyce shredded through his book.

Read, Forrest: *Pound/Joyce: The Letters of Ezra Pound to James Joyce, with Pound's Essays on Joyce* (New York: New Directions, 1967). A major chapter in literary history, impeccably edited.

Schutte, William M.: *Joyce and Shakespeare: A Study in the Meaning of 'Ulysses'* (New Haven, Conn.: Yale University Press, 1957).

Seidel, Michael: *Epic Geography: James Joyce's 'Ulysses'* (Princeton, NJ: Princeton University Press, 1976). A surprising exploration of how Joyce used the Homeric theories of Victor Bérard.

Senn, Fritz (ed.): *New Light on Joyce from the Dublin Symposium* (Bloomington, Ind., and London: University of Indiana Press, 1972). See especially Jack P. Dalton, 'The Text of *Ulysses*', pp. 99–119.

Staley, Thomas F. (ed.): *'Ulysses': Fifty Years* (Bloomington, Ind., and London: University of Indiana Press, 1974). See especially Fritz Senn, 'Book of Many Turns', pp. 29–46.

Staley, Thomas F., and Bernard Benstock (eds): *Approaches to 'Ulysses': Ten Essays* (Pittsburgh, Pa.: University of Pittsburgh Press, 1970). See especially David Hayman, 'The Empirical Molly', pp. 103–35.

Staley, Thomas F., and Bernard Benstock (eds): *Approaches to Joyce's 'Portrait': Ten Essays* (Pittsburgh, Pa.: University of Pittsburgh Press, 1976). See Hans Walter Gabler, 'The Seven Lost Years of *A Portrait of the Artist as a Young Man*', pp. 25–60.

Sultan, Stanley: *The Argument of 'Ulysses'* (Columbus, Ohio: Ohio State University Press, 1965).

Thornton, Weldon: *Allusions in 'Ulysses'* (Chapel Hill: University of North Carolina Press, 1968). Contexts of quotations, words of songs: a most useful work.

Toynbee, Philip: see Givens.

A Wake Newslitter (Colchester: A Wake Newslitter Press): mostly devoted to *Finnegans Wake*, but with frequent short notes on *Ulysses*. Bi-monthly since 1962.

Wilson, Edmund: *Axel's Castle* (New York: Charles Scribner's Sons, 1931). The chapter 'James Joyce' is an early attempt to locate and define Joyce's work and especially *Ulysses*.

INDEX

Adams, R. M. 133, 144, 153, 163, 172
AE 56*n*, 59, 60, 74–5, 115*n*
'Aeolus' 63, 100, 104, 112
Alain-Fournier 12
Ambrose, St. 40
Anderson, C. 71*n*12
Aristotle 111, 118
Arranger 61–71, 86, 91, 98, 101, 153, 172
Atherton, J. S. 108

Babbage, C. 150, 153
Barthes, R. 156
Beadle, M. 40*n*
Beckett, S. 156
Bérard, V. 29
Berlitz 123–4
Blamires, H. 19
Bloom, Leopold *and hat* 46–7; *and letter* 21–2; *and math* 166–8; *and newspaper* 32–3; *and silences* 48–51; *and style* 69; *and watch* 105; *as Jew* 43, 70, 103, 141, 152; *as Odysseus* 28–9, 106; *edits narrative* 101–2, 145; *finances* 44, 127, 141; *library* 73, 76, 143; *list of rivals* 142–3; *on water* 135–6; *sound of name* 87, 89; *stature* 44, 141
Bloom, Molly *and cards* 49; *and metempsychosis* 81–2; *as catechiser* 50, 101; *emergence of* 70; *soliloquy* 145–9
'The Boarding House' 17
Borges, J. L. 127
Bowen, Z. 172
Boylan, Blazes 20, 28, 47–51, 52, 53, 81, 88, 91, 105, 125, 132, 143, 148
Brémond, H. 85
Budgen, F. 4, 5, 15, 22, 71*n*4, 93*n*, 170
Butcher and Lang 83
Butler, S. 83, 105

'Calypso' 46–50, 66, 75
Cantos, The 3
catspeech 40, 45, 46, 68
character 45
Chiasmus 7–8, 68, 69, 129
Childs case 122
Chrysostomos 35, 38, 96, 98

'Circe' 26, 60, 76, 118–29
Clocks 72–3
Clockwork Orange 123
Un Coeur Simple 144
Collins, J. 3
Colum, P. 9
'Counterparts' 13
Countess Cathleen 118, 161
Count of Monte Cristo 30
Cronin, A. 133*n*
Curtius, E. R. 88
'Cyclops' 24, 92–103, 106, 112, 121, 141

Dalton, J. 164, 174
Dante 88
Darwin, E. 85, 92*n*6
Davenport, G. 121*n*, 155
Dedalus, Stephen *and bird-girl* 8–9, 11, 12, 26, 106; *and father* 10, 16–17, 19, 58, 110; *and Joyce* 6; *and money* 55–7; *and Shakespeare* 112–14; *and style* 7–9, 39–40, 68, cf. 148; *his day* 55–60; *his parable* 140; *hits Mulligan?* 115; *myopia* 38, 152
Determinism 149–51
DeValera, E. 103
Dionysius of Halicarnassus 84
Discontinuity 99–100
Disney, W. 89
Documentation 46
Don Giovanni 28, 90
Dowden, E. 112–13
Dubliners 12, 17, 49, 58, 61–3

Eden, 76–9
Egan, Kevin 39, 98, 162
Eglinton, J. 59, 60, 115*n*
Einstein 81, 153–4
Eliot, T. S. 2, 3, 112, 169, 170
Ellmann, R. 18*n*5, 42*n*3, 137*n*, 144*n*, 171–2
Emmet, R. 87, 93, 120
Empson, W. 85
Episodes 23–4, 101
'Eumaeus' 24, 55, 68, 129–33, 141

Faust, see Goethe
Finnegans Wake 13, 18*n*4, 28, 34, 41, 49, 57, 85, 90, 155, 156